מסורה

ArtScroll Mesorah Series

Rabbis Nosson Scherman/Meir Zlotowitz
General Editors

akdamus

akdamus

AKDAMUS MILLIN / WITH A NEW TRANSLATION
AND COMMENTARY ANTHOLOGIZED FROM THE
TRADITIONAL RABBINIC LITERATURE

Published by
Mesorah Publications, ltd.

Translated and compiled by
Rabbi Avrohom Yaakov Salamon

An Overview: Akdamus/Prelude to Torah
by
Rabbi Nosson Scherman

FIRST EDITION
First impression ...... May, 1978

Distributed by
Z. BERMAN / Books
1340 Fifty-third Street
Brooklyn, New York 11219

THE AKDAMUS MILLIN
Copyright © 1978
by Mesorah Publications, Ltd, Brooklyn, N.Y.

סדר במסדרת
חברת ארטסקרול בע"מ

Typography by CompuScribe at ArtScroll Studios, Ltd.
1969 Coney Island Avenue / Brooklyn, N.Y. 11224 / (212) 339-1700

Printed by Moriah Offset

מוקדש לכבוד אבי מורי

הרב מאיר שאלאמאן שליט״א

ולאמי מורתי

פרומעט שאלאמאן תחי׳

ואחרון אחרון חביב ליקיר ביתי אשתי

גאלדי רייזל תחי׳

לזכרון עולם

יזכר אלהים את נשמות זקני וזקנותי

הרבני מוה׳ ר׳ יוסף בן יעקב ז״ל הי״ד

ואשתו הצדקת מרת אסתר ע״ה בת אליהו ז״ל הי״ד
ונשמות

החסיד מוה׳ ר׳ אברהם יעקב בן אליהו ז״ל הי״ד

ואשתו הצדקת מרת גיטל ע״ה בת שמואל דוד ז״ל הי״ד
שנהרגו ונשרפו על קדוש השם
באושוויץ בשנת השואה תש״ד

השם ינקם את דמם

ת.נ.צ.ב.ה.

&

ולזכרון בהיכל ה׳

למזכרת נצח ולעילוי נשמות רב מרדכי ב״ר משה

ואלו שנהרגו על קידוש השם ע״י הרוצחים הנאצים ימ״ש
הי״ד

גאלדא פריידא ב״ר יואל; **אליהו וואלף** ב״ר מרדכי

העגדל לאה ב״ר מרדכי; **גיטל** ב״ר מרדכי

שמואל ב״ר משה; **ביילא** ב״ר משה

רבקה ב״ר יואל; **בעריש** ב״ר יואל; **יוסף** ב״ר יואל

אברהם ב״ר אפרים פישל

רייזל ב״ר לייבוש

ביישא ב״ר אברהם

וכל משפחת **פנסר** ו**ירוזולמסקי** כלם קדושים
שנהרגו על קידוש השם

ת.נ.צ.ב.ה.

מכתב ברכה
ממרן הגאון ר' שניאור קוטלר שליט"א

RABBI SHNEUR KOTLER
BETH MEDRASH GOVOHA
LAKEWOOD, N. J.

בע"ה

שניאור קוטלר
בית מדרש גבוה
לייקוואוד, נ. דז.

בע"ה

הנני לקדם בברכה את פעולתו החשובה של האברך הנעלה, יקר הרוח וחכם לב, חופש גנזי מטמונים, **הרב אברהם יעקב שלומון נ"י**, — לתרגם ולבאר את השיר שנתקבל בכל תפוצות ישראל כהקדמה לקריאת התורה ביום התקדש חג השבועות זמן מתן תורתנו, שיסודתו בהררי קודש, ותוכו רצוף רשפי אש ממדרשי חז"ל, המלהיבים לבבות לאהבת ה', קדושת התורה וסגולת ישראל. היקפו מראש מקדמי עולם בקו ישר עד אחרית הימים, ושורש הכל בתוה"ק אשר בה אסתכל וברא עלמא, רבותינו דישראל קראי בשמעתא, ועמידתם קבל אוה"ע וכל טובות העוה"ז, שהכל אוכם כלפי זוהר האור העליון המנצנץ לנו מן העתיד הקרוב.

וחשיבות יתירה נודעת ליזמתם הברוכה של סגל **חבורת המוציאים לאור והעורכים**, המזכים את הרבים ע"י שימת ד"ת שלחן ערוך ומוכן לאכול לפני האדם. וערמב"ן פ' כי תבא נכלל בברכת אשר יקים וכו' החזן המראה פני כתיבתו לעם וכו'. יזכו לראות בכבוד התורה והרמת קרנה בבוא גואל לציון ברנה בב"א.

הכו"ח לכבוד התורה, אור ליום ג', בעשור לח' ניסן, התשל"ח

יוסף חיים שניאור קוטלר
בלאאמו"ר הגר"א זצוק"ל

Preface

The Akdamus may well be Judaism's best known פִּיוּט, liturgical poem. No other poem has been more beloved and endeared in the hearts of the Jewish people. Composed as an introduction to the reading of the Ten Commandments on Shavuos, it is written in a terse, difficult Aramaic. In its ninety verses, the poem deals, in a most recondite and beautiful manner, with lofty and noble concepts in the Torah, the Jewish faith, and the Jewish people. The poet leads the reader through the great heights and depths of mystical understanding — from a description of God's creation of the world to a close look at the splendors of Paradise in the World to Come, from the angels' praising of the Almighty above to the greatness of the Jewish people and their suffering below.

Couched within the ninety short verses of the poem, lies such a wealth of spiritual knowledge and insight that the human imagination can hardly conceive how such magnificence could have been composed by a person of flesh and blood. Small wonder that Akdamus has been treated with reverence and awe, and regarded as the veil behind which lay the mysteries of Creation.

THE AUTHOR

The Akdamus was composed by Rabbi Meir ben Rabbi Yitzchak, Shliach Tzibbur (i.e., leader in prayer), ben Shmuel.

Very little is known about him. Even the dates of his birth and death are subjects of conjecture. It is commonly presumed that he was born between 1030-1040 C.E., and that he died in the year 1096 or earlier in the city of Worms. He was a towering figure in his native Jewish community. He was instrumental in the composition and adaption of many prayers, and selichos in his time. Much of the contents of Machzor Vitry, of Rabbeinu Simcha, and Siddur Rashi, two of the authoritative early prayer books, stemmed directly or indirectly from him. He was also the author of a book on Jewish synagogue liturgy and customs which, unfortunately, is no longer extant.

Rabbi Meir was also known as a great Torah scholar. Rashi quotes him frequently (see for example, Hosea 6:9; Amos 3:12; Psalms 73:12). He is also cited extensively in Siddur Rashi, Responsa of Rashi, Machzor Vitry, and Shibbolei HaLeket, as well as in the Tosafos to Rosh

HaShanah *11a* (רי״ה אלא). *It is known that he was the composer of forty-nine liturgical poems, forty in Hebrew, and nine in Aramaic.* (Davidson, Thesaurus of Medieval Hebrew Poetry, vol. *IV, 432). Only about fifteen of those poems are still known to exist.*

It is assumed that Rabbi Meir died in Worms sometime before 1096, the year of the First Crusade. Thus he was spared from the horrible massacre that occurred there when eight hundred Jews, among them his son, Yitzchak, were martyred in sanctification of the Name (Kobetz al-Yad, year 3, p. 5).

THE AKDAMUS

T*he Akdamus is written in Aramaic, and contains ninety verses. The first twenty-two pairs of verses are in double acrostic form, beginning with the twenty-two letters of the Hebrew Alphabet, in order. The first letters of the remaining forty-six verses spell out the name of the author and a blessing:* מאיר ביר רבי יצחק יגדל בתורה ובמעשים טובים אמן, וחזק ואמץ, — '*Meir, the son of Rabbi Yitzchak, may he grow in Torah and in good deeds. Amen. Be strong and of good courage' (cf.* Joshua *1:18).*

Each of the ninety verses concludes with the suffix תא, *the last and first letters of the Hebrew alphabet, to signify that the cycle of Torah study is endless, and that as soon as one completes the Torah once, he should begin his study anew* (Kitov, Sefer HaToda'ah).

As mentioned, the Akdamus was composed as an introduction to the reading of the Ten Commandments, its lofty and grandiose style having the effect of spiritually reawakening every Jew to reapply himself to the study of the Torah. Indeed, because it is related to the Ten Commandments, each of its verses contains ten voweled syllables, for example:

אַקְדָמוּת מִלִין וְשָׁרָיוּת שׁוּתָא:

אַוְלָא שָׁקִילְנָא הַרְמָן וּרְשׁוּתָא:

[*Note that* sheva *and* chatef *are not considered vocal syllables; hence a word like* עֲרֵי *is considered one syllable. According to some versions, however, there are occasional verses which do not conform to the rule of ten syllables.*]

Since the poem was composed as part of the Shavuos liturgy, the author makes extensive use of the Targum *to Haftaros of the two festival days. The Haftarah of the first day is from Ezekiel ch. 1, and that of the second day is from Habakuk 2:20 — 3:19 (see v. 5 of Akdamus). Since the chapter in Ezekiel deals with Ma'aseh Merkavah, the esoteric depiction of the angels giving homage to God, the poem contains much about the creation of the world and of the angel's recitation of Kedushah, Sanctification, before God (see v. 19).*

THE AKDAMUS IN JEWISH LITURGY

*T*he exact time when Akdamus *became widely accepted as part of the liturgy is in doubt.* It is first mentioned in Minhagei Maharil, *by Jacob ben Moses Moellin (1360-1427), that the Akdamus is to be recited on Shavuos immediately after the reading of the first verse of the Torah portion of the day. Indeed such was the custom throughout Europe for over four hundred years.*

Many of the leading scholars of the fifteenth and sixteenth centuries questioned the propriety of interrupting the reading of the Torah for the recitation of a liturgical poem. After nearly two centuries of halachic dis-putation, the recitation of the Akdamus *was moved up to precede the first benediction before the reading of the Torah. Although the matter was extensively discussed, final decision to change the order of reading can be credited primarily to* Turei Zahav *(David ben Shmuel haLevi, 1586-1667), the first major commentary to express wonder at the custom of interrupting the reading of the Torah with a poem. Nevertheless, although it is considered disrespectful to engage in any activity while the Torah waits to be read, the Akdamus is the only liturgical composition with the unique distinction of being recited after the Torah has been removed from the ark and before it is read. (See* Taz: Shulchan Aruch Orach Chaim, *494. See also* Responsa Sha'ar Ephraim *6).*

A POSSIBLE REASON

*I*t may be that the original custom of interrupting the Torah reading for *Akdamus was a not surprising outgrowth of a universal custom of olden times. Already in the time of Nehemia in the fifth century B.C.E. (see* Nedarim *37b), it was customary to employ a Meturgeman [מְתוּרְגְמָן = translator or interpreter] to explain the Torah reading to the congrega-tion. This was necessitated by the fact that Hebrew had ceased to be the spoken language of the people, who had adapted Aramaic during the Babylonian exile. Therefore, a scholar, the Meturgeman, would be ap-pointed by the synagogue, to give a verse-by-verse Aramaic translation of the Torah reading. The reader read one verse of the Torah and paused while the Meturgeman gave an Aramaic paraphrase of that verse, sometimes including brief* halachic *or* midrashic *commentaries. The reader would read the second verse, and the Meturgeman would translate that one as well, and so on (see the* Mishnah, Megillah *23b).*

These Aramaic translations were later codified and standardized into our Targum. *Targum Onkelos was written in Babylonian Aramaic, and* Targum Yonasan *and* Targum Yerushalmi *were written in Jerusalemite dialects of Aramaic.*

By the time of the Gaonic Period, (600 C.E.-1000 C.E.), Aramaic was giving way to Arabic as the spoken language of the Jewish people. Hence Rav Saadia Gaon (882-942) wrote most of his major works in Arabic, including an Arabic translation of the Torah. It should be emphasized, however, that Aramaic remained the scholarly language of the Gaonim, and was therefore the language used in the extensive writings of the foremost gaon of the period, Rav Hai ben Sharira Gaon (939-1038). The lives of Rav Hai Gaon and Rabbi Meir, the author of the Akdamus, *overlap, hence Aramaic was still very much a spoken language in Babylonia, and a literary language in the scholarly Jewish communities of Europe. Furthermore it has been speculated that the author of the* Akdamus *was born in Babylonia (Introduction: Shnei HaMe'oros). That fact was kept secret by the Jews of Worms, because relations between Arabs, who inhabited Babylonia, and Europeans, were extremely hostile; the Jews therefore feared that if Rabbi Meir's origin were known he might be accused of spying for the Arabs of his native land.*

Our hypothesis is that it was still common for the Torah to be read with the Aramaic Targum *in the tenth century when Akdamus was composed. Therefore, the insertion of the Aramaic poem was considered no more of an interruption than what the Meturgeman had been doing at the end of every verse, for over one thousand years. Indeed, old manuscripts of the* Akdamus *used this ancient format: the first verse of the Torah reading, then the entire text of the* Akdamus, *and then, after the final verse of the* Akdamus, *the Targum of the first verse of the Torah which had been read earlier. Afterwards the manuscript continues, interspersing one Torah verse with its Targum, until the conclusion. (See* Machzor Vitry).

By the twelfth and thirteenth centuries the practice of the reading of the Targum *during the reading of the Torah had been discontinued in Europe. The practice of reading the* Targum *to the Haftaros on festivals continued until well into the end of the 14th century, however (see* Sefer HaMachkim, Cracow, 1909; *by Nathan b. Judah, beg. 14th century; see also* Tosafos *to* Megillah 24a ד״ה ואם).

Hence we may conclude that, originally the Akdamus *was meant to be read after the first verse of the Torah. We may further surmise that Rabbi Meir realized that a poem of such length might be considered too lengthy an interval between the blessing and the rest of the Torah reading; he, therefore concluded* Akdamus *with an Aramaic rendering of the blessing for the Torah (vs. 89-90). In our time, however, since the* Targum *is no longer read, it would indeed be an interruption for the* Akdamus *to be read after the first verse of the Torah.*

[For further information on Akdamus, *the reader may consult the works listed in the bibliography.*]

THE COMMENTARY

The commentary is divided into two sections: LEXICAL NOTES and COMMENTARY.

The LEXICAL NOTES *define the words of the Akdamus. In cases where the word is difficult, or occurs infrequently in the* Targum, Talmud, *or* Midrash, *or if it is used in an unusual manner, examples of such usage are cited.*

Many words have been given a seemingly redundant variety of English equivalents because it was often impossible to find a single English word that is precisely equivalent to the Aramaic; hence several definitions are given which, in combination, better approximate the Aramaic. Furthermore, the varied definitions give the reader an insight into the many nuances of the original Aramaic. Thus the reader can derive a better 'feel' for the word than would be possible if only single, one-dimensional definitions were offered.

The definitions should by no means be considered a 'dictionary' in the sense that they indicate all senses of the words. The definitions offered are those that apply to the context of the particular verse; others are omitted.

The COMMENTARY *explains the broader meaning of the Akdamus. The author has consulted all available works on* Akdamus *and attempted to blend all major interpretations. The task was made possible by the fact that there are only twenty-one known commentaries to the poem.*

The COMMENTARY *aims to give the source of every verse in the* Akdamus, *from the* Scriptures, Targum, Talmud *and* Midrash. *The sources are often quoted, in their entirety followed by an English translation. Often a given verse of the Akdamus is virtually a word-for-word paraphrase of its source. By quoting the source verbatim, we allow the reader to see the similarity clearly, something that would have been extremely difficult if only the English translation had been provided.*

The COMMENTARY *aims to provide the 'plain' or 'simple' meaning* (פְּשַׁט) *of each verse. Homiletical interpretations have been generally avoided; otherwise the work could have been increased ten-fold. A clear understanding of the text, does not require a knowledge of the homiletical commentaries. Conversely, however, knowledge of the plain meaning is a prerequisite to an understanding of the wealth of Akdamus just as it is to any other part of the sacred literature.*

One should also be aware that the Akdamus was composed in such a manner that each pair of verses — an odd and an even-numbered-one — express a complete thought. Therefore each verse should be read in con-

junction with its companion verse to attain a full understanding of the couplet.

The publication of this work represents the culmination of three years of research and writing. The original manuscript was considerably longer, containing m ore direct quotes of sources and much material not directly pertaining to the simple understanding of the text. Such material was eliminated from the final version in order not to impose an inordinate burden upon the general readership.

For scholars seeking further elaboration or documentation on specific parts of the text and commentary, the author will be pleased to discuss questions and provide further material.

I thank the Almighty for having given me the ability and opportunity to fulfill my ten-year ambition of writing such a work and seeing it through to publication. I hope that it will in some small way contribute to the understanding of our Holy Torah, and to Israel's appreciation of the beauty of the liturgy. May God grant me the knowledge and understanding to be able to write other works for the sanctification of His Name.

Acknowledgements

I t is an honor to become a participant in the ArtScroll Series and thereby become a member of the distinguished group which has joined the ranks of the great Torah disseminaters.

I wish to express my deepest gratitude to RABBI NOSSON SCHERMAN who devoted long, hard hours to the final editing of the manuscript. His contributions to the translation as well as the entire manuscript of the commentary gave the work a degree of readability and flow that it would otherwise have lacked. I also extend my heartfelt thanks for his Overview. I feel privileged that the work has been enhanced by his erudition and insight.

I also wish to thank RABBI MEIR ZLOTOWITZ for the indefatigable energy and enthusiasm that inspired and pervaded all phases of the production of this work. He has the rare ability to see directly to the root of a given situation, whether it is an interpretation of a verse, a matter of esthetic taste, or the meeting of a publishing deadline. That the ArtScroll Series has become an international vehicle for the spread of Torah knowledge is due primarily to his scholarship and organizational ability.

My gratitude goes to RABBI ANSHEL BERMAN for his skillful editing of the manuscript during the initial stages of preparation. This work's internal appearance and structure is due to his skill, taste, and adept handling.

RABBI AVIE GOLD read the entire manuscript and ferreted out many errors that crept into the manuscript during writing and typesetting. Much of the work's accuracy can be attributed to his learning and understanding.

To REB SHEA BRANDER fell the difficult task of designing the printed page so that the book's various components — text, translation, notes, and commentary — would be esthetically pleasing and clear to the reader. His work continues his tradition of graphic excellence which has become a hallmark of ArtScroll productions. I am deeply grateful to him.

The ArtScroll staff, SHIMON SHAMILZADEH, ROCHEL BRISMAN, and LAURIE MENDELOWITZ, are to be commended for the dedication and competence with which they prepared the manuscript. The work was often difficult, requiring extra effort and time. They have my heartfelt gratitude.

My sincere thanks go to a good friend and master librarian, MISS ORA HAMELSDORF, who was always ready to help locate and obtain whichever books and information were required during the long period of research for this work. Much of the literature was made available only thanks to her skill and diligence. Also, I wish to thank my close friend ELAZAR STEINMETZ who allowed me unlimited use of his large personal library during the writing of this work.

I also wish to acknowledge my thanks to two good friends, RABBI EUGENE ZAVELOFF and my brother-in-law, MR. ABRAHAM M. PENZER, ESQ., for their encouragement and companionship throughout the arduous months when the book was written.

Last, but not least, I wish to thank my wife GOLDIE, who stood by me and gave me constant encouragement throughout the long period during which this book was written. To her should really go all the acknowledgements, for without her patience and understanding, this work could not have been undertaken.

Avrohom Yaakov Salamon

ערב פסח ה׳תשל״ח

❧ An Overview/
Akdamus — Prelude to Torah

An Overview/

Akdamus — Prelude to Torah

דָּרַשׁ רַבִּי סְמָאי בְּשָׁעָה שֶׁהִקְדִּימוּ יִשְׂרָאֵל נַעֲשֶׂה
לְנִשְׁמָע בָּאוּ שִׁשִּׁים רִבּוֹא שֶׁל מַלְאֲכֵי הַשָּׁרֵת וְכָל
אֶחָד וְאֶחָד קָשְׁרוּ לוֹ שְׁנֵי כְתָרִים אֶחָד כְּנֶגֶד נַעֲשֶׂה
וְאֶחָד כְּנֶגֶד נִשְׁמָע ...

*Rabbi Simai expounded: At the moment
that Israel said, 'We will do,' before saying
'We will hear,' [Exodus 24:7] sixty
myriads of ministering angels came. To
each [Jew] they wreathed two crowns, one
[in reward] for, 'We will do' and one for,
'We will hear' ...*

אָמַר רַבִּי אֶלְעָזָר ... יָצְאָה בַּת קוֹל וְאָמַר מִי גִלָּה
לְבָנַי רָז זֶה שֶׁמַּלְאֲכֵי הַשָּׁרֵת מִשְׁתַּמְּשִׁין בּוֹ דִּכְתִיב
בָּרְכוּ ה׳ מַלְאָכָיו גִּבֹּרֵי כֹחַ עֹשֵׂי דְבָרוֹ לִשְׁמֹעַ בְּקוֹל
דְּבָרוֹ בְּרֵישָׁא עוֹשֵׂי וַהֲדָר לִשְׁמֹעַ ...

*Rabbi Elazar said: [When Israel said the
above] a Heavenly voice came forth saying, 'Who revealed to My children this
secret which the angels use?' As it is written, His angels bless Hashem, powerful
ones who fulfill His word, to hear the
sound of His word [Psalms 103:20] — first
they fulfill, then they hear ...*

הַהוּא מִינָא ... אָמַר לֵיהּ ... עַמָּא פְּזִיזָא
דְּקַדְמִיתָא פּוּמָא לְאוּדְנַיְיכוּ ... בְּרֵישָׁא אִיבָּעֵי
לְכוּ לְמִשְׁמַע אִי מְצִיתוּ קַבְּלִיתוּ וְאִי לָא לָא
קַבְּלִיתוּ

*A certain heretic said [of Israel]: 'Impetu-
ous people! You preceded your mouths to
your ears. First you should have listened
[to ascertain] whether you could accept
[the Torah], and if not, you should not
have accepted it'. (Shabbos 88a)*

I. 'We Will Do'

The **W**hen Moses came to his people with the question
Logical whether they were willing to accept God's
Argument Torah, they answered נַעֲשֶׂה וְנִשְׁמָע, *we will do and we
will hear (Exodus* 24:7). They were ready to accept
the Torah in its entirety no matter what command-
First came the ments and restrictions it contained. First came the
resolve — we will do resolve — *we will do* — then there would be time to
— then there would
be time to listen and listen and learn what it was they were to do.
learn what it was
they were to do. To the heretic, it was an incomprehensive act of
national impetuosity; an entire people had lost its
senses in the enthusiasm of having been liberated by
God and given the chance to carry the banner of his
Torah. Can one reasonably accept a mission before
learning what it is? Is it logical to place one's 'mouth
before his ears', to sign a blank check, to abandon the
free-willed choice that is man's distinction, chal-
lenge, and protection?

That Yet, the Sages teach, that pronouncement placed
pronouncement
placed Israel at the Israel at the pinnacle of its glory. It raised them to the
pinnacle of its glory. level of the angels, made them privy to the divine
mystery of God's own 'powerful ones' whose very
being has no purpose other than to do God's will.
'Who revealed to My children this secret of the
angels?' God exclaimed. And an army of angels
descended to earth bearing crowns for Israel, the
people who had earned a heavenly coronation in
recognition of their devotion to God and faith in His
word.

But what of the reasonable argument of the
heretic? Wouldn't Israel have displayed even more
greatness if it had first listened and heard the commandments that frightened off all other nations —
and *then* announced its willingness to subordinate
license to God's will? Wouldn't their subsequent
obedience to God's will have been more meaningful
had it been based on wisdom rather than emotion?

Subjective Wisdsom

Of course, man should have the goal of exercising wisdom in his every choice. Israel knew that — and *acted upon it*. Human intellect is rooted in man's physical existence. It is indivisible from his need to nourish his body, satisfy his urges, and coexist with his environment. If doing the 'right' thing will result in pain, hunger, death, and doing the 'wrong' thing will result in gratification, prosperity, and health, then 'wisdom' may well decree that self-preservation overrides all values. Many of the great moral debates in human history have dealt with such questions. If man had no need to defend his borders and feed his children, then his intellect would decree courses of action far different from those typically chosen by reasonable people. Most of the so-called great debates that dominate the news of any week in history can be distilled into such questions. The protagonists will defend their opposing viewpoints on grounds of morality, wisdom, and need. And each will be right according to his own *particular* needs and the decisions that flow from them. Organized labor feels entitled to a higher standard of living for its people, industry cannot allow its competitive position to be undercut, government cannot allow the broader economy to suffer. Nations refuse to compromise their territorial integrity, and the world watches aghast as war breaks out and acreage becomes more important than blood. The arguments on all sides are eloquent and unyielding — and *logical* from the vantage point of the various parties to the conflict.

If man had no need to defend his borders and feed his children, then his intellect would decree courses of action far different from those typically chosen by reasonable people.

Neutral parties argue their positions passionately, as well, but even neutrality is based on commitment to values and obligation to needs. The neutral mediator may plead that the common weal takes priority over all else or that standards of decency prohibit a particular course of action, but even that eminently reasonable view is based on a perception — his own or society's — that is valid only to the point that it can gain sufficient acceptance to be enforcable. Weak countries, because they lack the strength

Even neutrality is based on commitment to values and obligation to needs.

to resist their strong neighbors, are more susceptible than powerful ones to high-minded declarations of principle. Dispensable workers are more loath to strike than are irreplaceable ones.

Dispensable workers are more loath to strike than are irreplaceable ones.

Frederick the Great put it crudely when he said that God is on the side of the more powerful army; unfortunately, however, there is a little bit of Frederick in most people. For them, life is a constant series of decisions that must be weighed in the balance of aspiration versus reality, reward-of-success versus cost-of-failure, morality versus exigency, conscience versus greed.

When man sees himself as a party to a social contract that functions for the benefit of the body politic — a body of which he is an organ — then laws and regulations have a force above and beyond the punishment that awaits an offender. The most effective deterrent to wrongdoing is not lashes, imprisonment, or execution, but the consciousness that every limb of society bleeds a little when the contract is violated. But when cynicism and selfishness change man's perception of society so that he sees it as an organized enemy, then why should its laws not be defied with impunity if there is no alert policeman on the corner and no vigilant judge on the bench? For when the 'greater good' is understood as nothing but a pernicious cliche, there is no compelling reason but fear to subordinate one's own interests to those of society.

The most effective deterrent to wrongdoing is the consciousness that every limb of society bleeds a little when the contract is violated.

It is true that the most successful people are highly motivated and single-minded in pursuit of their goal; but what goal: Torah knowledge, fear of God, financial success, power, gratification? Man should pursue truth; but *whose* truth — yours, mine, God's? Idealistic man can spend a lifetime in search of justice and, when he defines it, thrust himself into living according to its dictates. But as long as the definition is arrived at by human beings acting upon their instincts alone, it will be colored by all the considerations that make one man different from his fellows.

The Only Absolute Truth

Whenever one exercises his inherent right of choice, no matter how well he 'listens', what he 'hears' is filtered through infinite layers of experience and preconception. Inevitably, therefore, even the most objective choice is influenced to some extent by the one who does the choosing and, to that extent, it is colored.

Only one course of action is perfect by definition — that ordained by God.

Only one course of action is perfect by definition — that ordained by God. The person who submits himself unreservedly to God's will is freed from the fetters of human subjugation to emotion and desire. Israel said נַעֲשֶׂה, *We will do* as God commands, whatever He tells us, without deciding beforehand whether His will suits our taste. The nation, far from abandoning its freedom of choice, was *freeing* itself from the overlay of subjectivity which mankind imposes upon itself and which it dignifies with such high-sounding platitudes as culture, civilization, social order, justice and all the other inspiring terms by which human deeds, from the noblest to the basest, are defended.

'We will do!' — that was Israel's declaration of freedom.

'We will do!' — that was Israel's declaration of freedom. Even the Exodus and the crossing of the Sea of Reeds would not have freed the nation from Egypt if it had taken Egypt along with it in mind and heart.

The Jew who carries God in his heart and Torah in his mind wherever he goes, is always standing at Sinai.

The Jew who carries God in his heart and Torah in his mind wherever he goes, is always standing at Sinai and is forever ascending the Temple Mount in the most significant sense; the Jew who enters the study halls of Jerusalem with an inner longing for Spanish *filosophia*, German *Kultur*, or American constitutional democracy, is but carrying his personal exile along with him wherever he goes.

The heretic considered it incredibly impetuous that Israel could surrender its freedom of action without even an inquiry to a God Who said, 'Trust Me!' — as if it had to fear that God would swindle it once He had seduced it into His service.

Surely the heretic admired the judgment of Esau's descendants who, upon being offered the Torah asked 'What does it say?' Told that it contained the

injunction לֹא תִרְצָח, *You shall not kill* [*Exodus* 20:13], they refused, saying that they must live by the sword. The heretic nodded with approval when Ishmael's children spurned a Torah that commanded, *'You shall not steal'* [*ibid.*] Only for Israel which trusted God did the heretic feel contempt, for it blindly accepted a law that might make impossible demands.

Imperative Demands

Israel knew better. Impossible demands? God had created man for a purpose; surely the universe could not have been the product of Divine caprice. Man, as the ultimate creature in God's plan, was charged with carrying out that purpose. Indeed, the universe was tailored to man's role in the fulfillment of God's design (see *Overview* to *Bereishis I*, ArtScroll ed.). It is no more sensible for man to weigh God's will in his own scale of values than it is for a technician to rewire the innards of a complex electronic mechanism to conform to the esthetic taste of a sculptor. Whatever demands the Torah makes on man are based only on his ability to fulfill them and on the cosmic efficacy of their fulfillment. To base his obedience to God's will on his own predilections is like refusing to lift up the telephone receiver because one enjoys the sound of the ring but dreads the message.

It is no more sensible for man to weigh God's will in his own scale of values than it is for a technician to rewire the innards of a complex electronic mechanism to conform to the esthetic taste of a sculptor.

Israel's purpose was to carry out God's will. It recognized and accepted that purpose and thereby proved itself to be angelic — nay, even higher than the angels. For the angels, despite their power to move mountains and split seas, exist only to carry out God's will. The very word מַלְאָךְ, *angel*, means, literally, *agent*. An agent has no independent power. His legal status is determined solely by the fact that he acts on behalf of his employer. If that sanction is withdrawn, then his actions are invalid. An angel, too, is no more than a *mal'och*, an agent, of his Creator. God can intervene personally, so to speak, in the affairs of the universe, as He did on the fateful night when the Jews left Egypt — as the *Haggadah*

The very word מַלְאָךְ, angel, means, literally, agent. An agent has no independent power.

expounds: *I and not an angel, I and not a Seraph, I and not an agent* — or He can delegate an angel, a prophet, a storm, or an insect to carry out His will. However He chooses to effect His will, whatever occurs, happens only because He wills it. The most powerful angel has less ability to thwart the wisdom of God than has a child to change the direction of a hurricane by blowing at it — because the child's breath, slight though it is, has some minute force, but the angel's very existence is purely an extension of God's will to act.

The most powerful angel has less ability to thwart the wisdom of God than has a child to change the direction of a hurricane by blowing at it.

Thus, by definition, an angel is but an expression of God's will. If he is not that, he ceases to exist; he is like a thought without a thinker, a word without a speaker — a contradiction in terms. Man, however, *has* independent existence, for he was created to exercise his God-given freedom of choice — and given the option *even to defy God*. The very purpose of his creation was that he exercise that choice justly and fight the unending inner war to do so.

Man, however, has independent existence, for he was created to exercise his God-given freedom of choice — and given the option even to defy God.

How to Prevail Over Self

אֵיזֶהוּ גִבּוֹר? הַכּוֹבֵשׁ אֶת יִצְרוֹ

Who is the powerful one? He who conquers his own inclination. (Avos 4:1)

The Sages did not indulge in rhetoric when they said this. The struggle for righteousness within man is fiercer than war. It knows no lull, no armistice, no victory. It rages forever as long as man is alive. Everything is foreordained by God for the newly conceived embryo — whether it will be rich or poor, strong or weak, wise or foolish, influential or ignored — but one thing is left for each human being to decide for himself: Whether he will fear God or not *(Berachos* 33b).

Angels are God's agents by their very nature; man must raise himself to that pinnacle. If he succeeds, he is indeed superior to them because he had to fight for his achievement; indeed, he had to fight the most implacable enemy of all — himself.

How does one gain this greatest of all victories? By casting aside the Maginot Lines that blind him to the

truth. By recognizing that truth is an absolute value, not what happens to strike his fancy at any particular moment in life. By declaring in his heart of hearts that only by acknowledging God's mastery and by dedicating himself to unquestioning allegiance to God's word can he hope to perceive the truth when he sees it.

Had Esau's children done that, then they would not have been frightened off by a prohibition against murder. When sensible people are told that their favorite food is poisonous, they may be chagrined, but they will resolve never to eat it again. Fools will disregard the warning and deny the validity of the finding — and continue to gorge themselves with the instrument of their destruction.

When sensible people are told that their favorite food is poisonous, they may be chagrined, but they will resolve never to eat it again. Fools will disregard the warning.

Esau chose his own version of truth, over God's revealed truth. Israel said that it would *first* subordinate its own inclination to God's will, whatever that might be. Having so resolved, it would then be prepared to listen. But the word וְנִשְׁמָע, *we will listen*, implies more than taking in with the ear. It has the deeper connotation of understanding, of comprehending what is being heard. After first dedicating itself to the truth, Israel could accept the truth. After lifting itself — at least in its aspirations — to the level of angels by pledging itself to become agents of God's will, it could hope to hear and understand His word. To the spiritual person, commitment is the mother of wisdom. It is hardly surprising that people with a sword in their hands, plunder in their minds, and passion in their hearts cannot even comprehend — much less accept — a Torah that insists: 'You shall not kill, you shall not steal, you shall not commit adultery.'

After first dedicating itself to the truth, Israel could accept the truth.

To the spiritual person, commitment is the mother of wisdom.

'Who revealed this secret to My children?' God lovingly asked. It is the secret of the angels, for they, too, know that first comes the dedication to act upon God's will. The angels know it because it is created within them, but how can human beings know it unless they have aspired nobly, and uncompromisingly consigned their bodies to the service of their souls?

Armies of angels descended earthward bearing crowns of נַעֲשֶׂה and crowns of נִשְׁמָע, the heavenly recognition of earthly greatness.

There were six hundred thousand pairs of crowns, one pair for each Jewish soldier in God's army. Just as every person's passions and inclinations are unique so is his mission unique; and, therefore, the obstacles facing him are unique. Each Jew said, 'We will do and we will hear.' Each individual thereby achieved his own measure of greatness, and thereby created crowns of spiritual royalty that were distinctively his.

Each individual thereby achieved his own measure of greatness, and thereby created crowns of spiritual royalty that were distinctively his.

An Altered Way When Israel sinned by worshiping the Golden Calf, the angels returned and withdrew the crowns. By failing to maintain its commitment to God's will, Israel fell from its lofty estate. (The affair of the Golden Calf will be discussed in the Commentary and *Overview* to *Ki Sisa*, ArtScroll ed.). All was not lost, however.

אֲבַדְתֶּם נַעֲשֶׂה, הִזָּהֲרוּ בְּנִשְׁמָע

You have lost [your attainment] of we will do, be vigilant of we will hear.

Simply understood, this saying of the Sages indicates that the angelic pinnacle of total dedication was irretrievably lost, but that Israel should beware not to give up its obligation to hear and obey the commandments of the Torah. Not so, taught *Chiddushei Harim*. The mission of Israel remained the same, only the tactics to attain it had changed. In its finest hour, it had placed loyalty to God above every personal consideration and had thereby earned the approbation of God and the fealty of angels. That degree of selflessness became the vehicle by which the nation could attain an understanding of God's word, the Torah. A nation that could erect a golden calf could no longer aspire to such greatness. But Torah has a power of its own. It is God's word, God's will, God's wisdom. By obeying its dictates and immersing himself in its study, the Jew can elevate himself again toward the level of *'we will do'*.

By obeying its dictates and immersing himself in its study, the Jew can elevate hiself again toward the level of 'we will do'.

As he becomes so ennobled, his understanding of the Torah becomes deeper and broader. He can begin to see in it the mysteries of creation (see *Overview* to *Bereishis*, ArtScroll ed.). As he does, his dedication to God grows, thus, in turn, furthering his understanding of Torah. The spiral can continue upward as our greatest have proven by personal example. Or, if the individual fails to discharge his responsibilities to himself and the Torah, it can reverse and go downward.

[The above treatment was based primarily on *Maharal*, most prominently *Tiferes Yisrael* 29.]

II. God's Glory — Purpose of Creation

His Plan By its acknowledgment of the obligation to elevate itself to the level of the angels, Israel was fulfilling the purpose of creation to proclaim God's glory throughout the universe:

כֹּל מַה שֶׁבָּרָא הקב״ה בְּעוֹלָמוֹ לֹא בְּרָאוֹ אֶלָּא לִכְבוֹדוֹ שֶׁנֶּאֱמַר כֹּל הַנִּקְרָא בִשְׁמִי וְלִכְבוֹדִי בְּרָאתִיו יְצַרְתִּיו אַף עֲשִׂיתִיו וְאוֹמֵר ה' יִמְלֹךְ לְעֹלָם וָעֶד

Whatever the Holy One, blessed be He, created in this world, He created only for His glory, as it says: Everything that is called after My Name and that I have created for My glory have I formed and I have fashioned it (Isaiah 43:7). And it says: HASHEM shall reign forever (Exodus 15:18) (Avos 6:11, Yoma 38a, Avos d'Rabbi Nosson 41:16).

Everything in creation which exists to serve righteous man — from the mighty stars to microscopic amoebas — all were created only for God's glory. *Everything that is called after [God's] Name* — the righteous who are dedicated to His service and whose lives are sanctifications of His Name — and everything in creation which exists to serve righteous man — from the mighty stars to microscopic amoebas — all were created only for God's glory.

This is not even to suggest that God *requires* the glorification of man or angel. Before the creation of the universe He was alone and lacked nothing. There was a vacuum beyond our comprehension — no angel sang 'Holy', no man did His will — but He lacked nothing. By definition, God is perfect and without need for anything. That He desires to do good, or to be glorified by human beings, or that creation be perfected by the performance of His commandments — these are because He, in His infinite lovingkindness, *wishes* it to be so, not that He requires them in order to achieve fulfillment.

It serves no purpose to inquire why His will decreed this purpose for creation, just as it is useless to speculate on why the laws of physics must be what they are.

Therefore, it serves no purpose to inquire *why* His will decreed this purpose for creation, just as it is useless to speculate on why the laws of physics must be what they are. One may devise an intellectually compelling thesis for the annulment of the law of gravity, but he would be best advised not to act upon his conclusions by stepping over the edge of a canyon. Just as the scientist must tailor his thesis to reality rather than vice-versa, the inquisitive human being must tailor his goals in life to the reality of existence. That reality is the goal of God's glorification, and the steps to achieve it are outlined in the Torah. Most assuredly the steps could have been different had He so wished it. But the expression of His will is *this* world, *these* conditions, and *this* mission — and it is for us to study, understand, and fulfill His wish as He has given us the ability to do so.

Kingship — Final Manifestation

When man transforms himself into an expression of God's glory, the result is הי יִמְלֹךְ לְעֹלָם וָעֶד, *HASHEM shall reign forever* [*Exodus* 15:18]. In the *Ten Sefiras*, the ten stages by which God's will emanates and finds expression in creation, the final one is מַלְכוּת, *kingship*, the outward manifestation of His will. When man acts in such a way that God's glory is apparent on earth, then He is the acknowledged King. His Presence becomes a reality rather than a goal, and *Shechinah* rests on earth.

Holiness is not created by Physical Man; it exists

independently of him — it was there before him and it will survive him; it exists concurrently with him no matter what sort of life he lives. How can flesh-and-blood, physical, lustful, animalistic man create holiness? This is a question which has troubled philosophers down through the centuries. The answer is that man does not *create* holiness at all, he merely removes the obstructions that prevent it from reigning; he controls his body so that his soul can shine through. When he succeeds in doing so, and to the extent that he does so, he enthrones God over himself and over earth, and makes Him King. The Sages teach that had Israel proclaimed at the splitting of the sea מֶלֶךְ ה׳, HASHEM 'IS' King — not that He *will* be King at some undetermined future date — then the final and complete redemption would have come immediately. There would have been no further exiles or oppressions, and mankind's still unended travail prior to God's eventual coronation, would never have taken place. Israel reached an exalted height in perceiving that God would *one day* become King, but it fell somewhat short of recognizing the spiritual glory that already lay within each person and on each place on earth. For people can be either the throne of Divine glory, or the obstruction that prevents it from finding a place on earth.

The angels are the instruments of God's will in the universe. Therefore, שְׁמוֹ שֶׁל הקב״ה מְשֻׁתָּף עִם כָּל מַלְאָךְ וּמַלְאָךְ, The Name of the Holy One, blessed be He, is joined with that of every angel (Tanchuma Mishpatim 18); i.e., God's Name is alluded to in the suffix or numerical value of every angel's name. גַּבְרִיאֵל, Gavriel represents God's quality of strength (גְּבוּרָה=strength, אֵל=God); רְפָאֵל, Refael, His quality of healing (רְפוּאָה=healing); מִיכָאֵל, Michael, His matchlessness (מִי=who, כָּאֵל=is like God). [Indeed, Michael is uniquely the angel associated with Israel, because Israel's mission is to establish for all humanity that there is none like God.] The angelic songs of praise to God are the acknowledgement of spiritual greatness — the exaltation that stands ready

Man does not create holiness at all, he merely removes the obstructions that prevent it from reigning; he controls his body so that his soul can shine through.

Michael is uniquely the angel associated with Israel, because Israel's mission is to establish for all humanity that there is none like God.

to envelope the Jew who conquers his body; that stands ready to exalt the earth when the Jew says, feels, lives, epitomizes ה׳ מֶלֶךְ, *HASHEM is King.*

The Gift of Interdependence

There is no way to express fully the greatness of God, but whatever is possible is within Israel's power to accomplish.

As the poet says in *Akdamus,* there is no way to express fully the greatness of God. Were the heavens parchment, the seas ink, the forests quills, the people scribes, it still could not be done. The angels cannot do it, man cannot do it. Neither is Israel charged with accomplishing more than the conditions of creation render possible. But whatever *is* possible is within Israel's power to accomplish. By accepting the Torah and ascending to the angelic mystery of *we will do,* Israel became God's instrument on earth. It became *greater* than the angels, because while the angels can be the instruments that proclaim holiness on high and carry out His will below, only Israel can make earth the Chariot of His Presence; only Israel can achieve the fulfillment of creation.

God and Israel are partners, therefore — not that the two are equal in absolute terms, of course; even the thought is unthinkable. But since His will decreed that His desired purpose can be achieved only when His holiness becomes melded with Israel, the two must interact to achieve His goal.

It is axiomatic that whatever God decreed should be the goal of the universe, must be attainable.

It is axiomatic that whatever God decreed should be the goal of the universe, must be attainable. If He wished that Israel should perceive His holiness and become its Chariot on earth, then it is possible for the Jew to do so. Of course, this not to suggest that we can conceive of His *true* essence, but there is a minute portion which we can comprehend. God told Moses, לְפִי מַעֲשַׂי אֲנִי נִקְרָא, *I am called according to My deeds.* Sometimes I am perceived as the God of mercy, sometimes in judgment, sometimes in strength, sometimes in nature *(Sh'mos Rabbah* 3). Moses, who had hoped to know God's true essence, was not truly rebuffed; he was told what man's role is. Man is not expected to perceive God's essence — he cannot. But he *is* expected to recognize God as He manifests Himself in creation; recognize Him,

proclaim Him, and thereby create the conditions for His presence to rest on earth. Puny though he is, man can exercise a veto over the fulfillment of God's will, for only man can satisfy God's desire to be recognized on earth.

Puny though he is, man can exercise a veto over the fulfillment of God's will, for only man can satisfy God's desire to be recognized on earth.

Therefore God says of Israel:

יוֹנָתִי תַמָּתִי — תְּאוֹמָתִי

My dove, My complete one — My twin

רַב יַנַּאי אָמַר תְּאוֹמָתִי כְּבִיָכוֹל, לֹא אֲנִי גָדוֹל מִמֶּנָּה וְלֹא הִיא גְדוֹלָה מִמֶּנִּי

Rav Yanai said, [She is] My twin, as it were. I [God] am not greater than she nor is she greater than I (Shir HaShirim Rabbah 5:2)

Whatever conception we have of Him is possible only because He deigns to reveal Himself to us, and the purpose of our existence is so that He can make it possible for us to glimpse something of His holiness. Although the level of our perception is further from His ultimate truth than is an anthill from Everest, yet that is what He decreed for us, and on *that* level, God permits Israel to be His equal, as it were. In His mercy, there is an interdependence between man and God: without Him, all is nothing, but without our recognition of holiness, His purpose goes unfulfilled (*Nefesh HaChaim* 2:3).

Without Him, all is nothing, but without our recognition of holiness, His purpose goes unfulfilled.

As *Maharal* explains, this 'twin' relationship is constant and on-going. As man draws closer to God by performing commandments, God reveals His brilliance to man resulting in the sublime joy of the spirit. Let man draw away from God, and the conduits of his spiritual lot will slowly close, leaving him saddened and depressed. God's holiness remains undiminished — for man's deeds or misdeeds can effect no change in Him — but man affects himself. Just as he can pull down his shades and shut out the sun or open them and bathe himself in light, so he can allow God's Face to shine upon him, or cause It to turn away (*B'er Hagolah*).

Activated Potential The ability to receive holiness and to transform the universe into its receptacle is a gift. Animals don't have it; angels don't have it. Israel has it. This capacity is more than the performance of deeds; an Israelite who performs the Temple service instead of a priest, would bring no benefits to the world even if he were not specifically forbidden to do so. His act would be unavailing because it was not commanded by God. A person with the purest of motives who concocted a seemingly sacred religious observance would be deluding himself if he felt that he were doing more than providing himself with a distraction. Even Rabbinically ordained commandments are binding only because the Torah grants the right to the Sages to institute such enactments (see *Overview* to *Bereishis*).

Israel's ability to bring holiness into the world was granted it by God with the giving of the Torah. Israel's ability to bring holiness into the world was granted it by God with the giving of the Torah. True, the nation's capacity to do so, already existed. It was won by Abraham who picked up the human debris left by Adam's sin and the failure of subsequent generations to remedy its damage (see *Overview ibid.*), and transmitted to his descendants. But Abraham had but created the *potential* for Israel's future mission; thanks to Abraham's merit, his descendants received the ability to be the levers of the world's fulfillment. However, the carrying out of the mission was dependent upon the future revelation and — most importantly — God's designation of Israel as the nation which would receive the Torah. Until then, Abraham's spiritual greatness carried with it the *potential* of Israel's future greatness. It may be likened to one who is selected for high office based on his proven ability; the powers of office, however, are not his until the designated time. By giving the Torah, God activated the potential and made it a reality. Just as He daily renews creation, so He renews Israel's unique role within it.

By giving the Torah, God activated the potential and made it a reality. Just as He daily renews creation, so He renews Israel's unique role within it. This result of God's command is implicit in the Talmudic dictum: גָּדוֹל הַמְצֻוֶּה וְעוֹשֶׂה מִמִּי שֶׁאֵינוֹ מְצֻוֶּה וְעוֹשֶׂה, *One who is commanded and fulfills is*

greater than one who is not commanded but still fulfills (Kiddushin 31a). The Divine command confers validity upon a deed. As long as the act is voluntary, it is an expression of the personality of the doer; let the deed be done in response to God's command, however, and it becomes a lever that implements the goal of revealing holiness on earth.

As long as the act is voluntary, is an expression of the personality of the doer; let the deed be done in response to God's command, however, and it becomes a lever that implements the goal of revealing holiness on earth.

God did this at Mount Sinai. We say that Israel received 'the Torah' when it stood at the mountain — but it didn't. Only the Ten Commandments were given then, not the entire Torah. Other commandments were given during the year that Israel was encamped at the mountain, but many commandments were first conveyed to Israel only during its later years in the Wilderness. Nevertheless we speak of that fateful fiftieth day after the Exodus as the day the *Torah* was given, for it was then that the *power to receive the Torah and to implement its potential* were conferred. It was then that Israel became the nation that was and is מְצֻוֶּה וְעוֹשֶׂה, the nation that was *commanded*, and because it was, it had the ability to make its deeds efficacious in the revelation of holiness on earth. Then, Israel was granted the spiritual qualities that were to remain the tangible symbols of its chosenness.

Commandments were indeed given later, but *Torah* — God's blueprint for creation and Israel's plan in elevating the universe — was given then. This concept explains an apparent difficulty in the Passover *Haggadah*. In the *Dayeinu* song, we thank God for fifteen benefits which he bestowed on us from the time of the Exodus until the building of the Temple. Among the list are that He brought us to Sinai and, as a second gift, that He gave us the Torah. But the question is logically put forward: what purpose could there have been in coming to Sinai without having received the Torah? Would not the coming to Sinai have been meaningless without the Torah? The two *are*, in fact, separate. We thank God for bringing us to Sinai for it was there that He designated us as His people and His instruments; his 'twin' and the

We thank God for bringing us to Sinai for it was there that He designated us as His people and His instruments; his 'twin' and the agent of His fulfillment.

agent of His fulfillment. Some of the Torah was given there, some later — but the Torah is a gift entirely distinct from that presented at Sinai.

[The foregoing section is based primarily on *Da'as Tevunos*.]

III. Israel and the Nations

Rose and Thorns

Small wonder that the nations decry the impetuosity of Israel in pledging itself to cleave to the Torah without regard to any other consideration; 'How could they know?'

Small wonder that the nations decry the impetuosity of Israel in pledging itself to cleave to the Torah without regard to any other consideration; that they are aghast at Israel's stubborn refusal to give up its Godly heritage despite the suffering and degradation strewn in its path; that they offer blandishments and seductions to entice Israel to assimilate with them. As the poet of *Akdamus* exclaims, 'How could they know?' How could they understand that the tinsel of their lures has no value to the nation that spoke face to face with God, that walks hand in hand with Him, that alone fulfills the goal of His creation.

כְּמַעֲשֵׂה אֶרֶץ מִצְרַיִם אֲשֶׁר יְשַׁבְתֶּם בָּהּ לֹא תַעֲשׂוּ וּכְמַעֲשֵׂה אֶרֶץ כְּנַעַן אֲשֶׁר אֲנִי מֵבִיא אֶתְכֶם שָׁמָּה לֹא תַעֲשׂוּ

Like the deeds of the land of Egypt in which you dwelled, do not do; and like the deeds of the land of Canaan to which I bring you, do not do (Leviticus 18:3).

As Israel was encamped in the Sinai Desert, poised to enter *Eretz Yisrael*, God commanded them against the various forms of immorality. In introduction to the chapter, He warned them not to indulge in the immorality they had observed in Egypt and to which they would be exposed in Canaan. Surrounded by nations steeped in lust, Israel had to remain pure. It was, indeed, a שׁוֹשַׁנָּה בֵּין הַחוֹחִים, *a rose among the thorns!*

Rabbi Azariah said in behalf of Rabbi Yehudah ben Simon: It is like the parable

of a king [*whose beautiful orchard was neglected until it was overgrown with weeds and thorns*]. *The king brought workmen and ordered them to cut down all the overgrowth. He peered at the thorns and saw a single rose. He took it and smelled it and was refreshed. The king said, 'Because of this rose, the entire orchard will be saved.' Such was the world. It was created only for the sake of the Torah. After the passage of twenty-six generations [from creation to the exodus] the Holy One, blessed be He, peered at His universe to know what He had wrought ... [It had sinned and grown corrupt, and God saw fit to destroy it.] Then He saw one rose — Israel. He took it and smelled it when He presented it with the Ten Commandments. He was refreshed by it when it said, 'We will do and we will hear'. [God] said, 'Because of this rose, the orchard was saved; because of the Torah and Israel, the world will be saved' (Vayikra Rabbah 23).*

The continued existence of the world — the thorns that had overgrown a once pristine creation — was in jeopardy.

But there was a rose — Israel.

As the commentators explain, the continued existence of the world — the thorns that had overgrown a once pristine creation — was in jeopardy. It corrupted its deeds further and further until the 'King' was ready to destroy it completely. But there was a rose — Israel. If Israel would accept the Torah the world would be saved. If not, then it, too, would become no different from the thorns and there would be no purpose in preserving an impossibly flawed universe. Israel was tested at Sinai. It accepted the Torah and the world was preserved.

The Thorns Are Needed

But why, asks *Sifse Tzaddik*, did the king find it necessary to preserve the loathsome thorns for the sake of the precious rose — why did he not destroy the thorns and preserve the rose? Although the flesh-and-blood king of the parable could not salvage the one while destroying the others, surely the King of

Kings could do as He wished. Had He not distinguished between the seed of Israel's first-born and the seed of Egypt's? Furthermore, the human king was surprised and chagrined at the sight of his once beautiful orchard which had become an almost unredeemed wilderness, but God knew when He created them that the nations would become thorns. Why did He create them if He did not want them?

The *Midrashic* parable reveals the mission of Israel and the hope of creation; all is part of God's plan. It was no happenstance that Israel's formative years were spent amid the moral filth of Egypt and Canaan; that the rose had to grow among the thorns. Abraham, Isaac, and Jacob were holy. Their seed was holy. Israel was holy. But that was not enough. *Everything* that God created had the mission to be holy — or, better said, to let the ever-present holiness seep into itself and turn the universe into God's throne, the open proclamation that He *is* King. Israel's mission was to live among the thorns and *still be a rose.* The nations were Israel's obstacles; its mission was to surmount them. In order for Israel to fulfill its purpose and utilize the tool of Torah and the spirituality granted it at Sinai to perfect the universe, it required the impediments of hostile societies. Just as Adam needed the serpent and the fruit as the test which he should have, but failed to, overcome; just as Noah's generation and the generation of the Dispersion had their challenges which, if overcome, could have been the means to the final attainment of the Divine goal, (see *Overview* to *Bereishis)*, Israel was given its own set of challenges.

The hostility and blandishment of the nations are not extraneous to Israel's mission; they constitute the terms of the mission. *'Live among them. Be challenged by them. Withstand them. Save them. Perfect them. And thereby bring about the final redemption.'* That is the mission.

Israel may long for the luxury of emerging from the thorns and serving God freely, but were it to do so, its mission would be diminished, for it was meant

to elevate the world along with itself. That was the test of the Ten Commandments. God offered the Torah to the nations, but they were incapable of subordinating their natures to its demands. However verdant their exteriors may have appeared, they thereby proved themselves to be sterile thorns, able to hinder but not help; to strangle, but not flower. Had Israel, too, valued its body over its soul, the king's orchard would have lost all hope of producing fruit, and creation would have been ended. But Israel was ready. It accepted the Ten Commandments and showed itself to possess to capacity to refresh its *Maker* by rising to the lofty level of the angels. 'Who taught my children this secret?' Who enabled them to live among thorns yet remain a rose?

However verdant their exteriors may have appeared, they thereby proved themselves to be sterile thorns, able to hinder but not help; to strangle, but not flower.

Because they responded by rising to greatness, God proclaimed Israel as מַמְלֶכֶת כֹּהֲנִים וְגוֹי קָדוֹשׁ, *a kingdom of priests and a holy nation (Exod. 19:6)*. Vestments and pomp do not make a priest. The *Kohain*, the priest, is the one who has the ability to carry out what others only *long* to do. The Jew can consecrate an animal and bring it to the Temple. He can lay his hands upon it and pour out his heart in remorseful repentance for his sin, but without the *Kohain* to perform the service, the Jew's acts and thoughts remain but unfulfilled aspiration. A *Kohain* is one who completes a service and who elevates potential into fact, hope into holiness. Israel, as a *nation* of priests, became to all mankind what the *Kohain* is to Israel. It gained the mission of bringing the potential of the universe to fruition.

Israel, as a nation of priests, became to all mankind what the Kohain is to Israel. It gained the mission of bringing the potential of the universe to fruition.

We were brought close to Mount Sinai. Independent of the individual commandments, we were given the quality of priesthood to the universe.

Inner Perfection

There is a rose among outer thorns; there is a rose among *inner* thorns. Every human being has personal obstacles that stand in the way of achievement. Each has his unique set of thorns, and his life's work is to overcome and ennoble them. The nation is charged with being holy, and so is the individual.

וְהִתְקַדִּשְׁתֶּם וִהְיִיתֶם קְדֹשִׁים

Hallow yourselves, and be holy (Leviticus 20:7)

To the extent that you labor at the unceasing task of bringing holiness into yourselves, you become holy — and, indeed, you make the universe holy. All the visions of the future await the world that permits itself so to become sanctified and perfected.

All the visions of the future await the world that permits itself so to become sanctified and perfected.

The *Holy Zohar* teaches that Israel, before the Torah was given, was like a woman who is unable to nurse, because, until the Torah was given, Israel lacked good deeds. Until the Torah was given, Israel had been perfecting itself, climbing the rungs from the forty-ninth level of impurity to the august level of Sinai. Those were great and inspiring days, yet the *Zohar* could still say that Israel had no good deeds — why? And the simile of the ability to nurse — are we to infer that Israel lacked the capacity to nourish others? What of Abraham who was the epitome of goodness and selfless generosity? What of the hundreds of people whom he taught in Charan and in Canaan, whom he and Sarah *'made'* in the spiritual sense? What of Israel in Egypt which had ignored the ire of its task-masters to help one another in times of affliction and suffering?

Every creature has the capacity to receive and to give. It derives benefits from its betters and provides for those beneath it.

Avnei Nezer explains that every creature has the capacity to receive and to give. It derives benefits from its betters and provides for those beneath it. During its days of preparation to receive the Torah, Israel achieved high levels of greatness: a nation does not divine the mysteries of the angels without intensive efforts. But it was not *giving* — it was perfecting itself, not providing for others. The capacity to nourish the world, to provide sustenance to the barren thorns — was as yet beyond it. Perhaps we may go even further. Without the direction and guidance of Torah, even generosity is lacking in substance, for it is an expression of instinct rather than an embodiment of God's will. Abraham's own instinctive knowledge of Torah, a product of his own unfathomable holiness, was sufficient to sanctify his

own deeds, but not to remove the dangers posed to lesser people by uncurbed generosity (see *Overview* to *Lech Lecha*, ArtScroll ed. for a lengthy discussion of this concept). Israel's unselfishness in Egypt was one of the merits which led to its rescue, but kindness alone had not been enough to prevent it from sinking to the forty-ninth level of impurity by the time the redemption arrived.

Kindness alone had not been enough to prevent it from sinking to the forty-ninth level of impurity by the time the redemption arrived.

When would Israel attain the quality of providing nourishment to others? When would it be able to perfect the world as it was perfecting itself, and when would the warmth, love, and kindness that were Abraham's legacy become elevated to the point where Israel could be said to be fulfilled?

— When the Torah was given. Until then Israel was like a woman who could not nurse. It could receive but not give. It was part of the twenty-six generations which had benefited from God's largesse, but it was not yet able to share in its responsibility as His 'twin.' Then, Israel came to Sinai. It was fulfilled and with it, the world could be relieved, for by its readiness to proclaim *We will do*, it saved the thorns for the time when they would blossom and become the garlands around God's throne.

By its readiness to proclaim We will do, it saved the thorns for the time when they would blossom and become the garlands around God's throne.

Within the *Akdamus*, the sublime song of holiness, are contained all of these concepts. The poet speaks of the impossibility of reciting all of God's praises — yet the obligation not to fall short of whatever it is in our power to do. To do more is beyond man's ability; to do less is to forfeit his opportunity to give purpose to creation. Angels by the myriads, the millions, sing His praises in an inferno of holiness, but every expression of their purest spirituality is but to create the conditions for Israel to raise its free-willed voice in the praise which God craves — for the voice of 'His twin' is the only meaningful complement to His labor for continuous creation.

The poet speaks of the impossibility of reciting all of God's praises — yet the obligation not to fall short of whatever it is in our power to do.

The rose is surrounded by thorny diatribes and blandishments: 'How foolish you are that you worship a God who forsakes you! Join us. We will

Israel answers:
'How can you know,
you nations who
found His Torah too
demanding, His
service too onerous?

honor you, give you position, power, pleasure.'

Israel answers knowing that its reply falls upon uncomprehending ears: 'How can you know, you nations who found His Torah too demanding, His service too onerous? How, as you wallow in your selfish lust, can you perceive the rays of the splendor that awaits us when deeds are measured and recompense apportioned? When the *Shechinah* will return to Jerusalem and the righteous will sit before its splendor? Then we shall rejoice with Him as He shall prepare the Banquet of the End of Days, the feast for which He made the world and placed His Behemoth upon the earth and His Leviathan within the deep.'

The Akdamus *is*
Israel's awakening
to the mission of
Sinai, its ascension
above the song of
the angels and the
impediments of the
thorns, its resolve to
stand ready at Sinai.

The *Akdamus* is Israel's awakening to the mission of Sinai, its ascension above the song of the angels and the impediments of the thorns, its resolve to stand ready at Sinai — the annual Sinai of Shavuos when the emanations of that sacred day are felt again — there to stand and say again 'We will do'; again to rise above the angels and be worthy of the mission of Him Whose holiness is within us.

Rabbi Nosson Scherman

מוקדש לעילוי נשמת

מנחם מענדל מרדכי בן צבי הירש הלוי מַרְדֶר זצ"ל

תלמיד חכם וצדיק, עניו ומאמין,

אוהב תורה ואהוב על הבריות מקבל יסורים באהבה

נצחו אראלים את המצוקים ונשבה הארון

ביום כ"ג ניסן אסרו חג דפסח תשל"ח

יהי זכרו ברוך

אקדמות מלין

א אַקְדָּמוּת מִלִּין,

וְשָׁרָיוּת שׁוּתָא.

ב אַוְלָא שָׁקִילְנָא,

הַרְמָן וּרְשׁוּתָא:

ג בְּבָבֵי תְּרֵי וּתְלָת,

1. אַקְדָּמוּת — *Introduction;* beginning, or opening words; from the root קָדַם, *to be first, to precede.*

מִלִּין — *Words;* the plural of מִילָא (see notes to verse 88), used here to mean utterances as in *Daniel 7:25,* וּמִלִּין לְצַד עִלָּאָה יְמַלֵּל , *and he shall speak (great) words against the Most High (Bais Levi, Yad Aharon, M'vo HaShir).* See also *Daniel 7:11,* מִלַּיָּא רַבְרְבָתָא, *great words.* The word often refers to the commandments of the Torah, as in מִילֵי דְאוֹרַיְיתָא, *the words of the Torah (Zohar III, 268a).*

וְשָׁרָיוּת — *And the beginning; commencement.* As in *Ezra 5:2,* וְשָׁרִיו לְמִבְנֵא בֵּית אֱלָהָא, *and they began to build the house of God;* and *Targum Onkelos to Deut. 16:9,* מִדְּשָׁרָיוּת מַגְּלָא בַּחֲצַד, *from the beginning of the sickle's cutting.* [It is noteworthy that the name of the first, or beginning, month of the year — *Tishrei* (תִּשְׁרֵי) — is derived from the same root as שָׁרָיוּת (*Ibn Ezra,* סֵפֶר הָעִבּוּר, *Mekize Nirdamim,* Lyck 1874, 4b).]

1. אַקְדָּמוּת מִלִּין — *In introduction to the Words.*

The Words, are the words of the Ten Commandments, which are to be read after the recital of this poem. *Akdamus* was composed as an introduction to the *Meturgeman's* verse-by-verse translation and explanation of the Ten Commandments. Verses 1-4 are the poet's request for *permission* from Hashem and from his listeners to explain the Torah's words [see Introduction].

וְשָׁרָיוּת שׁוּתָא — *And (the) commencement of my speech.*

This phrase can also be translated as *and to the beginning of the speech,* or *and before I begin my speech.* In all three versions, the word *speech* refers to a). the poem about to be read, and b). the poet's subsequent interpretation of the Ten Commandments. This interpretation was to be given in conjunction with the reading of the *Targum* to the Ten Commandments. Both the *Targumic* translation and its interpretation were customarily given as part of the reading of the Torah during the morning service (see Introduction). The poet thus begins this poem by

I n introduction to the Words,

and commencement of my speech,

² First I take

authorization and permission.

³ With two and three sections,

שׁוּתָא — *Speech*, as in a conversation or discourse. The word is most accurately translated by the German and Yiddish words *gesprach*, and *rede*.

2. אוּלָא — *Firstly; at the beginning; at the outset*; as in the *Targum Yonasan* on *Genesis* 1:1, מִן אַוְולָא, *from the beginning* [*of the creation of the world*]. See also *Targum* on *Isaiah* 43:18.

שָׁקְלְנָא — *I* (wish to) *take*; contraction of שָׁקֵל אֲנָא, *I take. (Berger).*

הַרְמָן — *Authorization*; also, *decree; command*. Used in the *Talmud* to denote the royal authorization or decree issued by a king; as in *Bava Metzia* 83b: הַרְמָנָא דְמַלְכָּא, *the authorization of the king* (See also *Rashi, Chulin* 57b).

3. בְּבָבֵי — The plural of בָּבָא, *section, clause*; also: *door, gate*.

asking for permission to speak.

[The poet's complete Aramaic translation and interpretation of the Ten Commandments can be found in *Machzor Vitry* of *Rabbeinu Simcha*, pp. 338-344.]

2. הַרְמָן וּרְשׁוּתָא — *Authorization and permission.*

At the outset the poet requests הַרְמָן, *authorization*, from Hashem, the King of the Universe, and also רְשׁוּתָא, *permission* to speak from his congregation of listeners. Hence the double use of two basically synonymous words *(M'vo HaShir).*

3. בְּבָבֵי תְּרֵי וּתְלָת — *With two and three sections.*

This verse is both a continuation of the previous passage and a part of the subsequent verse. The poet is

saying that with the two major and three subordinate sections of the work (see below), he asks for authorization and permission to go on to the reading of the Ten Commandments and its interpretation.

The phrase *two and three sections* refers to the two major and three subordinate themes into which the poem is divided. The major themes are:
1) the greatness of the Creator of the universe, blessed be His name (verses 5-14); and
2) the virtuousness of the Jewish people in keeping their faith in God and in fulfilling the commandments of the Torah despite the oppression and ridicule of the nations around them (verses 31-52).

דְּאֶפְתַּח בִּנְקָשׁוּתָא.

ד בִּבְרֵי דְבָרֵי וְטָרֵי,
עֲדִי *לְקַשִׁישׁוּתָא: לְקַשִּׁישׁוּתָא

ה גְּבוּרָן עָלְמִין לֵיהּ,

LEXICAL NOTES

בִּנְקָשׁוּתָא — *With trembling*; from the root נְקַשׁ, *to knock, to strike against*; as in *Daniel* 5:6, וְאַרְכֻּבָּתֵהּ דָּא לְדָא נָקְשָׁן, *his knees were knocking one against the other* [because of great fear and trepidation] (*Bais Levi*, and *M'vo HaShir*).

4. בִּבְרֵי — *With the permission* [of God]; as in *Succah* 45b, דְעָיֵילִי בְּבָר, *they may go up* [to the place of the Shechinah only] *with permission* (ibid. *Rashi*; also *Sanhedrin* 97b).

דְבָרֵי — *Who created*; from בְּרָא, *to create.*

וְטָרֵי — *Protects, guards*; from the root נְטַר *to guard, protect, shield, oversee*; also *to hold back*, as to hold back one's anger as in *Bereishis Rabbah* 55:3 on the verse in *Leviticus* 19:18.

COMMENTARY

The three subordinate themes are:
1) a description of the heavenly angels, praising Hashem (verses 15-30);
2) the greatness of the Torah (a theme which pervades the entire poem); and,
3) a description of the reward awaiting the righteous in Paradise for upholding the Torah, (verses 62-88) (*T'yul B'gan*).
Another interpretation of the poet's use of the words תְּרֵי וּתְלַת, *two and three*, is in accord with the following passage:
וַיִּצְעַק מֹשֶׁה אֶל ה' לֵאמֹר אֵ-ל נָא רְפָא נָא לָהּ. בָּא הַכָּתוּב לְלַמֶּדְךָ דֶּרֶךְ אֶרֶץ שֶׁכָּל זְמַן שֶׁאָדָם רוֹצֶה לְבַקֵּשׁ שְׁאֵלוֹתָיו צָרִיךְ שֶׁיֹּאמַר שְׁנַיִם שְׁלֹשָׁה דִּבְרֵי תַּחֲנוּנִים וְאַחַר כָּךְ יְבַקֵּשׁ שְׁאֵלוֹתָיו

— *And Moses cried to God saying, 'Heal her, O God, I beg You'* (*Numbers* 12:13). *This verse teaches you proper manners — that whenever a person wishes to make a request, he should first say two or three words of supplication, and then ask for what he desires* (*Sifrei, Numbers, Piska* 105).

Since the poet too, is asking God for permission to speak, he first offers prayers of praise to the Holy One (*Yad Aharon*).

[For a complete explanation of the use of such terms as *two and three*, see *Tosafos, Succah* 2b s.v. אמה וחמשים וארבעים עד (*Yad Aharon*).]

דְּאֶפְתַּח — *By which I begin* (my discourse).

The poet, in his use of the word אֶפְתַּח, hints at the following dictum

by which I begin with trembling,

⁴ *With permission from Him Who created all and shields it*

till its hoary age.

⁵ *Eternal strength is His*

LEXICAL NOTES

עֲדֵי לְקַשִּׁישׁוּתָא — *Till its* [the world's] *hoary age* from עַד, *until*; and קַשִּׁישׁוּתָא, *Old age*. [See for example: *Bava Basra* 142b].

5. גְּבוּרָן — *Strength; power.*

עָלְמִין — I. *Eternal, infinite* or *limitless* (in time or in strength). II. *Worlds,* from the plural of עָלְמָא, *world.*

לֵיה — *To Him* (God).

COMMENTARY

(*Berachos* 4b): Rav Yochanan said: At the beginning [i.e., before commencing the recitation of the *Shemoneh Esrei*], one should recite the following verse, אֲדֹנָי שְׂפָתַי תִּפְתָּח וּפִי יַגִּיד תְּהִלָּתֶךְ — *O Lord, open my lips, so that my mouth may declare Your praise* [*Psalms* 51:17] (*Kinyan Tov* 1, and *Eshel Avraham*).

4. בְּבָרֵי דְבָרֵי וְטָרֵי — *With permission from Him Who created all and shields it* [i.e., the world].

In the first three verses the poet makes no mention of whom he asks permission from. This point is clarified in this verse (*Yad Aharon*).

The verse is an Aramaic paraphrase of *Isaiah* 46:4:

וְעַד זִקְנָה אֲנִי הוּא וְעַד שֵׂיבָה אֲנִי אֶסְבֹּל אֲנִי עָשִׂיתִי וַאֲנִי אֶשָּׂא וַאֲנִי אֶסְבֹּל וַאֲמַלֵּט — *Until old age I am He; until your extreme old age I will bear you; I have made* [Israel] *and I will carry,* sustain and deliver her. While the verse plainly refers to the Jewish people, the *Talmud* and *Mishnah* interpret it as referring to God's creation and sustenance of the world. Though the world is old and lacking in good deeds, God, in His mercy; hotds back His anger, protecting and maintaining the universe, allowing it continued existence (*Sanhedrin* 38b; *Sh'mos Rabbah* 36; *Vayikra Rabbah*, 4, *Tanchuma*, *Bereishis* 9; and elsewhere.)

5. גְּבוּרָן עָלְמִין לֵיה — *Eternal* (or *infinite*) *strength is His.*

God's strength never weakens nor ages with the passing of time.

The word עָלְמִין can also be translated *world* or *universe*. Accordingly, the phrase could be rendered: *The strength of the world* (or *universe*) *is His.* God has ab-

[51]   *Akdamus*

סְפֵק

וְלָא *סְפֵק פְּרִישׁוּתָא.

ו   גְּוִיל אִלּוּ רְקִיעֵי,

קְנֵי כָּל חוּרְשָׁתָא:

ז   דְּיוֹ אִלּוּ יַמֵּי,

וְכָל מֵי כְנִישׁוּתָא.

LEXICAL NOTES

וְלָא סְפֵק — From סְפַק, to supply; to furnish; also to be sufficient, to have enough.

פְּרִישׁוּתָא — Explicit explanation; a complete description; from פֵּירוּשׁ.

6. גְּוִיל — Parchment; see Targum Yonasan on Deuteronomy 31:24.

אִלּוּ — If that; or would they be.

רְקִיעֵי — The skies, the heavens.

COMMENTARY

solute power over the totality of the universe.

Both interpretations convey a sense of the strength and greatness of God.

[This phrase is taken from the *Targum* of *Habakuk* 3:6: גְּבוּרַת עָלְמָא דִּילֵיהּ, *Eternal strength is His*; or, alternatively, *the strength of the world is His*. Similarly, the *Targum ibid.* 3:3 is בִּגְבוּרַת עָלְמִין אִתְחֲפִיאוּ שְׁמַיָּא, *The heavens were covered with His eternal strength* (*Yad Aharon; Shnei Ha'me'oros*). This concept is expressed three times daily, during the *Shemoneh Esrei* prayer: אַתָּה גִבּוֹר לְעוֹלָם, *You are mighty forever*. The Hebrew text of *Habakuk* reads הֲלִיכוֹת עוֹלָם לוֹ, *All the workings of the world are under His direction* (*Rashi, Habakuk* 3:6): An alternate translation is, *His ways are everlasting*, i.e., God has not changed His ways since the giving of the Torah at Sinai, and the Exodus from Egypt.

Note that *Habakuk* 2:20 to 3:19 is read as the *Haftarah* of the second day of Shavuos. The poet paraphrases *Habakuk* and *Ezekiel* I extensively because they are read as the Haf-

toros of the second and first days of Shavuos respectively. (See *Introduction*.)]

וְלָא סְפֵק פְּרִישׁוּתָא — *Beyond description;* [literally, *and which cannot be given adequate description.*]

There is no being and there are no words that can adequately describe God's strength and greatness. The poet alludes to the following Midrash:

מִי יְמַלֵּל גְּבוּרוֹת ה' יַשְׁמִיעַ כָּל תְּהִלָּתוֹ. וְכִי יֵשׁ אָדָם בָּעוֹלָם שֶׁהוּא יָכוֹל לְמַלֵּל גְּבוּרָתוֹ שֶׁל הַקָּדוֹשׁ בָּרוּךְ הוּא אוֹ לְהַשְׁמִיעַ כָּל תְּהִלָּתוֹ. אֲפִילוּ מַלְאֲכֵי הַשָּׁרֵת אֵינָן יְכוֹלִין לְסַפֵּר אֶלָּא מִקְצָת גְּבוּרָתָיו

— Who can utter the mighty acts of God, and who can enunciate His praise (Psalms 106:2)? Is there any man in the world who can express the strength and greatness of the Holy One, blessed be He, or who

אקדמות   [52]

beyond description —

6 *Were all the skies parchment,*

were all the forests quills,

7 *Were all the seas ink,*

and all the gathered waters,

קְנֵי — *Quills;* literally *reeds* from which pens are made. A quill is usually called קוֹלְמוֹס, see *comm.* to verse 8 below.

חוּרְשָׁנָא — *Forests, dense forests or thickets;* from חוֹרְשָׁא, as in the *Targum* of *Psalms* 80:14 (Hebrew text: יַעַר, *forest, wood*).

קְנֵי כָל חוּרְשָׁתָא — *A dense, impassable forest;* as חוֹרְשָׁא שֶׁל קָנִים, *a dense forest of reeds* (*Shir HaShirim Rabbah* 1:8; *Koheles Rabbah* 2:14).

7. כְּנִישׁוּתָא — *Gatherings,* the plural of כְּנִישְׁתָּא: from the root כְּנַשׁ, *to gather, collect.*

can enunciate His Praise? — Even the ministering angels are able to recount only a small fraction of His greatness (*Pirkei d'Rabbi Eliezer,* 3).

Similarly, *Rashi* to *Exodus* 15:1 states:

עַל כָּל הַשִּׁירוֹת וְכָל מַה שֶׁאֲקַלֵּס בּוֹ עוֹד
יֵשׁ בּוֹ תּוֹסֶפֶת וְלֹא כְּמִדַּת מֶלֶךְ בָּשָׂר וָדָם
שֶׁמְקַלְּסִין אוֹתוֹ וְאֵין בּוֹ

— *Above all the songs and whatever I can praise him more can always be added. Unlike a flesh and blood king, who is praised though it is not in him* (i.e., the compliments are but empty flattery).

Rashi's comment is based on the *Mechilta, Piska d'Shiratha,* 2; and *Tanchuma, B'Shallach* 11, on כִּי גָאֹה

גָאָה, *for He is highly exalted,* (*Exodus* 15:1).

6. גְּוִיל אֵלוּ רְקִיעֵי — *Were all the skies parchment.*

If all the skies were parchment, and all the forests pens, they would nevertheless be inadequate to describe fully God's strength and greatness. This verse as well as verses 7 and 8, are parenthetical. The main thought, that God's strength and glory are beyond description, begins in *v.* 5 and continues in *v.* 9. Vs. 6-9 elaborate, saying that even if unlimited resources were available to aid in the attempt, the depiction of God's greatness would still be an impossible task.

ח דָּיְרֵי אַרְעָא סָפְרֵי,

וְרָשְׁמֵי רַשְׁוָתָא:

ט הֲדַר מָרֵי שְׁמַיָּא,

וְשַׁלִּיט בְּיַבֶּשְׁתָּא.

הֲקֵם; יְחִידָאֵי י *הֲקֵם עָלְמָא יְחִידָאֵי,

LEXICAL NOTES

8. דָּיְרֵי — *Inhabitants, dwellers; from* דַּיּוֹר.

אַרְעָא — *Land, earth.*

סָפְרֵי — *Writers, scribes; the plural of* סַפְרָא.

וְרָשְׁמֵי — *And recorders of,* [literally; *and markers of;*] *from the roots* רָשַׁם, *to mark* (characters of writing), *and* רִישׁוּם, *record, engrave. As in the Targum to Ezekiel* 9:4, וְתִרְשׁוּם תְּוָא — *and you should engrave a mark.*

רַשְׁוָתָא — *The first letter of every word; the first letter or word of each chapter* (רָאשֵׁי פְּרָקִים); *from* רֵישְׁתָא, *beginning, first (M'vo HaShir).*

COMMENTARY

8. וְרָשְׁמֵי רַשְׁוָתָא — *And recorders of the initials* (of every chapter!)

Were all the world's inhabitants scribes, writing only the initials of chapters depicting God's greatness, and all its waters ink, it would still be impossible to record all the praises of the Holy One, blessed be He *(Yad Aharon; Zos Nechemosi).*

[This simile appears many times in *Talmud* and *Midrash*, as for example in *Sabbath* 11a:

וְאָמַר רָבָא בַּר מְחַסְיָא אָמַר רַב חָמָא בַּר גּוּרְיָא אָמַר רַב: אִם יִהְיוּ כָּל הַיַּמִּים דְּיוֹ וַאֲגַמִּים קוּלְמוֹסִים וְשָׁמַיִם יְרִיעוֹת וְכָל בְּנֵי אָדָם לַבְלָרִין אֵין מַסְפִּיקִים לִכְתּוֹב חֲלָלָה שֶׁל רְשׁוּת

— *Said Rava the son of M'chasya, in the name of Rav Chama son of Gurya in the name of Rav: If all the seas were ink, and all the fields were overgrown with quills and all the heavens were folios and all the people scribes — they would still be insufficient to describe the complexities of administering a*

government. The Talmud speaks of the complexities of running the government of a king of flesh and blood. How infinitely more complex is the universe of the King of the World! *(Yad Aharon; M'vo HaShir).* Other examples are: *Shir HaShirim Rabbah* 1:20; *Sofrim* 16:8; *Avos d'Rabbi Nassan* 25. Also the liturgical poems *Chasdei Hashem* and *Ayom v'Nora* of the seventh and eighth days of Passover, respectively.]

9. הֲדַר מָרֵי שְׁמַיָּא — *The glory of the Master of heaven.*

This verse continues the theme beginning with *v.* 5 (see *comm.* to *v.* 6), and is a paraphrase of *Psalms* 145:12. Even if all the world were indeed filled with ink, pens, paper and scribes, it would still not be possible *to make known to the sons of Man His mighty acts, and the glorious majesty of His kingdom* (*Eshel Avraham*).

⁸ *The dwellers of earth, scribes*

        and recorders of initials —

⁹ *The glory of the Master of heaven*

        and Ruler of earth.

¹⁰ *Who established earth in Oneness*

9. הֲדַר — *Glory, beauty*; see also notes to *v.* 88.

מָרֵי — *Lord, master.*

וְשַׁלִּיט — *And the ruler of*; from שָׁלַט, *to rule, to have dominion over.*

בְּיַבֶּשְׁתָּא — *Upon the earth*, [literally: *dry land*] as in *Daniel* 2:10, לָא אִיתַי אֱנָשׁ עַל יַבֶּשְׁתָּא, *there is not a man upon the earth* [who can interpret a dream without having heard it first] (*M'vo HaShir*).

10. הֲקֵם — *He erected, put up*, the past tense of הֵקִים.

עָלְמָא — *The world.*

יְחִידָאֵי — *Alone; single-handedly*; from יָחִיד.

וְשַׁלִּיט בְּיַבֶּשְׁתָּא — *And Ruler of earth.*

The phrase is a brief allusion to *Psalms* 145:13: — *Your kingdom is an everlasting kingdom and Your dominion extends throughout all generations* (*Eshel Avraham*).

10. The poet now proceeds to speak of God's greatness after having made clear his realization that an adequate description is beyond human capability.

הֲקֵם עָלְמָא יְחִידָאֵי — *Who established earth in Oneness.*

God created the world by Himself without the help or advice of anyone. This phrase alludes to *Bereishis Rabbah* 1:

When were the angels created?

Rav Yochanan says on the second day [of creation] … and Rav Chanina says on the fifth day … All agree that they were not created on the first day, so that it should not be said that Michael stretched [the world] from the south, and Gabriel from the north, and the Holy One, blessed be He, was always in the middle. I am God Who created all things. I alone stretched forth the heavens, I spread out the earth [מֵאִתִּי] *by Myself (Isaiah 44:24). The word* מֵאִתִּי *is spelled* מי אתי [lit. *who is with Me*]: i.e., to include who* (מִי) *was a partner with Me* (אִתִּי) *at the creation of the world (Yad Aharon).*

[See also *Bereishis Rabbah* 3; *Tanchuma Buber, Bereishis,* 1 and 12; *Midrash Tehillim* to 24; 86; and 104; and *Yalkut Tehillim* 836.]

וְכַבְּשֵׁיהּ בְּכַבְּשׁוּתָא:

יא   וּבְלָא לֵאוּ שַׁכְלָלֵיהּ,
וּבְלָא תְּשַׁשׁוּתָא.

וְכַבְּשֵׁיהּ — There are three possible definitions: I. *To suppress; to conquer;* (see comm. below); II. *to press, to squeeze;* III. *to conceal;* as in *Leviticus* 20:4: וְאִם הַעְלֵם יַעְלִימוּ, *if they will conceal* which *Onkelos* renders וְאִם מִכְבַּשׁ יְכְבְּשׁוּן.

11. וּבְלָא — *And without.*

לֵאוּ — The word derives from the Hebrew לָאָה and the Aramaic לָאִי, and has two definitions: I. *Fatigue,* as in וַיִּלְאוּ לִמְצֹא הַפָּתַח, *and they tried vainly* [lit. *wearied themselves*] *to find the entrance* (Gen. 19:11); II. *Toil, labor;* (See also notes to verse 35). *(Berger).*

וְכַבְּשֵׁיהּ בְּכַבְּשׁוּתָא — *And suppressed it with constraint.*

This translation is in accordance with the following Talmudic passage:

וְאָמַר רַב יְהוּדָה אָמַר רַב בְּשָׁעָה שֶׁבָּרָא הקב"ה אֶת הָעוֹלָם הָיָה מַרְחִיב וְהוֹלֵךְ כִּשְׁתֵּי פְקָעִיּוֹת שֶׁל שְׁתִי עַד שֶׁגָּעַר בּוֹ הקב"ה וְהֶעֱמִידוֹ. שֶׁנֶּאֱמַר: עַמּוּדֵי שָׁמַיִם יְרוֹפָפוּ וְיִתְמְהוּ מִגַּעֲרָתוֹ.

— *And Rav Yehuda said in the name of Rav: When the Holy One, blessed be He, created the world, it continuously expanded outwards [the world being very eager to obey God's command when it was ordered into existence (M'vo HaShir)] as the two spools of thread extend from the two ends of a warp, until the Holy One, blessed be He, overpowered and halted it. As it says, The pillars of Heaven tremble, and are astonished at His reproof (Job 26:11) [Chagigah 12a] (M'vo HaShir).*

An alternative translation is: *And [He] pressed it (together) firmly.*

The heavens were *pressed* together in the same way that one presses and squeezes something in order to make it hard and firm. This expression is based on the following Midrash:

וַיֹּאמֶר אֱלֹקִים יְהִי רָקִיעַ ... רַב אָמַר לַחִים הָיוּ מַעֲשֵׁיהֶם בַּיּוֹם הָרִאשׁוֹן, וּבַשֵּׁנִי קָרְשׁוּ. יְהִי רָקִיעַ יֵחָזֵק הָרָקִיעַ.

— *And God said, Let there be a firmament (Genesis 1:6) ... Rav says: On the first day of creation the heavens were yet moist, [i.e., soft], and on the second day they hardened. Thus, Let there be a firmament means Let the firmament become hardened (Bereishis Rabbah, 4; see also Rashi to Genesis 1:6).*

A third translation is: *And hid it in concealment.* Only God knows all the intricate workings of the world, for He alone was present when the world was created. As is stated in *Job* (38:4), אֵיפֹה הָיִיתָ בְּיָסְדִי אֶרֶץ הַגֵּד אִם יָדַעְתָּ בִינָה, *Where were you when I laid the foundations of*

and suppressed it with constraint.

¹¹ *Then without fatigue did he perfect it,*

and without weariness,

LEXICAL NOTES

שַׁכְלְלֵיהּ — *Did He finish it,* from שַׁכְלֵל, as in *Ezra* 4:12; 5:3; and 6:14. The word usually designates perfecting the construction of a building *(Kohut, Aruch HaShalem).* It can also mean *to establish.*

וּבְלָא תְשָׁשׁוּתָא — *From* תָּשַׁשׁ, *to be weak,* and תּוֹשֵׁשׁ, *to weaken.*

COMMENTARY

the earth? Declare if you have any understanding! Also as in *Eccle.* (3:11), גַּם אֶת הָעֹלָם נָתַן בְּלִבָּם מִבְּלִי אֲשֶׁר לֹא יִמְצָא הָאָדָם אֶת הַמַּעֲשֶׂה אֲשֶׁר עָשָׂה הָאֱלֹהִים מֵרֹאשׁ וְעַד סוֹף — *He has also put an enigma into their minds so that Man cannot comprehend what God has done from beginning to end* [see *Rashi ibid.* and *Koheles,* ArtScroll Ed. p. 87]. *(Yad Aharon; M'vo HaShir).*

... הָקֵם עָלְמָא — *Who established earth ...*

This entire verse is a paraphrase of *Job* (9:8): נֹטֶה שָׁמַיִם לְבַדּוֹ וְדוֹרֵךְ עַל בָּמֳתֵי יָם, *He spreads out the heavens alone, and treads upon the heights* [i.e., *waves*] *of the sea* [Cf. *Amos* 4:13].

[*Midrash Tanchuma Chukas* says in regard to the above verse that when God commanded the waters of the heavens to separate into the waters above and the waters below, the waters on earth began to cry and complain that they should not be required to remain in the profane world below. They proceeded to rise in order to join the Heavenly water above. The Holy One, blessed be He, restrained and trod upon them, forcing them to remain below. [*Tanchuma,* beginning of *Chukas:* מַה עָשָׂה הקב״ה? כְּבָשָׁן וְדִרְכָן]. This *Midrash* supports our first definition of כָּבַשׁ above *(Yad Aharon).*

See *Midrash Tanchuma* to *Chukas;*

Pirkei d'Rabbi Eliezer, Ch. 5; *Seder Rabbah de Bereishis,* 9 in *Batei Midrashos,* Wertheimer Vol. I; *Midrash Koren,* in *Bais Hamikdash,* Jellinek Vol. II; page 24-25; *Midrash Asseros HaDibros, Dibbur* I; *Sefer Haddar Zekeinim* to Genesis 1:4; and the *Rashi* to *Job* 9:8.]

11. שַׁכְלְלֵיהּ לָאו וּבְלָא — *Then without fatigue did He perfect it,* or: *did He establish it* [the world].

This phrase is based upon *Isaiah* 40:28: ה' בּוֹרֵא קְצוֹת הָאָרֶץ לֹא יִיעַף — ... *God, Creator of the ends of the earth, does not tire nor grow weary.* The *Targum* renders the above verse: לָא בַעֲמַל וְלָא בְלִיאוּ, *without toil and without fatigue.*

[The above verse concludes: וְאֵין חֵקֶר לִתְבוּנָתוֹ, *there is no searching of His understanding,* i.e., the purpose of, and the reasons for, the creation of the world have been hidden from Man's understanding. God's actions are hidden in mystery and none can fathom His understanding *(Yad Aharon; Mateh Levi).* This idea is also in harmony with the last definition of כָּבַשׁ in the previous verse.]

This verse also alludes to *Bereishis Rabbah* 3:2: רַב יְהוּדָה בֶּן רַב סִימוֹן אָמַר: לֹא בַעֲמַל וְלֹא בִּיגִיעָה בָּרָא הקב״ה אֶת עוֹלָמוֹ אֶלָּא בִּדְבַר ה' וּכְבָר שָׁמַיִם נַעֲשׂוּ — *Rav Yehuda the son of Rav*

יב וּבְאָתָא קַלִילָא,

דְּלֵית בַּהּ מְשָׁשׁוּתָא:

יג זַמֵּן כָּל עֲבִידְתֵּיהּ,

בְּהַךְ יוֹמֵי שַׁתָּא.

LEXICAL NOTES

12. וּבְאָתָא — *And with a letter*; from the Aramaic אָתָא, and the Hebrew אוֹת.

קַלִילָא — *Slight*, from קַל, *easy to achieve*.

דְּלֵית בַּהּ — *In which there is no . . .*

מְשָׁשׁוּתָא — *Tangibility, substance*; from מְשַׁשׁ, מַמָּשׁ, as in *Genesis 31:34*.

COMMENTARY

Simon said: Without toil and without weariness did the Holy One, blessed be He, create His world, only — By the word of God — and immediately ... the heavens were made [*Psalms 33:6*] (*Yad Aharon*, See also *comm.* to the next verse).

וּבְלָא תְּשָׁשׁוּתָא — *And without weariness,*

God did not become weakened by the exertions of having created the universe (*Yad Aharon*).

12. וּבְאָתָא קַלִילָא — *And with a letter, slight.*

This verse continues the previous stanza. God created the world as effortlessly as a person pronouncing the letter *he*, ה. The letter *he* is the easiest of all letters to enunciate, requiring the mere exhalation of breath for its articulation. The poet refers to *Midrash Tehillim 62:1*:

אֵלֶּה תוֹלְדוֹת הַשָּׁמַיִם וְהָאָרֶץ בְּהִבָּרְאָם׳ אַל תִּקְרִי ׳בְּהִבָּרְאָם׳ אֶלָּא ׳בְּהֵ״א בְרָאָם׳ וְלָמָה נִבְרָא הָעוֹלָם הַזֶּה בְּהֵ״א לוֹמַר . . .

לָךְ מָה הֵ״א כְּשֶׁאָדָם מוֹצִיאָהּ מִתּוֹךְ פִּיו אֵין בָּהּ לֹא רִיחוּשׁ שְׂפָתַיִם וְלֹא חֲרִיצַת לָשׁוֹן כַּךְ בְּלֹא עָמָל וּבְלֹא יְגִיעָה בָּרָא אוֹתָהּ

— These are the generations of the heavens and earth when they were created (*Genesis 2:4*): *Read not* (בְּהִבָּרְאָם) when they were created, *but* (בְּהֵ׳ בְּרָאָם) *with [the letter]* 'he' *He created them ... And why was this world created with the letter* 'he'? *To tell you that just as Man utters the sound* 'he', *letting it slip from his mouth without movement of his lips and without pressure from his tongue, so did God create the world without toil and without effort.* [See also *Menachos 29b*; *Bereishis Rabbah 3:2*; *Yerushalmi Chagigah 2:1*; *Tanchuma Buber Bereishis 16*; *Midrash Lekach Tov, Bereishis 2:4*].

All letters involve some effort in their pronunciation — (such as) the curving of the mouth, and the moving of the tongue and lips. The pronunciation of the letter '*he*',

אקדמות [58]</cite>

¹² *And with a letter, slight*

and lacking substance.

¹³ *He readied all His work*

in those very six days.

LEXICAL NOTES

13. זַמֵּן — *Readied* or *prepared, arranged;* from זְמַן. Also *to designate for use.*

עֲבִידְתֵּיה — *His work, labor;* from עֲבוֹדָה.

בְּהַךְ — *In those,* from הַךְ *that (those); this (these).*

יוֹמֵי שִׁתָּא — *Six days* [of creation]; שִׁתָּא, *six.*

COMMENTARY

however, requires no movement whatsoever [*Midrash Lekach Tov, Bereishis* 2:4] (*Yad Aharon*).

דְּלֵית בַּהּ מְשָׁשׁוּתָא — *And lacking substance.*

The letter *he's* lack of substance, is specifically referred to in the following Midrash:

וּמַה נִשְׁתַּנָּה ה"א יַתִּיר מִכָּל אוֹתִיוֹת ... מִפְּנֵי שֶׁאֵין בּוֹ מַמָּשׁ ... ה"א כְּשֶׁאָדָם מוֹצִיאוֹ מִפִּיו אֵינוֹ מַרְגִּישׁ בָּהּ ...

— *Why is the letter 'he' different from all the other letters ? ... Because it has no substance ... when someone pronounces it, he does not feel it* (*Osios d'Rabbi Akiva,* version A as quoted in *Batei Midrashos,* Wertheimer ed. vol. II p. 363. See *comm.* there).

13. זַמֵּן כָּל עֲבִידְתֵּיה — *He readied all His work in those very six days.*

All miracles, that is, all events that transcend natural physical law, which have occurred and shall occur until the end of time, were preordained and designated during the six days of Creation to happen in their proper place and time. Therefore, no miracle can truly be deemed a contradiction of the laws of Nature, for God had already decreed, during the first six days, that these miracles should happen as part of the natural course of events (*Rambam,* see below). This concept accords with *Ecclesiastes* 1:9: וְאֵין כָּל חָדָשׁ תַּחַת הַשָּׁמֶשׁ, *And there is nothing new under the sun.* That is, God has not altered the physical laws since Creation. This thought is further expressed in *Avos* 5:6:

עֲשָׂרָה דְבָרִים נִבְרְאוּ בְּעֶרֶב שַׁבָּת בֵּין הַשְּׁמָשׁוֹת וְאֵלּוּ הֵן: פִּי הָאָרֶץ, פִּי הַבְּאֵר, פִּי הָאָתוֹן, הַקֶּשֶׁת, וְהַמָּן ...

— *Ten things were created during the twilight of Sabbath eve, namely: the mouth of the earth* [which swallowed Korach], *the mouth of the well* [which supplied the Israelites with water in the desert], *the mouth of the ass* [which spoke to Balaam], *the rainbow* [sign of the flood], *the manna* [from heaven], ... [*Avos* 5:6.]

יד   זְהוֹר יְקָרֵיהּ עֲלִי,

כּוּרְסְיֵהּ   עֲלֵי *כָּרְסְיֵהּ דְּאֶשָׁתָא:

טו   חַיָל אֶלֶף אַלְפִין,

וְרִבּוֹא לְשַׁמְּשׁוּתָא.

LEXICAL NOTES

14. זְהוֹר — *Brilliance, splendor.*

יְקָרֵיהּ — The Aramaic equivalent of the Hebrew כְּבוֹדוֹ, a word which denotes *brilliance, splendor, glory, His majesty, honor.* It is often used by the *Targum* to refer to the majesty of God's presence (*Shechinah*), the brilliance that radiates from God as in the *Targum Onkelos* to *Exodus* 16:7 יְקָרָא דַה' (Hebrew text: כְּבוֹד ה') *the glory of God. Targum Yonasan* renders: יְקָר שְׁכִינְתָּא דַה', *the splendor of God's Shechinah.* Compare with verses 20, 25, and 54, see also verse 47 for another meaning of the word.

זְהוֹר יְקָרֵיהּ — *His brilliant majesty* is often used in *Targum* as a metaphor for God, as in *Deuteronomy* 33:2 and *Psalms* 18:13.

עֲלִי — I. *Ascended;* from עֲלִי and עֲלָא. II. *To be exalted, to be elevated.*

עֲלִי — *Upon;* root — עַל.

COMMENTARY

Rambam further points out, that the list of miracles cited in the above *Mishnah*, is by no means a complete listing, but is rather, only a record of the things created at the twilight of the sixth day. [From *Rambam's* commentary on the *Mishna Avos* 5:5]. (*Yad Aharon, T'yul B'gan;* see also *Tosfos Yom Tov*, and *Midrash Shmuel* to *Avos ibid.* , as well as *Aggados Maharsha* to *Pesachim* 54a and b.

14. . . . זְהוֹר יְקָרֵיהּ עֲלִי — *Then the splendor of His majesty made ascent upon His fiery throne.* Alternatively: *His brilliant majesty was then exalted upon His fiery throne.*

This verse paraphrases the morning Sabbath prayer: לָאֵל אֲשֶׁר שָׁבַת מִכָּל הַמַּעֲשִׂים בַּיּוֹם הַשְּׁבִיעִי, הִתְעַלָּה

וַיֵּשֶׁב עַל כֵּס כְּבוֹדוֹ, *To God who rested from all work of Creation on the seventh Day; He ascended and sat upon His throne of glory.* The same description is found in the following *Midrash:* גָּמַר אֶת כָּל מַעֲשָׂיו, וְנִתְעַלָּה וְיָשַׁב בִּמְרוֹמָיו שֶׁל עוֹלָם, [*On the sixth day of Creation, God*] *completed all His works and ascended and sat in the heights of the universe* (*Avos d'Rabbi Nathan,* 1:8).

Zohar Chadash (17b) discusses these ideas in fuller detail:

— *Rav Yehuda said in Rav's name: The Holy One, blessed be He, did not sit upon His throne of glory, until the Sabbath arrived and He was (thereby) exalted [or He ascended] and sat upon His throne*

¹⁴ *Then the splendor of His majesty made ascent*

upon His fiery throne.

¹⁵ *With an army of a thousand thousands*

and myriads to serve Him

LEXICAL NOTES

בָּרְסְיֵהּ — *His throne*, from כּוּרְסְיָא.

דְּאֶשָׁתָא — *Of fire*, from אֶשָׁא, אֵשׁ.

עֲלִי בָּרְסְיֵהּ דְּאֶשָׁתָא — *Upon His fiery throne*, from Daniel 7:9, בָּרְסְיֵהּ שְׁבִיבִין דִּי נוּר, *His throne was [made] of fiery flame (Heidenheim).*

15. אֶלֶף — *Thousand;* plural: אַלְפִּין, *thousands.*

וְרִבּוֹא — *Myriad, an unspecified very large number;* also translated as *ten thousand,* the Aramaic equivalent of the Hebrew רְבָבָה.

לְשַׁמְּשׁוּתָא — *To serve Him;* or *to minister to Him,* from שַׁמֵּשׁ.

COMMENTARY

... *Until the world's creation, there were none to offer praises to the Holy One, blessed be He, and to recognize Him. But upon the creation of the world, the angels, the Holy beings, the heavens and their hosts, and Man — all were in readiness to praise and glorify their Creator. However, they did not glorify and praise Him, until the arrival of the Sabbath, when all were at rest. Then they all burst forth in song and praise ... and it was then that God sat upon His throne of glory (Yad Aharon; Shnei Ha-Me'oros).*

15. The poet now proceeds to tell of the greatness of God, by describing the angels in Heaven, and the awe and reverence with which they praise Him (verses 15-30).

— חֵיל אֶלֶף אַלְפִּין וְרִבּוֹא לְשַׁמְּשׁוּתָא

With an army of a thousand thousands and myriads to serve Him.

This verse is taken almost verbatim from *Daniel* (7:10): אֶלֶף אַלְפִין יְשַׁמְּשׁוּנֵּהּ וְרִבּוֹ רִבְבָן קָדָמוֹהִי יְקוּמוּן, *Thousands of thousands ministered into Him, and ten thousand times ten thousand (or: 'myriad of myriads') stood before Him.*

The *Talmud* (*Chagigah* 13b) elaborates on the above verse, as follows: רַבִּי אוֹמֵר מִשּׁוּם אַבָּא יוֹסִי בֶּן דּוֹסַ(תָּ)אי: אֶלֶף אַלְפִין יְשַׁמְּשׁוּנֵּהּ — מִסְפַּר גְּדוּד אֶחָד וְלִגְדוּדָיו אֵין מִסְפָּר — *Rabbi says in the name of Abba Yossi ben of Dos(d)ai: A thousand thousands ministered into Him — [this is but the number] of one troop [of angels]. However, the actual number of troops is innumerable (Shnei HaMe'oros; Eshel Avrohom; Heidenheim).*

טז חַדְתִּין נְבוֹט לְצַפְרִין,
סַגִּיאָה טְרָשׁוּתָא:

16. חַדְתִּין — *New ones*; plural of חַדְתָּא, *new*.

נְבוֹט — *Sprout forth*; or, *spring forth* as water from a spring; from נְבַט.

לְצַפְרִין — *Each morning* [literally: *to the mornings*]; plural of צַפְרָא, *morning*.

סַגִּיאָה — *Great*; the feminine form of סַגִּי.

טְרָשׁוּתָא — *Trustworthiness, righteousness*.
This word does not appear in this sense anywhere else in Jewish literature. Most commentators arrive at the above definition by recognizing this verse as a paraphrase of *Lamentations 3:23*, חֲדָשִׁים לַבְּקָרִים רַבָּה אֱמוּנָתֶךָ, *New ones are created every morning, great is your trustworthiness*. Consequently, they infer that the Hebrew אֱמוּנָתֶךָ, must correspond to טְרָשׁוּתָא in this verse.
[Two possible derivations of this word may be proposed:
I. טְרַשׁ, *rock, hard craggy ground*; also: *to harden*, and *solidity* in general. *Berger* points out that טְרַשׁ conveys the meaning of *solidity*, as does the word אָמֵן, *to be firm* and *enduring*, and the word אֱמוּנָה, *firm, faith, honesty*. Hence, the words share a common meaning.

16. חַדְתִּין נְבוֹט לְצַפְרִין סַגִּיאָה טְרָשׁוּתָא — *New ones* [i.e., angels] *sprouting every morning — How great is your trustworthiness.*

This verse is a paraphrase of the verse and *Targum to Lamentations 3:23*, נִיסִין חֲדַתִּין מַרְחִישׁ בְּצַפְרַיָא — *He brings about new miracles every morning, great is your faithfulness.*

The poet is referring to the following passage from *Chagigah 14a*: כָּל יוֹמָא וְיוֹמָא נִבְרָאִין מַלְאֲכֵי הַשָּׁרֵת מִנְּהַר דִּינוּר וְאָמְרִי שִׁירָה וּבְטֵלִי, שֶׁנֶּאֱמַר: חֲדָשִׁים לַבְּקָרִים רַבָּה אֱמוּנָתֶךָ — *There are ministering angels created each and every day from the river Dinur (di-nur = דִּי־נוּר, of fire), and they say praises (to God) and are abo-*

lished, as is stated: New ones are created every morning, great is your faithfulness (Lamentations 3:23).

A similar passage appears in *Sh'mos Rabbah 15:6*: הַמַּלְאָכִים מִתְחַדְּשִׁין בְּכָל יוֹם וּמְקַלְסִין להקב״ה וְהֵן חוֹזְרִין לְנָהָר אֵשׁ שֶׁיָּצְאוּ מִמֶּנּוּ וְשׁוּב הָאֱלֹהִים מְחַדְּשָׁן וּמַחֲזִירָן כְּשֵׁם שֶׁהָיוּ בָּרִאשׁוֹנָה שֶׁנֶּאֱמַר: חֲדָשִׁים לַבְּקָרִים ... — *Angels are created new every day and they offer praises to the Holy One, blessed be He, and thereupon return to the river of fire from whence they came. The Lord then renews them once again, and re-stores them to their original state, as it says: New ones ...*

[See also: *Bereishis Rabbah 78:1* and *Eichah Rabbasi 3:23*.

¹⁶ New ones sprouting every morning —

How great is Your trustworthiness —

II. טַרְשָׁא, a sale on credit to be paid for at the future market price which will be higher than the current cash price. For example, *one sells beer in Tishrei when it is abundant, to be paid for at the Nisan price when beer will be scarce and therefore, more expensive (Rashi, Bava Metziah 65a)*. *Shnei HaMe'oros* points out that the above practice is an act of faith in that the seller trusts that the product he sells *will* increase in price in the future; knowing full well that if it does not, he must incur a loss. This situation is analogous to stock market investment; when one buys a stock he 'believes' that the price will be higher in the future.

It is also possible that the word טְרָשׁוּתָא is a form of the Aramaic word תְּרִיצוּתָא, *trustworthiness, faithfulness.*]

The commentary on *Akdamus* usually found in *Machzor Mateh Levi*, notes that the *Targum* renders אֱמוּנָתֶךָ, *(Lam. 3:23)* into מטרשא. However, no such Targumic rendering is presently known to exist. It is quite possible that such a version of the Targum did at one time exist, but is now lost, the commentary having been written well over 450 years ago, and found in Machzorim printed as early as 1557.

COMMENTARY

See also: *Yedai Moshe* to *Sh'mos Rabbah* ad loc. and *Tosafos* to *Chagigah* 13b, s.v. מזיעתן של חיות, for an explanation of why the angels are sent back to the river of fire and destroyed.]

סַגִּיאָה טְרָשׁוּתָא — *Great is your trustworthiness.*

The wonders of the heavenly angels above, and the vastness and intricacy of the workings of the u-niverse, all attest that God is able to provide and perform all the things that He promised us. The explana-tion of this phrase may be found in the following Midrash:

ר' שִׁמְעוֹן בְּשֵׁם ר' סִימוֹן אוֹמֵר מִמַּה שֶׁאַתָּה מְחַדְּשֵׁנוּ לַבְּקָרִים אָנוּ מַאֲמִינִים וּמַכִּירִין שֶׁאַתָּה מַחֲזִיר לָנוּ נִשְׁמוֹתֵינוּ לִתְחִיַּית הַמֵּתִים. ר' אַלֶכְּסַנְדְּרִי אוֹמֵר מִמַּה שֶׁאַת מְחַדֵּשׁ אוֹתָנוּ לַבְּקָרִים שֶׁל

גָּלִיּוֹת. אָנוּ יוֹדְעִים שֶׁאֱמוּנָתְךָ רַבָּה לְגָאֲלֵנוּ

— *Rabbi Simeon said in the name of Rabbi Simon: Because You renew us every morning* [when we arise from sleep], *we therefore believe and recognize that You will return our souls to us at the time of the resurrection of the dead. Rabbi Alexandri said: In that You renew us in our exile at the dawn of each new kingdom* [i.e., in that the Jewish people remain despite the rise (and fall) of the governments around them, and despite con-tinuous persecutions], *we therefore, know that Your faithfulness is great that You will redeem us from exile* [speedily in our time] *(Midrash Tehillim 25:2).*

יְקִירִין יז

טְפֵי*יְקִידִין שְׂרָפִין,
כְּלוֹל גַּפֵּי שִׁתָּא.
יח   טַעַם עַד יִתִיהֵב לְהוֹן,
שְׁתִיקִין בְּאַדְשְׁתָּא:

LEXICAL NOTES

17. טְפֵי — There are three possible meanings: I. *Greater in quantity;* II. *Greater in quality;* III. *Furthermore.*

יְקִידִין — *Flaming,* from יָקַד.

Some editions read: יְקִירִין, *Important, precious;* from יְקָר. According to this version, טְפֵי יְקִירִין, is rendered: *Even greater in importance* (חֲשִׁיבוּת) *are the flaming Seraphim* (M'vo HaShir). This follows the second definition in the above note. See the second entry in the *commentary.*

שְׂרָפִין — *Seraphim; a class of flaming angels,* the highest in the hierarchy of notability of all angels, possessing six wings, as opposed to lesser angels which have two or four wings (see *Isaiah* 6:2 and *Ezekiel* 1:6).

כְּלוֹל — *All, every one;* from כּוֹל, כָּלַל, *to be comprised of, to consist of, to include.*

COMMENTARY

17. טְפֵי יְקִידִין שְׂרָפִין — *More numerous even are the flaming Seraphim.*

The flaming angels are even more numerous than the heavenly army of angels enumerated in verse 15 above, of which this verse is a continuation (*Yad Aharon; Heidenheim*).

An alternative translation: *More wondrous are the flaming Seraphim.* The Seraphim are superior to the angels described earlier for the Seraphim are permanent and are not destroyed at the end of each day. Furthermore, they are a wonderous sight to behold because of their flaming brilliance (*Shnei HaMe'oros; Yad Aharon*).

A third translation: *Moreover* [*i.e., besides the angels mentioned in verses 15-16*] there are also the flaming Seraphim (*Eshel Avrohom*).

כְּלוֹל גַּפֵּי שִׁתָּא — *Each one six-winged* or: *all of them six-winged.*

This verse is based upon the following verse in *Isaiah* (6:2): שְׂרָפִים עֹמְדִים מִמַּעַל לוֹ שֵׁשׁ כְּנָפַיִם שֵׁשׁ כְּנָפַיִם לְאֶחָד בִּשְׁתַּיִם יְכַסֶּה פָנָיו וּבִשְׁתַּיִם יְכַסֶּה רַגְלָיו וּבִשְׁתַּיִם יְעוֹפֵף, *Seraphim stood above Him, each having six wings; with two he covers his face, with two he covers his feet, and with two he flies.*

The *Midrash* says that the angels use two wings to cover their face so as not to see God's *Shechinah,* and two wings to cover their feet so as

¹⁷ *More numerous even are the flaming Seraphim,*

each one six-winged,

¹⁸ *Until the command is given them,*

they remain in total silence.

גַּפֵּי — *Wings, plural of* גַּפָּא.

18. טְעֵם — *Command, decree as in Ezra* 4:21: כְּעַן שִׂימוּ טְעֵם, *give you now the command. See also ibid.* 4:9; *Jonah* 3:7 *and Daniel* 3:10., An alternative rendering is *permission.*

עַד יִתְיְהֵב לְהוֹן — *Until it is given to them, from* יְהַב, *to give.*

שְׁתִיקִין — *They are silent, from* שְׁתַק.

בְּאַדְשְׁתָא — *In silence, or with silence, from* אֲדַשׁ, *to be silent; as in Sanhedrin* 7a: טוּבֵיהּ דְּשָׁמַע וַאֲדִישׁ — *Happy is he who hears [himself insulted] and remains silent.* (See *Rashi* there).

שְׁתִיקִין בְּאַדְשְׁתָא — *They remain quiet, in (total) silence.* The two words are synonyms repeated for emphasis.

not to remind Hashem of Israel's sin of the Golden Calf, the Seraphim's feet having the appearance of a calf's hoof [*Midrash Vayikra Rabbah* 27:3]. (See also *Ezekiel* 1:7, *Chagigah* 13b; and *Tanchuma Tzav* 13).

18. ... טְעֵם עַד יִתְיְהֵב לְהוֹן — *Until the command is given them they remain in (total) silence,* or alternatively: *Until permission is given them* ...

Until (the) permission or command to praise God is given, the angels are compelled to remain silent. They are not permitted to offer their daily hymns to God, until Israel has completed its psalms of praise to the Lord.

This thought is expressed in the following Midrash:

בְּשָׁעָה שֶׁמַּלְאֲכֵי הַשָּׁרֵת מְבַקְשִׁים לוֹמַר שִׁירָה לְמַעְלָה ... אוֹמֵר לָהֶם הקב״ה הַחֲרִישׁוּ אֵלַי כָּל מַלְאָךְ וּמַלְאָךְ ... עַד שֶׁאֶשְׁמַע וְאַאֲזִין תְּחִלָּה קוֹל שִׁירָאָן וְתִשְׁבְּחָתָן שֶׁל יִשְׂרָאֵל ... שֶׁאֵין רְשׁוּת לְמַלְאֲכֵי הַשָּׁרֵת לוֹמַר שִׁירָה עַד שֶׁפּוֹתְחִין תְּחִלָּה יִשְׂרָאֵל בְּשִׁירָה
— *At the time when the ministering angels above, desire to sing their praises (to God) ... the Holy One blessed be He tells them: be silent for Me all you angels ... until I first listen to, and hear, the voice [sound] of the songs and praises of Israel ... for the ministering angels are not permitted to say praise, until Israel has first commenced with its praises* [*Pirkei Heichalos* cited by *Bais*

יט   יְקַבְּלוּן דֵּין מִן דֵּין,

שָׁוֵי דְּלָא בְשַׁשְׁתָּא.

LEXICAL NOTES

19. יְקַבְּלוּן — *They accept [permission or sanction]; from* קַבֵּל.

דֵּין — *This, that.*

מִן — *From.*

דֵּין מִן דֵּין — *One from the other.*

COMMENTARY

Hamidrash, Jelinek III p. 161; *Ozar Midrashim*, Eisenstein I p. 221, *Seder Rabbah* of *Bereishis Batei Midrashos*, *Wertheimer* I p. 45; and *Siddur ha'Sh'loh*, *Shaar Hashamaim* to *Yotzer Or*] (*Yad Aharon*; *Shnei HaMe'oros*).

See also *Chaggiga* 12b and *Rashi* there. Also: *Chullin* 91b, 92a; and *Bereishis Rabbah* 65:21.

19. In the subsequent verses (19-30), the poet describes in minute detail, the Angels' daily recitation of Kedushah, the Sanctification of God. The text of the Kedushah recited by the angels is composed of the following three verses:

1. וְקָרָא זֶה אֶל זֶה וְאָמַר: קָדוֹשׁ קָדוֹשׁ קָדוֹשׁ ה' צְבָאוֹת מְלֹא כָל הָאָרֶץ כְּבוֹדוֹ — *And one (angel) called to the other and said; 'Holy, holy, holy is HASHEM of Hosts, the whole earth is full of His glory' (Isaiah 6:3).*

2. בָּרוּךְ כְּבוֹד ה' מִמְּקוֹמוֹ — *Blessed be the glory of HASHEM from His place (Ezekiel 3:12).*

3. יִמְלֹךְ ה' לְעוֹלָם אֱלֹהַיִךְ צִיּוֹן לְדֹר וָדֹר הַלְלוּיָהּ, — *HASHEM shall reign for ever, your God, O Zion, for all generations. Praise the Lord (Psalms 146:10).*

יְקַבְּלוּן דֵּין מִן דֵּין — *They accept [permission] from one another.*

The angels accept permission from one another and signal to each other in order to coordinate their recitation of the Kedusha at *exactly* the same instant. [See the notes to the other half of this verse] (*Yad Aharon; Shnei HaMe'oros*).

This phrase is taken nearly verbatim from the first four words of the *Targum Yonasan*'s rendering of the Kedusha in *Isaiah* 6:3 (above):
וּמְקַבְּלִין דֵּין מִן דֵּין וְאָמְרִין קַדִּישׁ בִּשְׁמֵי מְרוֹמָא עִלָּאָה בֵּית שְׁכִנְתֵּיה קַדִּישׁ עַל אַרְעָא עוֹבַד גְּבוּרְתֵּיה קַדִּישׁ לְעָלַם וּלְעָלְמֵי עָלְמַיָּא ה' צְבָאוֹת מַלְיָא כָל אַרְעָא זִיו יְקָרֵיה
— *And they accept permission from one another, and say: Holy, in the lofty heavens, from the place of His Shechinah; holy, upon the earth, the work of His might; holy, forever and ever is HASHEM of hosts; the whole world is full of the radiance of His glory (Berger).*

That the angels wait to accept permission from one another, prior to their saying of Kedushah, is to be found in the following passage:
וּמִנַּיִן שֶׁיְּרֵאִים זֶה אֶת זֶה וּמְכַבְּדִין זֶה אֶת זֶה וְעוֹנְתָנִין מִבְּנֵי אָדָם — שֶׁבְּשָׁעָה

¹⁹ They accept permission from one another, then all together without delay:

LEXICAL NOTES

שְׁוֵי — I. *Simultaneously, equally*; also *immediately*, from the root שְׁוֵי, or שְׁוָא, *to be alike, to be equal; to be even or alike*, or II. *Anxiously*, or *tremblingly*, from the root שְׁוֵי. See the notes to אֶשְׁוְתָא, in *v* 24 below *(Heidenheim)*.

דְּלָא — *Without* [literally: which not].

בְּשִׁשְׁתָּא — *Delay*, from the Hebrew בּוֹשֵׁשׁ, *to tarry*. As in *Exodus* 32:1: כִּי בֹשֵׁשׁ מֹשֶׁה לָרֶדֶת, *that Moses delayed to descend*.

COMMENTARY

שֶׁפּוֹתְחִין אֶת פִּיהֶם וְאוֹמְרִים שִׁיר זֶה אוֹמֵר לַחֲבֵירוֹ פְּתַח אַתָּה שֶׁאַתָּה גָדוֹל מִמֶּנִּי וְזֶה אוֹמֵר לַחֲבֵירוֹ פְּתַח אַתָּה שֶׁאַתָּה גָדוֹל מִמֶּנִּי . . . וְיֵשׁ אוֹמְרִים כִּתּוֹת כִּתּוֹת הֵן כַּת אַחַת אוֹמֶרֶת לַחֲבֶרְתָּה פְּתְחִי אַתְּ שֶׁאַתְּ גְדוֹלָה מִמֶּנִּי שֶׁנֶּאֱמַר וְקָרָא זֶה אֶל זֶה וְאָמַר — *And from where do we know that [the angels] revere one another, respect one another, and are humbler than human beings? When they are about to open their mouths to sing hymns, one says to the other: 'You begin, for you are greater than I,' and the other replies: 'You begin, for you are greater than I'. ... Some say that there are groups [of angels] and each group says to the other, 'You begin for you are greater than we.' As it is stated: (Isaiah 6:3), And one called to the other [Avos d'Rabbi Nosson, 12:6].*

The result of the above cited dialogue among the angels is that they consequently all recite the *Kedushah* simultaneously. [See *Tosafos* in *Chagigah* 13b cited in comm. to *v.* 16 above, and also the notes below.]

שְׁוֵי דְּלָא בְּשִׁשְׁתָּא — *All together*

without delay, or *immediately without delay*.

All the angels hasten to signal and give permission to one another so that all should be able to utter their praise simultaneously. The angels do this in great fear and awe, for, any angel that recites his praise earlier or later than his peers is immediately destroyed in flames. *Yad Aharon* notes that this thought is explained in the following *Midrash*: וְקָרָא זֶה אֶל זֶה וְאָמַר — נוֹטְלִין רְשׁוּת זֶה מִזֶּה שֶׁלֹּא לְהַקְדִּים הָאֶחָד וְיַתְחִיל וְיִתְחַיֵּב שְׂרֵפָה. אֶלָּא פָּתְחוּ כֻלָּם כְּאֶחָד וְעוֹנִין (קָדוֹשׁ . . .) — *And one called to the other, and said: (Isaiah 6:3) They take permission, one from another, so that one should not precede [another] and begin [saying Kedushah], and consequently be subject to incineration. Rather, all begin [singing praise] simultaneously and reply: Holy ... (Tanchuma Tzav 13). See Rashi to Isaiah 6:3; for more on this subject. See also the sources cited in verse 18.*

יְקַבְּלוּן דֵּין מִן דֵּין . . . — *They accept (permission) from one another ...*

The angels accept permission

[67]   *Akdamus*

כ יְקָר מְלֵי כָל אַרְעָא,
לִתְלוֹתֵי קְדוּשְׁתָּא:

כא בְּקָל מִן קֳדָם שַׁדַּי,
בְּקָל מֵי נְפִישׁוּתָא.

LEXICAL NOTES

20. מְלֵי — *Is filled, or fills*; from מְלֵי or מְלָא.

לִתְלוֹתֵי — *Threefold, triple*; from תְּלָתָא.

קְדוּשְׁתָּא — *Holiness*, referring to the triple utterance of קָדוֹשׁ, *Holy*, during *Kedushah*.

COMMENTARY

from, and signal to, one another in order that they should all be able to begin the *Kedushah* simultaneously without any angel delaying. [*Yad Aharon; Shnei HaMe'oros*].

The contents of verses 18 through 23 are expressed in full detail in the daily morning prayers, which describe the angels' recitation of *Kedushah* to the Almighty:

— *And they [the angels] all take upon themselves the yoke of the Kingdom of Heaven one from the other, and give permission to one another to declare the holiness of their Creator. In serene spirit, with pure speech and holy melody they all respond in unison, and exclaim with awe: 'Holy, holy, holy is* HASHEM *of hosts, the whole earth is full of His glory' (Isaiah 6:3). And the Ofanim and the holy Chayos with a noise of great rushing, up-raising themselves opposite the Seraphim, thus opposite them offer praise and say: 'Blessed be the glory of* HASHEM *from His place' (Ezekiel 3:12).*

20. יְקָר מְלֵי כָל אַרְעָא — *[Saying:] With His glory is filled the entire earth.*

This verse is taken almost word for word from the *Targum* to *Isaiah* 6:3: מַלְיָא כָל אַרְעָא זִיו יְקָרֵיהּ which is the translation of the Hebrew מְלֹא כָל הָאָרֶץ כְּבוֹדוֹ, *The entire earth is filled with His glory.* See the notes to *v.* 19 for the complete text of the verse in *Isaiah* and the *Targum.*

לִתְלוֹתֵי קְדוּשְׁתָּא — *After threefold sanctification,* or: *after thrice uttering, 'Holy.'*

The angels begin their recital of *Kedushah* with the words: '*Holy, holy, holy, ...*' (See verse 19). Then they say, '*The whole earth is filled with His glory*' [*Isaiah* 6:3] (*Yad Aharon*).

As is described in *Chulin* 91b:

אָמַר רַב חֲנַנְאֵל אָמַר רַב שָׁלֹשׁ כִּתּוֹת שֶׁל מַלְאֲכֵי הַשָּׁרֵת אוֹמְרוֹת שִׁירָה בְּכָל יוֹם אַחַת אוֹמֶרֶת קָדוֹשׁ וְאַחַת אוֹמֶרֶת קָדוֹשׁ וְאַחַת אוֹמֶרֶת קָדוֹשׁ ה' צְבָאוֹת ...

— *Rav Chananel said in the name of Rav: Three groups of angels utter*

²⁰ *'With His glory is filled the entire earth'*
— after threefold sanctification.

²¹ *As the voice of the Almighty,*
as the sound of roaring waters ...

LEXICAL NOTES

21. בְּקָל — *As the voice;* from קוֹל, *voice.*

שַׁדַּי — *The Almighty, the Omnipotent One.* This Name denotes God's power.

מֵי — *Waters,* the construct form of מַיִם.

נְפִישׁוּתָא — *Great, vast,* from נְפִישׁ.

COMMENTARY

hymns of praise daily. One says, [only the word] 'Holy!' *Another says,* 'Holy!' *and the third says,* 'Holy is HASHEM of hosts!' — The *Talmud* goes on to dispute the above description of the manner in which the angels recite the *Kedushah,* and comes to the following conclusion: אֶלָּא אַחַת אוֹמֶרֶת קָדוֹשׁ וְאַחַת אוֹמֶרֶת קָדוֹשׁ קָדוֹשׁ וְאַחַת אוֹמֶרֶת קָדוֹשׁ קָדוֹשׁ קָדוֹשׁ — *Rather [the angels recite the Kedushah as follows:] one [group] says,* 'Holy!', *another says,* 'Holy! Holy!', *and the other says,* 'Holy, holy, holy is HASHEM of hosts! Yad Aharon).*

יְקָר מְלִי כָל אַרְעָא ... — *[Saying:] With His glory is filled the entire earth.*

This verse should be understood as follows: After the angels have said, 'Holy!', three times, they thereupon say, 'The whole earth is filled with His glory!' (*Yad Aharon*).

Eshel Avrohom interprets the verse differently: The angels accept

permission from one another to say the *Kedushah* simultaneously, without delay (*v.* 19). They do so: [*Because of Him*] *whose glory fills the whole earth, with threefold holiness.* The *threefold holiness,* refers to the three aspects of God's holiness as expressed by *Targum Yonasan* to *Isaiah* 6:3: 1) holy, in the heavens on high; 2) holy, upon the earth below; and 3) holy, forever, for all eternity. See the text of the *Targum* in the *comm.* to *v.* 19.

21. בְּקָל מִן קֳדָם שַׁדַּי — *As the voice of the Almighty.*

This phrase is taken verbatim from the *Targum Yonasan* to *Ezekiel* 1:24, בְּקָלָא מִן קֳדָם שַׁדַּי, *as the voice of the Almighty.*

בְּקָל מֵי נְפִישׁוּתָא — *As the sound of roaring* [lit. *great, numerous*] *waters.*

The sound of the angels praying in unison is like the thunderous roar of the ocean's waves. (See next verse).

כב כְּרוּבִין קֳבֵל גַּלְגַּלִין, גַּלְגְּלִין

מְרוֹמְמִין בְּאוּשָׁתָא:

כג לְמֶחֱזֵי בְּאַנְפָּא עַיִן,

כְּוָת גִּירֵי קַשְׁתָּא.

LEXICAL NOTES

22. כְּרוּבִין — *Cherubim*; plural of כְּרוּב, *cheruv*, an angel possessing a childlike face as in *Chagigah* 13b, וּמַאי כְּרוּב — כְּרַבְיָא, *What is meant by 'cheruv'?* — *As* (the face of) *a child.* The *Cherubim* are identical to the *Chayos* in *Ezekiel* 1:5. As Yechezkel says: וַיֵּרֹמוּ הַכְּרוּבִים הִיא הַחַיָּה אֲשֶׁר רָאִיתִי בִּנְהַר כְּבָר, *And the Cherubim were lifted up. This is the Chayah that I saw by the river of Chebar* (*Ezekiel* 10:15).

קֳבֵל — *Opposite; corresponding to.* *Targum Yonasan* translates לְעֻמָּתָם, as לְקָבְלֵהֶן (*Ezekiel* 1:20, and *ibid.* 3:13). See also *v.* 38.

גַּלְגְּלִין — *Galgalim*, [lit. *wheels*]; the name of a type of angel also known as *Ofanim* in *Ezekiel* 1:15-16. As Yechezkel says: לָאוֹפַנִּים לָהֶם קוֹרָא הַגַּלְגַּל בְּאָזְנָי, *The Ofanim I heard being addressed as Galgalim* (*Ezekiel* 10:13).

מְרוֹמְמִין — *Exalt* [*Him*] from רוֹמֵם.

COMMENTARY

... בְּקָל מִן קֳדָם — *As the voice of the Almighty* ... This paraphrases *Ezekiel* 1:24, וָאֶשְׁמַע אֶת קוֹל כַּנְפֵיהֶם בְּקוֹל מַיִם רַבִּים כְּקוֹל שַׁדַּי, *And I* [*Ezekiel*] *heard the sound of their wings, like the sound of great waters, like the sound of the Almighty* ... (Cf. *Ezekiel* 10:5; 43:2; and *Psalms* 29).

The angels beat their wings when praising the Almighty, causing a sound similar to the roar of the vast oceans. The sound of the angels' wings heard by Ezekiel was the sound of the angels saying *Kedushah*, as *Tanchuma* (*Kedoshim* 6) says:

And what is meant by, 'When they stood they let down their wings' (*Ezekiel* 1:24)? *When Israel praises the Almighty, the minister-*

ing angels relax their wings and halt their recitation of praises. For it is with their wings that they utter praises.

וָאֶשְׁמַע אַחֲרַי קוֹל רַעַשׁ גָּדוֹל מַהוּ אַחֲרַי — אָמַר יְחֶזְקֵאל מִשֶּׁקִּלַּסְתִּיו אֲנִי וַחֲבֵרַי שָׁמַעְתִּי שֶׁמַּלְאֲכֵי הַשָּׁרֵת מְקַלְסִין אוֹתוֹ אַחֲרַי וְאוֹמְרִים בָּרוּךְ כְּבוֹד ה' מִמְּקוֹמוֹ *And I heard* [אַחֲרַי] *behind me the sound of great noise* (*Ezekiel* 3:12): *What is meant by* אַחֲרַי, [*behind me, which can also be translated after me*]? *Ezekiel said: After I and my companions had recited praises, I heard the ministering angels praising Him after me saying: 'Blessed be the glory of* HASHEM *from His place'* (*ibid.*) (*Yad Aharon*).

22. כְּרוּבִין קֳבֵל גַּלְגְּלִין — *Cherubim great noise* [*saying*]: '*Blessed be the*

²² Cherubim correspond to galgalim,

exalting in a crescendo.

²³ Appearing before the eye,

as arrows flashing from a bow.

בְּאוּשְׁתָּא — *Shouting loudly,* [literally, *with great noise*] from אָשׁ, or אֲוָשׁ, *to shout, to cause a din,* as in *Berachos* 50a, אַיְידֵי דְּאָוְושׁוּ כּוּלֵי עָלְמָא לָא שָׁמַע, *Since everyone* [*responded*] *in a very loud voice* [בְּקוֹל רָם (Rashi)], *it* [the saying of grace] *could not be heard.*

23. לְמֶחֱזֵי — *Appearing;* or *to see them,* from חֲזֵי, *to see;* and מֶחֱזֵי, *to look like.*

בְּאַנְפָּא — *Before, in sight of,* (Hebrew בִּפְנֵי), from אַפָּא, *face.*

לְמֶחֱזֵי בְּאַנְפָּא עֵין — *Appearing before the eye* ... or alternately: *to see them before one's eye* ... This phrase is from *Targum Yonasan* to *Ezekiel* 1:14, בְּאַנְפָּא עֵינָא לְמֶחֱזֵי, *to the appearance of one's eye* or: *to see them with one's eye* (see notes to *v.* 24 for the complete *Targum.*

גִּירֵי — *Arrows;* plural of גִּירָא, *arrow, projectile.*

קַשְׁתָּא — *Bow;* also: *rainbow,* from the Hebrew קֶשֶׁת (see below).

Cherubim opposite the Galgalim.

Wherever and whenever the *Chayos* [the Cherubim] give praise to Hashem, the *Ofanim* [Galgalim] follow correspondingly in order to offer their praises in unison. This is based on *Ezekiel* (1:19), וּבְלֶכֶת הַחַיּוֹת יֵלְכוּ הָאוֹפַנִּים, *And when the Chayos went, the Ofanim went along with them.* Also, in the next verse: וְהָאוֹפַנִּים יִנָּשְׂאוּ לְעֻמָּתָם, *And the Ofanim were lifted up over against them* [the Chayos], (see Rashi ibid.).

See also the *Rashi* to *Ezekiel* 3:13, and the additional notes to verse 19. (Heidenheim).

מְרוֹמְמִין בְּאוּשְׁתָּא — *Exalting in a crescendo.* This phrase is based on *Ezekiel* 3:12, וַתִּשָּׂאֵנִי רוּחַ וָאֶשְׁמַע

אַחֲרַי קוֹל רַעַשׁ גָּדוֹל בָּרוּךְ כְּבוֹד ה' מִמְּקוֹמוֹ, *And a wind lifted me up, and I heard behind me the sound of great noise* [saying]: *Blessed be the glory of HASHEM from His place.'*

23. לְמֶחֱזֵי בְּאַנְפָּא עֵין — *Appearing before the eye.*

Both this verse and the next one paraphrase *Ezekiel* 1:14 and the *Targum Yonasan* thereon.

The complete *Targum* and translation are given in the *comm.* to *v.* 24.

כְּנָת גִּירֵי קַשְׁתָּא — *As arrows flashing from a bow.*

The angels, when sent to carry out a command, move with such great speed that, metaphorically, they appear to the eye as an arrow

כד לְכָל אֲתַר דְּמִשְׁתַּלְּחִין,
זְרִיזִין בְּאֵשְׁוָתָא:

כה מְבָרְכִין בְּרִיךְ יְקָרֵיהּ,
בְּכָל לְשָׁן לְחִישׁוּתָא.

LEXICAL NOTES

24. דְּמִשְׁתַּלְּחִין — *To which they are sent*; from שָׁלַח, *to send.*

זְרִיזִין — *They [the angels] hasten*; from זְרַז.

בְּאֵשְׁוָתָא — *With anxiety*; or alternatively, *with trembling, with haste*, from the root
שָׁוֵי, *to be anxious, to be frightened. (Kohut, Aruch HaShalem,* VIII, p. 38, n. 4). As
in וְחָרֵד עַל דְּבָרִי, *and who tremble at My word* (Isaiah 66:2) which *Targum Yonasan*
renders: וּמַשְׁתְּוֵי לְקַבֵּל פִּתְגָּמִי. See also *ibid.* 66:5. Thus, אֵשְׁוָתָא is the Aramaic
equivalent of the Hebrew חֲרָדָה, *anxiety, trembling (Yad Aharon; Shnei
HaMe'oros; Heidenheim).*

COMMENTARY

shot from a bow *(Yad Aharon; Heidenheim).*

There are also two other interpretations of this phrase as follows:

1. The commentary in the *Kol Bo Machzor* translates: *as lightning bolts from a cloud* [lit. *rainbow*, which is a cloud] since lightning bolts are like the 'arrows' of a cloud. This interpretation is based on Ezekiel 1:14: וְהַחַיּוֹת רָצוֹא וָשׁוֹב כְּמַרְאֵה הַבָּזָק, *And the Chayos ran and returned as the appearance of a flash of lightning.* See also Ezekiel 1:28 cited below, and the notes to the next verse.

2. *Heidenheim* and *Mateh Levi* render: *as the brightness of a rainbow.* Their complete translation of this verse is as follows: לְמֶחֱזֵי בְּאַנְפָּא עֵין, *For the eye to see their faces, is* בְּוַת גִּירֵי קַשְׁתָא, *as the eye trying to perceive the brightness of a rainbow* [whose brightness makes it impossible to see directly *(Targum Yonasan)*]. Both commentators perhaps understand the word גִּירֵי, *arrows*, as being a form of the Hebrew word נֹגַהּ, *brightness.* Their interpretation is based on Ezekiel 1:28, כְּמַרְאֵה הַקֶּשֶׁת אֲשֶׁר יִהְיֶה בֶעָנָן בְּיוֹם הַגֶּשֶׁם כֵּן מַרְאֵה הַנֹּגַהּ סָבִיב הוּא מַרְאֵה דְּמוּת כְּבוֹד ה', *As the appearance of the rainbow that is in the cloud on the day of rain, so is the appearance of the brightness all around. This is the vision of the likeness of the glory of HASHEM.*

24. זְרִיזִין בְּאֵשְׁוָתָא — *They hasten anxiously*, in fear of Hashem and in their extreme eagerness to carry out His commands.

Given the other possible meanings of אֵשְׁוָתָא [see Notes], this phrase can also be translated as follows:

24 *To whichever place they're sent,*

they hasten anxiously.

25 *Blessing: 'Blessed be His glory' —*

in every whispered language —

LEXICAL NOTES

25. מְבָרְכִין — *They recite the blessing* or *they praise* from בָּרַךְ.

בְּרִיךְ יְקָרֵיה — *Blessed be His glory,* from the *Targum* paraphrase of the second verse of the *Kedushah* prayer: בְּרִיךְ יְקָרָא דַה' מֵאֲתַר בֵּית שְׁכִינְתֵּה, *Blessed be the glory of HASHEM from the dwelling place of His Shechinah (Targum Ezekiel 3:12).* The Hebrew text may be found in the *comm.* to *v.* 19.

לְשָׁן — *Language, tongue.*

לְחִישׁוּתָא — *Whispered* or: *in a whisper.* [Possibly it is a conjunction of the two words לְחִי, *jaw, cheeks;* and שׁוּתָא, *speech,* (see *v.* 1), hence לְחִי־שׁוּתָא, *the speech emerging from the jaws or cheeks,* hence: *in every form of spoken expression.*]

COMMENTARY

I. *They hurry with great haste,* or:
II. *They hasten with trembling.*

Both this verse and the preceding one are based almost verbatim on the *Targum Yonasan* to Ezekiel 1:14:

וּבְרִיָתָא בְּאִשְׁתַּלְחוּתְהִין לְמֶעְבַּד רְעוּת רִבּוֹנְהֶן דְּאַשְׁרֵי שְׁכִינְתֵּיה בִּמְרוֹמָא עֲלָא מִנְהֶן בַּאֲנָפָא עֵינָא לְמֶחֱזֵי חֶזְרָן וּמַקְפָן וּמְכַסָן יַת עַלְמָא וְתָיְבִין בְּרִיָתָא כַּחֲדָא וְקָלִילָן כְּחֵיזוּ בַרְקָא.

— *And when the Chayos are sent to carry out the will of their Master, whose Shechinah rests in the heavens above them, they surround, encircle, and cover the world, and return in unison. To see them before one's eyes, [their movement is] as the appearance and swiftness of a flash of lightning.*

25. מְבָרְכִין בְּרִיךְ יְקָרֵיה — *Blessing: 'Blessed be His glory' (Targum to Ezekiel 3:12).*

The poet is continuing his description of the angels' recital of the *Kedushah.* Having spoken of the Seraphim's uttering of *Kedushah* in verses 19-20, the poet now proceeds to describe the verses sung by the Cherubim and the Galgalim. The second verse of the *Kedushah* (Ezekiel 3:12), is recited by the Chayos and Ofanim, as expounded in *Chullin* 91b-92a and *Yalkut Tehillim* 743 (Yad Aharon).

Some commentators translate מְבָרְכִין בְּרִיךְ יְקָרֵיה: *they praise His blessed glory* or: *they praise His holy Name.* According to either translation, however, the basic meaning is the same (Heidenheim; Eshel Avrohom).

בְּכָל לְשָׁן לְחִישׁוּתָא — *In every whispered language* or: *in every spoken language.*

This is a poetic way of saying

כו מֵאֲתַר בֵּית שְׁכִינְתֵּיה,
דְּלָא צְרִיךְ בְּחִישׁוּתָא:

כז נְהִים כָּל חֵיל מְרוֹמָא,
מְקַלְּסִין בַּחֲשַׁשְׁתָּא.

26. שְׁכִינְתֵּיה — *His [God's] Shechinah; from* שָׁכַן, *to dwell. Hence:* שְׁכִינָה, *is a dwelling or royal residence.*

בְּחִישׁוּתָא — *Seeking, from the root* בָּחַשׁ.

27. נְהִים — *Roar, rumble (as thunder), from the Biblical* נַהַם, *to roar, growl, as in the Targum Yonasan to Isaiah 5:29,* נִיהוֹמֵי לֵיה כְּאַרְיָא, *their roaring shall be like a lion. See also Isaiah 5:30. The word* נְהִים *may be most accurately rendered as: a very loud droning hum.*

COMMENTARY

that the angels utter praise to Hashem in all languages (*Shnei HaMe'oros; Heidenheim*). That the angels know all languages [except Aramaic] is seen in *Sota* 36b where it is taught that Gabriel came to Joseph in Egypt and taught him all seventy languages (*Eshel Avrohom*).

Mateh Levi renders: *in all languages in a whisper.* However, such a translation would contradict verse 22 which states that the angels say the *Kedushah* very loudly.

Another possible translation of this verse would be *in all languages that are whispered in prayer* or: *in every language of prayer.* This translation is based on Isaiah 26:16: צָקוּן לַחַשׁ, *they poured out [their prayers] in a whisper.* Thus, לַחַשׁ means *silent prayer* (*M'vo HaShir*).

26. מֵאֲתַר בֵּית שְׁכִינְתֵּיה — *From the place of His Shechinah's house.*

The poet completes his excerpt from the *Targum* version of the *Kedushah* which he began in the previous verse. This phrase quotes *Targum Yonasan* to *Ezekiel* 3:12: מֵאֲתַר בֵּית שְׁכִינְתֵּיה (See *comm.* to the previous verse; see also the *comm.* to verse 19 for the complete Hebrew text and *Targum* with translation).

דְּלָא צְרִיךְ בְּחִישׁוּתָא — *Which needs no seeking.*

The Divine Presence of Hashem need not be sought, since Hashem is everywhere. This refers back to the first verse of the *Kedushah*: מְלֹא כָל הָאָרֶץ כְּבוֹדוֹ, *the whole earth is filled with His glory* (Isaiah 6:3) which the Midrash (*Sh'mos Rabbah* 2:9) expounds: לָמָה מִתּוֹךְ הַסְּנֶה — לְלַמֶּדְךָ

26 *From the place of His Shechinah's house*

which needs no seeking.

27 *Roaring — the whole heavenly host —*

praises in fear:

LEXICAL NOTES

חֵיל — *Army, host.*

מְרוֹמָא — *Above, on high; the heavens* (see *Psalms* 75:6 and *Targum Yonasan* there).

מְקַלְּסִין — *They praise;* from קָלַס.

בַּחֲשַׁשְׁתָּא — *In* or *with fear, anxiety;* from חֲשָׁשָׁא.

COMMENTARY

שָׁאֵין מָקוֹם פָּנוּי בְּלֹא שְׁכִינָה אֲפִילוּ סְנֶה, Why [did Hashem manifest His Presence] from within a bush? (See Exod. 3:2). To teach you that no place is devoid of the Divine Presence, not even a bush (Shnei HaMe'oros).

27. נְהִים כָּל חֵיל מְרוֹמָא — *Roaring, the whole heavenly host,* or: *All the celestial legions roar.*

The sound of all the angels saying the *Kedushah* is as a roaring sound throughout the heavens. The poet's choice of words in this verse parallels that used by *Midrash Tehillim* 146:10 and *Pesikta Rabbasi* 20:

וּבְשָׁעָה שֶׁיַּגִּיעַ כֶּתֶר כָּל חַיָּלֵי מַעֲלָה מִזְדַּעְזְעִים וְחַיּוֹת דּוֹמְמוֹת וְנֶהָמוֹת כְּאֲרִי ... וְאוֹמְרִים קָדוֹשׁ קָדוֹשׁ ... בְּשָׁעָה שֶׁהוּא עוֹבֵר עַל כָּל חַיְלֵי מָרוֹם פּוֹתְחִים פִּיהֶם וְאוֹמְרִים בָּרוּךְ כְּבוֹד ה' מִמְּקוֹמוֹ ... בְּשָׁעָה שֶׁמַגִּיעַ כֶּתֶר לְרֹאשׁוֹ ... כָּל

חַיּוֹת וּשְׂרָפִים וְאוֹפַנִּים וְגַלְגַּלֵי הַמֶּרְכָּבָה וְכִסֵּא הַכָּבוֹד בְּפֶה אֶחָד אוֹמְרִים יִמְלֹךְ ה' לְעוֹלָם אֱלֹהַיִךְ צִיּוֹן לְדֹר וָדֹר הַלְלוּיָהּ — *And when the crown [of Israel's prayers] reaches [the Chayos], all the heavenly armies tremble, and the [heretofore] silent Chayos roar like lions … and say: 'Holy, holy …'* (Isaiah 6:3) … *At the time that [the crown] passes over all the heavenly armies, they open their mouths and say: 'Blessed be* HASHEM *from His place'* (Ezek. 3:12) … *At the time that the crown reaches His head, all the Chayos, the Seraphim, the Ofanim, the Galgalim of the chariot and the throne of glory, say in unison:* 'HASHEM *shall reign forever, your God, O Zion, for all generations, Praise God!' Psalms* 146:10) (Yad Aharon).

[The text of the Pesikta has been translated according to the Parma manuscript No. 1240, and Casanata manuscript No. 3324. See

כח נְהִירָא מַלְכוּתֵיהּ,
לְדָר וְדָר לְאַפְרַשְׁתָּא:

כט סְדִירָא בְּהוֹן קְדוּשְׁתָּא,
וְכַד חָלְפָא שַׁעְתָּא.

LEXICAL NOTES

28. נְהִירָא — I. *Light, glow* from נְהַר, *to shine, to be bright;* II. *Memory, to recall,* as in *Chulin* 54a: וְלֹא נְהִירָא לֵיהּ לְאוֹתוּ תַּלְמִיד, *Do you not remember that student?*

מַלְכוּתֵיהּ — *His kingdom.*

לְדָר וְדָר — *For all generations,* Literally, *for generation and generation.*

לְאַפְרַשְׁתָּא — *Eternally;* from אַפְרֵשׁ, *a time to be specified in the future* (see *comm.*) as in *Targum Yonasan* to *Isaiah* 57:16, וְלָא לְאַפְרֵשׁ יְהֵי רוּגְזִי, *nor will I be wroth forever.* See also *Targum* to *II Samuel* 2:26.

29. סְדִירָא — *Arranged, ordered, (in time and/or in place);* from סָדַר.

COMMENTARY

comm. to *v.* 37 for a full explanation. See also *Chagigah* 13b.]

28. נְהִירָא מַלְכוּתֵיהּ — I. *May His kingdom glow,* or: *May His kingdom shine brightly* (Heidenheim). Similarly, some translate this phrase like the Hebrew הֲדַר מַלְכוּתוֹ, *the glory of His kingdom* [see notes to *v.* 9] (Heidenheim; Emunos Machzor).

According to definition II, the verse is rendered: *That the memory of His kingdom be for all generations unto eternity* (Mateh Levi; Yad Aharon).

נְהִירָא מַלְכוּתֵיהּ לְדָר וְדָר ... — *May His kingdom glow for all generations ...*

This is a paraphrase of the third and final verse of the *Kedushah* prayer, יִמְלֹךְ ה' לְעוֹלָם אֱלֹהַיִךְ צִיּוֹן לְדֹר וָדֹר הַלְלוּיָהּ, *HASHEM shall reign forever, your God, O Zion, for all generations. Praise God!* See also notes to *v.* 19. [Shnei Ha-Me'oros].

[Compare this verse with *Psalms* 145:4: *One generation to another shall praise Your works.*]

This verse may also be interpreted as a continuation of the previous one: *All the heavenly armies roar, praising in fear, the brilliance of His kingdom, for all generations unto eternity* i.e., the angels praise the Holy One for all eternity without ceasing.

Still other commentators interpret לְאַפְרַשְׁתָּא as a derivation of

אקדמות [76]

²⁸ *'May His kingdom glow*

for all generations eternally.'

²⁹ *Arranged among them is Kedushah,*

and when the time has passed

קְדוּשְׁתָּא — *The Kedushah*, the series of hymns and prayers of sanctification recited to the Holy One every day by both the angels and Israel; mentioned in *Sotah* 49a; see also the notes to *v.* 19.

חֲלְפָא — *Passed by, gone*, from חֲלַף.

שַׁעְתָּא — *Time; hour.*

the root פָּרַשׁ, *to explain clearly; to describe*. Accordingly, they translate the verse as follows: *They [the angels] describe the brilliance of Hashem's kingdom from generation to generation throughout all time (M'vo HaShir; Yad Aharon; Eshel Avrohom)*.

29. סְדִירָא בְּהוֹן קְדוּשְׁתָּא — *Arranged among them is (the saying of) Kedushah.*

The specific time that each class of angel is permitted to sanctify and praise God, is prearranged and fixed. See the notes to לְתְלוֹתֵי קְדוּשְׁתָּא of *v.* 20 above. Even the very number of words that they are allowed to utter before the Holy One is specified for them.

This point is derived from the following passages in *Chullin* 91b: וַיֹּאמֶר שַׁלְחֵנִי כִּי עָלָה הַשַּׁחַר אָמַר לוֹ גַּנָּב אַתָּה אוֹ קוּבְּיוּסְטוֹס אַתָּה שֶׁמִּתְיָרֵא מִן

הַשַּׁחַר אָמַר לוֹ מַלְאָךְ אֲנִי וּמִיּוֹם שֶׁנִּבְרֵאתִי לֹא הִגִּיעַ זְמַנִּי לוֹמַר שִׁירָה עַד עַכְשָׁיו. — *And he said, 'Let me go, for day is breaking!' (Gen. 32:27). He (Jacob) said to him: 'Are you a thief or a kidnapper' [(Rashi); Tosafos translates dice-player] that you are afraid of daybreak?' He replied, 'I am an angel, and from the day that I was created, my time for saying hymns of praise[to the Lord]did not arrive until today' (Bereishis Rabbah 78:2; Pirkei d'Rabbi Eliezer 37)*. See also the notes to the next verse *(Yad Aharon)*.

וְכַד חֲלְפָא שַׁעְתָּא — *And when the time has passed.*

Once their turn for the saying of the *Kedushah* has passed, as the next verse continues, some angels are never again given the opportunity to recite it.

ל סִיּוּמָא דִלְעָלַם,

וְאוּף לָא לִשְׁבוּעֲתָא:

לא עֲדַב יְקַר אַחֲסַנְתֵּיה,

חֲבִיבִין דִּבְקַבְעֶתָא.

LEXICAL NOTES

30. סִיּוּמָא — *At an end*, from סַיֵּים.

דִלְעָלַם — *Forever*; literally, *from forever*.

לִשְׁבוּעֲתָא — *After* (or: *upon*) *seven years*; from שְׁבוּעֲתָא, *a period of seven years*, which is the span of time between Sabbatical years.

COMMENTARY

30. סִיּוּמָא דִלְעָלַם . . . — *It is forever ended* . . .

In this verse and in the previous one, the poet refers to the following passage from *Chulin* 91b:

חֲבִיבִין יִשְׂרָאֵל לִפְנֵי הַקָּדוֹשׁ בָּרוּךְ הוּא יוֹתֵר מִמַּלְאֲכֵי הַשָּׁרֵת שֶׁיִּשְׂרָאֵל אוֹמְרִים שִׁירָה בְּכָל שָׁעָה וּמַלְאֲכֵי הַשָּׁרֵת אֵין אוֹמְרִים שִׁירָה אֶלָּא פַּעַם אַחַת בַּיּוֹם וְאָמְרִי לָה פַּעַם אַחַת בְּשַׁבָּת וְאָמְרִי לָה פַּעַם אַחַת בַּחוֹדֶשׁ וְאָמְרִי לָה פַּעַם אַחַת בְּשָׁנָה וְאָמְרִי לָה פַּעַם אַחַת בַּשָּׁבוּעַ וְאָמְרִי לָה פַּעַם אַחַת בַּיּוֹבֵל וְאָמְרִי לָה פַּעַם אַחַת בְּעוֹלָם

— *Israel is more beloved to the Holy One, blessed be He, than are the ministering angels. For Israel says praise at all times, while the ministering angels say praise only once a day. And some [say the Kedushah] once a week, and some once a month. Some say it only once a year, and some say but once in seven years. And some say it once*

in fifty years (lit., a Jubilee), and some say it only once ever [Yad Aharon; Heidenheim; et al.] See also the two following verses.

31. עֲדַב יְקַר אַחֲסַנְתֵּיה — *His precious inheritance's lot is dearer.*

This refers to Israel which is God's own portion, selected from all the nations of the world.

This phrase is taken from *Targum Onkelos* and *Yonasan* to *Deut.* 32:9: כִּי חֵלֶק ה' עַמּוֹ יַעֲקֹב חֶבֶל נַחֲלָתוֹ which the *Targum* renders: אֲרֵי חֻלָקָא דַה' עַמֵּהּ יַעֲקֹב עֲדַב אַחֲסַנְתֵּהּ, *For the portion of HASHEM is His people, Jacob, the lot of His inheritance.*

The poet's reference to the people of Israel as Hashem's lot, is in accordance with *Tanchuma Ha'azinu* 6:

כְּשֶׁבָּא הַקָּדוֹשׁ בָּרוּךְ הוּא לְבַלְבֵּל דּוֹר הַפְּלָגָה אָמַר הַקָּדוֹשׁ בָּרוּךְ הוּא לַמַּלְאָכִים

³⁰ *It is forever ended,*

not even after seven years.

³¹ *But His precious inheritance's lot,*

is dearer for with regularity

LEXICAL NOTES

31. עֲדַב — *Lot, share, portion.*

יְקַר — *Precious, honored.*

אַחֲסַנְתֵּיה — *His inheritance, from* אַחֲסַנְתָּא.

דְּבִקְבַעְתָּא — *With regularity; from* קְבַע, *to fix, to permanently establish a time or place.*

COMMENTARY

שָׁרֵי כָּל הָאֻמּוֹת בָּאוּ וְנָטִיל גּוֹרָלוֹת לְמִי
יַעֲלוּ הָאֻמּוֹת אָמְרָה לְכָל אֶחָד מִמֶּנּוּ וְאֵיזֶה
יַעֲלֶה לְחֶלְקִי לְחֶלְקִי הִטִּילוּ גּוֹרָלוֹת וְנָפַל יִשְׂרָאֵל
לְחֶלְקוֹ שֶׁל הַקָּדוֹשׁ בָּרוּךְ הוּא כְּדִכְתִיב:
בְּהַנְחֵל עֶלְיוֹן גּוֹיִם . . . וְכֵן הוּא אוֹמֵר: כִּי
חֵלֶק ה' עַמּוֹ יַעֲקֹב חֶבֶל נַחֲלָתוֹ.
— When the Holy One, blessed be
He, came to confuse the [languages
of the] Generation of the Dispersion
(Gen. 11:1-9), the Holy One, blessed
be He, said to the angels in
charge of the nations: 'Come let us
cast lots [to determine] to whom the
nations will be assigned, one nation
for each of us, and which nation
shall be My portion.' So they cast
lots and Israel came out as the lot of
the Holy One, blessed be He, as it is
written: When the Most High gave
to the nations their inheritance,
(Deut. 32:8) and it also says (ibid.
32:9): For the portion of HASHEM is
His people, Jacob the lot (חֶבֶל) of
His inheritance. [See also Pirkei

d'Rabbi Eliezer 24; and Midrash
Tehillim 16:6.] (Yad Aharon).

[Our translation of חֶבֶל as *lot* follows
Sifrei 312 to Deut. 32:9, אֵין חֶבֶל אֶלָּא גּוֹרָל,
the word חֶבֶל means only 'lot'].

חֲבִיבִין — *Is dearer (than the angels).*
Israel is more beloved to the Holy
One than the angels in heaven. The
poet refers to the Talmudic passage
quoted in the previous verse. See
comm. to the next verse for further
explanation.

דְּבִקְבַעְתָּא — *For with regularity,* (i.e,
daily, at permanently established
and fixed intervals of time at morning and evening prayers).

The Jewish people pray to
Hashem three or more times daily,
every single day, as opposed to the
angels who are permitted to offer
their praises not more than once a
day, and sometimes only once in a
lifetime.

עֲבְדִין; חֲטִיבָא לב עֲבִידִין לֵיה חֲטִיבָה,

בְּדְנַח וּשְׁקַעְתָּא:

LEXICAL NOTES

32. עֲבִידִין — *They make,* from עֲבַד.

עֲבִידִין לֵיה — *They make Him [Hashem].*

חֲטִיבָה — *Object of love,* (according to *Mateh Levi*), from חֲטִיב, *to select [as the object of one's love], to betroth to.*

Torah Temimah (Deut. 26:17 n. 82) translates: *something set aside because of its special value or praiseworthiness,* from חֲטַב, *to chop off.*

Aruch, quoting Rav Hai Gaon, translates: *a unique concept in the world,* i.e., something recognized as unique.

COMMENTARY

32. עֲבִידִין לֵיה חֲטִיבָה — *They make Him their sole desire* or: *they make Him the sole object of their praise.*

This verse is based on the following passage from *Berachos* 6a and *Chagigah* 3a:

אֶת ה' הֶאֱמַרְתָּ הַיּוֹם (לִהְיוֹת לְךָ לֵאלֹהִים)
(וּכְתִיב) זַה' הֶאֱמִירְךָ הַיּוֹם (לִהְיוֹת לוֹ
לְעָם) אָמַר לָהֶם הַקָּדוֹשׁ בָּרוּךְ הוּא
לְיִשְׂרָאֵל אַתֶּם עֲשִׂיתוּנִי חֲטִיבָה אַחַת
בָּעוֹלָם וַאֲנִי אֶעֱשֶׂה אֶתְכֶם חֲטִיבָה אַחַת
בָּעוֹלָם אַתֶּם עֲשִׂיתוּנִי חֲטִיבָה אַחַת
בָּעוֹלָם דִּכְתִיב שְׁמַע יִשְׂרָאֵל ה' אֱלֹהֵינוּ ה'
אֶחָד וַאֲנִי אֶעֱשֶׂה אֶתְכֶם חֲטִיבָה אַחַת
בָּעוֹלָם שֶׁנֶּאֱמַר: וּמִי כְּעַמְּךָ יִשְׂרָאֵל גּוֹי
אֶחָד בָּאָרֶץ

— [*It is written*], You have avouched HASHEM this day [to be Your God], *and it is written:* And HASHEM has avouched you this day [to be His own treasured people] (*Deut.* 26:17-18 see *Onkelos* there). *The Holy One, blessed be He, said to Israel: 'You have made Me the sole object of your love in the world, and I shall make you the sole* object of My love in the world. You have made Me a unique object of your love, as it is written: 'Hear O Israel, HASHEM our God, HASHEM is one!' (Deut. 6:4). And I shall make you a unique object of My love, as it says: 'And what one nation in the earth is like Your people Israel?' [I Chronicles 17:21]* (Heidenheim; see *Bamidbar Rabbah 14:11; Tanchuma Ki Savo 2; Tanchuma Buber ibid. 4; Pirkei d'Rabbi Eliezer 4.*)

עֲבִידִין לֵיה חֲטִיבָה ... — *They make Him their sole desire, at sunrise and sunset.*

This refers to Israel's morning and evening recitation of the *Shema* (*Deut.* 6:4 see above), Israel's declaration of the oneness and uniqueness of Hashem in the universe. Israel's love for Hashem is declared in the second verse of the *Shema* ... וְאָהַבְתָּ אֵת ה' אֱלֹהֶיךָ, *And you shall love HASHEM your God* ... [Shnei Ha-Me'oros].

32 They make Him their sole desire,
at sunrise and sunset.

בְּדְנַח — *At sunrise*, from דְּנַח, *to shine*, as in the *Targum* to *Gen.* 32:32, וּדְנַח לֵיהּ שִׁמְשָׁא, *and the sun rose* (lit. *shone*) *upon him*.

וּשְׁקַעְתָּא — *And sunset*, from שְׁקַע, *to sink* as in שְׁקִיעַת הַחַמָּה, *sunset*, literally: *sinking of the sun*.

[In the last three verses, the poet has cited the two reasons given in the Talmud for Israel's being more beloved to the Holy One, blessed be He, than the angels. The first reason is that Israel utters the *Kedushah* to Hashem twice daily, while some angels utter it but once in their existence. The second is that Israel declares the oneness of Hashem, and its love for Him, twice daily. See also *Targum Yonasan* to *Deut.* 26:17-18, and to *I Chron.* 17:21).]

The poet is referring to the passage (*Chulin* 91b) quoted in the *comm.* to *v.* 30, which continues: וְיִשְׂרָאֵל מַזְכִּירִין אֶת הַשֵּׁם אַחַר שְׁתֵּי תֵּיבוֹת שֶׁנֶּאֱמַר שְׁמַע יִשְׂרָאֵל ה' ... וּמַלְאֲכֵי הַשָּׁרֵת אֵין מַזְכִּירִין אֶת הַשֵּׁם אֶלָּא לְאַחַר ג' תֵּיבוֹת כְּדִכְתִיב קָדוֹשׁ קָדוֹשׁ ה' צְבָאוֹת.

— *And [another reason why Israel is more beloved to Hashem than the angels is that] Israel utters Hashem's name after [saying] two words, as is said: 'Hear O Israel, HASHEM ... '. (Deut. 6:4). While the ministering angels mention His Name only after three words, as is written: 'Holy, holy, holy, is HASHEM of hosts' (Isaiah 6:3)* [*Chullin* 91b; see also the notes to *v.* 30] (*Yad Aharon*).

Yad Aharon points out that the poet identifies Israel's twice-daily reading of the Shema as that which makes Israel more beloved than the angels to Hashem, rather than their twice-daily recital of the *Kedushah*. This is because the *Shema* is recited at all times without the need of a *minyan* (i.e., a quorum of ten), while the *Kedushah* may be recited only with a *minyan*.

With regard to the usage of the phrase 'at sunrise and sunset' see *Malachi* 1:11; and also the *comm.* to *v.* 36.

Compare this verse also with Rashi's commentary (based on *Menachos* 110a) to *Malachi* 1:11, כָּל תְּפִלּוֹת יִשְׂרָאֵל שֶׁמִּתְפַּלְלִין בְּכָל מָקוֹם הֲרֵי הֵן לִי כְּמִנְחָה טְהוֹרָה, [*Hashem says:*] *All the prayers that Israel prays in all places, I consider to be as a pure meal-offering to Me* (*Yad Aharon*).

לג **פְּרִישָׁן לְמָנָתֵיהּ,**
לְמֶעְבַּד לֵיהּ רְעוּתָא.
לד **פְּרִישׁוּתֵיהּ שְׁבָחֵיהּ,** פְּרִישְׁתֵּי
יְחַוּוֹן בִּשָׁעוּתָא:

LEXICAL NOTES

33. פְּרִישָׁן — *He set them aside* or alternatively: *They [Israel] are set aside,* from פֵּרֵשׁ, *to set aside, or separate something because of its special importance.*

לְמָנָתֵיהּ — *As (for) His portion,* from מָנָה.

לְמֶעְבַּד — *To do,* from עֲבַד, *to do, to make,* the Aramaic equivalent of לַעֲשׂוֹת.

רְעוּתָא — *Will, desire;* from רְעִי, *to desire,* and from רַעֲנָא, *will.*

COMMENTARY

33. פְּרִישָׁן לְמָנָתֵיהּ — *Separated as His portion.*

Hashem set Israel aside from all the people of the world as His special portion. This phrase again refers to *Deut. 32:9:* כִּי חֵלֶק ה' עַמּוֹ יַעֲקֹב חֶבֶל נַחֲלָתוֹ, *For the portion of HASHEM is His people, Jacob, the lot if His inheritance,* and to *Lev. 20:26:* וָאַבְדִּל אֶתְכֶם מִן הָעַמִּים לִהְיוֹת לִי, *And I have set you apart from the peoples that you should be Mine (Shnei HaMe'oros).* Comp. also with *I Kings 8:53,* כִּי אַתָּה הִבְדַּלְתָּם לְךָ לְנַחֲלָה מִכֹּל עַמֵּי הָאָרֶץ, *For You separated them from amongst all the people of the earth, to be Your inheritance (Shnei Ha-Me'oros).*

לְמֶעְבַּד לֵיהּ רְעוּתָא — *To execute His will* or: *that they should do His will.*

Zvi V'Chamed, M'vo HaShir, and *T'yul B'gan* point out that the reason why Israel is more beloved than the angels to the Holy One, blessed be He, is not because Israel says the *Kedushah* more often than the angels; nor because they recite the *Shema* twice daily. Rather, the greatness of Israel lies in the fact that it praises and prays to Hashem *of its own free will,* and obeys Hashem's commandments despite the constant urging of the evil inclination to the contrary.

Such is not the case with angels. Angels have no free will and were created only to carry out Hashem's commands. Furthermore, angels have no evil inclination, consequently they can neither do wrong nor be rewarded for doing what is commanded of them. In addition, the angels are totally and constantly aware of Hashem's greatness, since they are near His Presence. We, on the other hand, must rely on our faith, for we are removed from Hashem's Presence, both physically and spiritually. Still, despite all obstacles, we pray to, and praise Hashem constantly. (See the notes to the next verse).

אקדמות [82]

³³ *Separated as His portion*

to execute His will.

³⁴ *His wonders and His praises,*

they recount at every hour.

LEXICAL NOTES

34. פְּרִישׁוּתֵיהּ — *His wonders,* from פְּרִישָׁא, *wonder, wonderful deed;* as in *Targum* to *Job* 37:14: פְּרִישׁוּתָא דָאֱלָהָא, *the wonders of the Lord.* (Cf. the *Onkelos* to *Exod.* 3:20; 33:16; and *Targum Yonasan ibid.* 13:8).

שְׁבָחֵיהּ — *His praises,* from שָׁבַח, *to praise.*

יְחַוּוֹן — *They recount, show* from חַוֵּי. (See also *v.* 42).

בְּשָׁעוּתָא — *At [every] hour* or *moment,* from שָׁעָה, *moment, hour.*

COMMENTARY

34. פְּרִישׁוּתֵיהּ שְׁבָחֵיהּ — *His wonders (and) His praises.*

Israel prays and gives thanks to Hashem constantly, as cited in *Tanchuma, Bamidbar* 4:

אֲבָל יִשְׂרָאֵל לְהַקָדוֹשׁ בָּרוּךְ הוּא הַנָּאָה לוֹ בָּהֶן קוֹרִין קְרִיאַת שְׁמַע וּמִתְפַּלְלִין וּמְבָרְכִין שְׁמוֹ בְּכָל יוֹם וּבְכָל שָׁעָה עַל כָּל דָּבָר וְדָבָר לְפִיכָךְ הֵם נִמְנִין בְּכָל שָׁעָה וּלְכָךְ נִמְשְׁלוּ בְּחִטִּים בִּטְנֵךְ עֲרֵמַת חִטִּים.

— *But Israel [is unlike the other peoples], because the Holy One, blessed be He, [as it were], derives satisfaction from them, (because) they recite the Shema, and they praise, and bless His name every day and at every moment concerning each and every matter. Therefore, they are counted [by Hashem] at all times, and are likened to wheat [which, because it is valuable, is constantly weighed and reweighed]: 'Your stomach is like a heap of wheat' (Shir HaShirim 7:3).*

Another translation for בְּשָׁעוּתָא is *at desirable times,* as is expounded by *Tanchuma Miketz* 9:

רַבִּי יוֹסִי בַּר חֲלַפְתָּא אוֹמֵר עִתִּים הֵם לַתְּפִלָּה שֶׁנֶּאֱמַר וַאֲנִי תְפִלָּתִי לְךָ ה' עֵת רָצוֹן. אֵימָתַי עֵת רָצוֹן? — בְּשָׁעָה שֶׁהַצִבּוּר מִתְפַּלְּלִין

— *Rabbi Yossi the son of Chalafta says: There are times for praying, as the verse states 'But as for me, my prayer is to you, HASHEM, an acceptable time' (Psalms 69:14) When is an acceptable time? At the time when the congregation prays (Yad Aharon).*

In this connection, *Yad Aharon* also cites *Aggados Bereishis* 76:

לְכָל דָּבָר נָתַן הַקָדוֹשׁ בָּרוּךְ הוּא זְמַן וְעֵת חוּץ מִן תְּפִלָּה אֵימָתַי שֶׁיִּתְפַּלֵל נַעֲנֶה שֶׁנֶּאֱמַר כִּי לְכָל חֵפֶץ יֵשׁ עֵת וּמִשְׁפָּט לָמָה שָׁאֲלוּ הָיָה אָדָם יוֹדֵעַ אֵימָתַי הוּא מִתְפַּלֵל וְנַעֲנֶה הָיָה מַנִיחַ כָּל הַיָמִים וְלֹא הָיָה מִתְפַּלֵל אֶלָּא בְּאוֹתוֹ יוֹם. אָמַר הקב"ה לְפִיכָךְ אֵינִי מוֹדִיעַ לָךְ אֵימָתַי אַתָּה נַעֲנֶה כְּדֵי שֶׁתְּהֵא מִתְפַּלֵל בְּכָל שָׁעָה שֶׁנֶּאֱמַר בִּטְחוּ בוֹ בְּכָל עֵת ...

— *For all things the Holy One, blessed be He, designated a time and duration, except for prayer: whenever one prays he will be*

וְחַמֵּד: וְרַגֵּג לה צְבֵי וְחָמִיד וְרָגִיג,
דִּילָאוּן בְּלָעוּתָא.
לו צְלוֹתְהוֹן בְּכֵן מְקַבֵּל,

35. צְבֵי — *He desired*, from צְבֵי, as in *Targum Yonasan* to חָפֵץ, *(Gen.* 34:19) and *Onkelos* to חָשַׁק *(Deut.* 7:7). Also *to find pleasure in, to choose.*

וְחָמִיד — *And longed, coveted,* from the Aramaic and Hebrew חָמַד, as in *Targum Onkelos* to Gen. 31:30.

וְרָגִיג — *And coveted, longed* from רְגַג equivalent to the Hebrew חָמַד, (as in *Ps.* 68:17) and to the Hebrew אִוָּה (as in *Ps.* 132:13-14).

COMMENTARY

answered. As is stated: Because to every purpose there is a time and a judgment *(Koheles* 8:6). *Why* [is this so?] — For if man knew at which time his prayers would be answered, he would wait daily and not pray except on that (specific) day. The Holy One, blessed be He, said, I will not inform you as to when (precisely) you will be answered in order that you should pray at all times; *as is stated:* Trust in Him at all times *(Psalms* 62:9).

[See also: *Pesikta d'Rav Kahana* (Buber), 157b; *Midrash Tehillim* 65:4; *Bamidbar Rabbah* 2:12; *Yerushalmi Makkos,* 2:6.]

35. צְבֵי וְחָמִיד וְרָגִיג — *He desired, longed, and coveted.*

Yad Aharon suggests that possibly the poet employs these three essentially synonymous words as an allusion to *Midrash Tehillim* 2:22: אָמַר ר' שִׁמְעוֹן בֶּן לָקִישׁ בְּשָׁלֹשׁ לְשׁוֹנוֹת שֶׁל חִיבָּה חִיבֵּב הַקְבָּ"ה אֶת יִשְׂרָאֵל אֵלּוּ הֵן — בִּדְבֵיקָה בַּחֲשִׁיקָה בַּחֲפִיצָה. בִּדְבֵיקָה 'וְאַתֶּם הַדְּבֵקִים', בַּחֲשִׁיקָה 'חָשַׁק ה' בָּכֶם' בַּחֲפִיצָה 'כִּי חָפֵץ ה' בָּךְ' — *R. Shimon ben Lakish said:* With

three expressions of affection did the Holy One, blessed be He, express His love for Israel; with 'cleaving, longing and desiring.' — With cleaving, [as it is written], 'And you that cleaved (הַדְּבֵקִים) to Hashem' *(Deut.* 4:4); with longing [as it is written], 'HASHEM longed (חָשַׁק) for you' *(ibid.* 7:7); *and with desire* [as it is written], 'For HASHEM desired (חָפֵץ) you' *(Isaiah* 62:4).

צְבֵי וְחָמִיד ... — *He desired, longed ...*

It is Hashem's will that Israel should study the Torah, as the *Sifra* comments: אִם בְּחֻקֹּתַי תֵּלֵכוּ מְלַמֵּד שֶׁהַמָּקוֹם מִתְאַוֶּה שֶׁיִּהְיוּ יִשְׂרָאֵל עֲמֵלִים בַּתּוֹרָה, *If you will walk in my statutes (Lev.* 26:3). *From here we learn that the Lord desires that Israel should labor in the study of the Torah* (*Yad Aharon*).

The study of the Torah is Israel's labor of love, the rewards of which are reaped in this world, but more especially in the world to come. As Ben Hai Hai says (*Avos,* 5:23):

³⁵ *He desired, longed, and coveted*

that they labor in the study

³⁶ *Their prayers He therefore listens to;*

LEXICAL NOTES

דִּילְאוּן בְּלָעוּתָא — *That they should toil [diligently] in the study [of Torah]*, from לָאֵי, and לָעֵי, *to labor, toil*; which often have the connotation of toiling in the study of Torah. For example, see *Targum to Job* 5:7, בַּר נָשׁ לְמִלְעֵי בְּאוֹרַיְתָא אִתְבְּרִי, *Man was created in order that he should study [labor in] the Torah*, and *Targum to Psalms* 73:5, בְּלִיעוּת גַּבְרִין דְּמִסְעַסְקִין בְּאוֹרַיְתָא, *[the wicked know not] of the labor of the men who occupy themselves with the study of the Torah*. [See also *Yerushalmi Shabbos* 6:1; and *ibid. Sanhedrin* 2:6: לָעֵין בְּאוֹרַיְתָא, *studying the Torah*] (Berger).

36. צְלוֹתְהוֹן — *Their prayers*, from צְלוֹתָא.

מְקַבֵּל — *Accepts*; from קַבֵּל.

COMMENTARY

לְפוּם צַעֲרָא אַגְרָא, *according to the labor is the reward (for the study of the Torah)*. [In *Avos d'Rabbi Nassan* 12:11, this statement is attributed to Hillel the Elder.]

God desires that Jews should exert themselves in the study of the law, so that their consequent reward shall be increased as it says: הַשּׁוֹנֶה וְאֵינוֹ עָמֵל כְּאִישׁ זוֹרֵעַ וְלֹא קוֹצֵר, *One who studies without effort, is like a man who sows but does not reap [since the rewards of study come from the labor invested].* (*Tosefta, Para*, 3).

This verse expresses another reason for Israel's superiority to the angels. Israel must toil and strain in order to understand the fine points of the Torah. It thereby merits reward for its labors. The angels, on the other hand, are neither obligated to study the Torah, nor need they exert themselves to do so (*Yad Aharon*).

36. צְלוֹתְהוֹן בְּכֵן מְקַבֵּל — *Their prayers He therefore listens to*, or: *are therefore accepted*.

Yad Aharon comments that because Israel diligently studies and upholds the Torah, Hashem pays heed to its prayers and requests. As is expressed in the following passages: אָמַר הַקָּדוֹשׁ בָּרוּךְ הוּא בִּזְכוּת הַתּוֹרָה שֶׁאַתֶּם עוֹסְקִין בָּהּ הָיִיתִי מַקְשִׁיב וְשׁוֹמֵעַ תְּפִלוֹתֵיכֶם, *The Holy One, blessed be He, says:'Because you occupy yourselves with the study of the Torah, I hearken and listen to your prayers.'* (*Tanchuma Emor* 16, see *Malachi* 3:16);

כָּל הָעוֹסֵק בְּתוֹרָה הַקָּדוֹשׁ בָּרוּךְ הוּא עוֹשֶׂה לוֹ חֶפְצִין, *Whoever is engaged in the study of the Torah, the Holy One, blessed be He, fulfills all his desires* (*Avodah Zarah* 19a);

מָאן דְּבָעֵי דִקב"ה יְקַבֵּל צְלוֹתֵיהּ יִשְׁתַּדֵל בְּאוֹרַיְיתָא, *He who desires that the Holy One, blessed be He, should accept his prayers, should strain*

וְהַנְיָא בָעוּתָא:

לז קְטִירָא לְחֵי עָלְמָא,
בְּתָגָא בִּשְׁבוּעָתָא.

LEXICAL NOTES

וְהַנְיָא — Efficacious, or: and it aids, from הַנְיָא (הֲנָאָה), benefit, pleasure; and from הֲנִין, to aid, as in Targum to Jeremiah 2:8, וּבָתַר דְּלָא יְהַנּוּן לְהוֹן אַזָלוּ, and they go after things that will be of no efficacy to them (Kinyan Tov).

בָעוּתָא — Prayer, supplication, from the root בְּעָא.

COMMENTARY

himself in the study of the Torah 202b];
אָמַר הקב״ה אִם שָׁמַעְתָּ לְמִצְוֹתַי אַף אֲנִי שׁוֹמֵעַ תְּפִלָּתֶךָ, The Holy One, blessed be He, says: If you listen to My commandments, then I too will listen to your prayers (Devarim Rabbah 7:4).

וְהַנְיָא בָעוּתָא — Their prayer is efficacious, or: and it benefits their supplications.

The merit that Israel gains from studying the Torah is helpful in achieving Hashem's acceptance of their prayers and requests.

This verse, along with verses 32, 33, and 35, is based on the following passage from Targum:
אֲרֵי מִמַּדְנַח שִׁמְשָׁא וְעַד מַעֲלֵיהּ רַב שְׁמִי בֵּינֵי עַמְמַיָּא וּבְכָל עִדָן דְּאַתּוּן עָבְדִין רְעוּתִי אֲנָא אֲקַבֵּל צְלוֹתְכוֹן וּשְׁמִי רַבָּא מִתְקַדַּשׁ עַל יְדֵיכוֹן וּצְלוֹתְכוֹן כְּקוּרְבַּן דְּכֵי קֳדָמַי
— Because from sunrise until sunset My name is great amongst the na-

tions. Whenever you do My will, I will accept your prayers and My great name will be sanctified through you. Your prayers are as a pure offering before Me [Targum Malachi 1:11; see also Targum Isaiah 49:8] (Yad Aharon).

37. קְטִירָא לְחֵי עָלְמָא ... — (The prayers are) wreathed for the Eternally Living, i.e., wreathed and bound to God like a crown.

The poet is referring to the following passages in the Talmud and Midrash. We cite them with the caution that they are allegorical and mystical and beyond our ability to comprehend:
מַלְאָךְ אֶחָד שֶׁהוּא עוֹמֵד בָּאָרֶץ וְרֹאשׁוֹ מַגִּיעַ לְבֵין הַחַיּוֹת. בְּמַתְנִיתָא תָּנָא סַנְדַּלְפוֹן שְׁמוֹ ... וְעָמַד אַחֲרֵי הַמֶּרְכָּבָה וְקוֹשֵׁר כְּתָרִים לְקוֹנוֹ. אִינִי וְהָא כְּתִיב: בָּרוּךְ כְּבוֹד ה' מִמְּקוֹמוֹ מִכְּלָל דִּמְקוֹמוֹ לֵיכָּא דְּיָדַע לֵיהּ אֶלָּא דְקָשַׁר לֵיהּ לְכֶתֶר וּמַשְׁבִּיעוֹ בְּשֵׁם הַמְפוֹרָשׁ וְאָזַל תַּגָּא וְיָתִיב בְּדוּכְתֵּיהּ

³⁷ *Wreathed for the Eternally Living*

into a crown, with an oath.

37. קְטִירָא — *Wreathed, bound* from קְטַר.

לְחֵי עָלְמָא — *To the Eternally living,* an expression for Hashem commonly found in the *Zohar,* and used in the *Zohar's* account of the quotations below. See *Zohar I,* 167b (*Yad Aharon*).

בְּתָגָא — *Into a crown,* literally, *with a crown,* from תָגָא.

בִּשְׁבוּעֲתָא — *With an oath.*

COMMENTARY

— *There is an angel who stands on the earth and whose head reaches among the Chayos. In a Braisa we learned that Sandalfon is his name ... And he stands behind the Merkavah* [see *Overview* to *Yechezkel,* ArtScroll ed.] *and binds (or: wreathes) crowns for his Maker [out of Israel's prayers] — But this is not so! It is written: Blessed be the glory of HASHEM from His place (Ezekiel 3:12), implying that His place is known to no one! — Only [it is as follows:] that he [Sandalfon] binds [the prayers] for Him into a crown and adjures it* (וּמַשְׁבִּיעוֹ) *with the Divine Name.* [I.e. He utters the Four-Letter Name upon the crown. This is what is literally meant by the words שְׁבוּעָה (oath) and מַשְׁבִּיעוֹ, *to cause to swear* (i.e., to utter the Divine Name). The poet uses the word בִּשְׁבוּעֲתָא, in the same sense.] *Then the crown goes and sets itself in its place* (*Ayin Yaakov*

to *Chaggigah* 13b; see also gloss of *Bach*).

The following Midrash further expands on the above:

מֵאַחַר שֶׁכָּל הַכְּנֵסִיּוֹת גּוֹמְרוֹת כָּל הַתְּפִלּוֹת נוֹטֵל כָּל הַתְּפִלּוֹת שֶׁהִתְפַּלְלוּ בְּכָל הַכְּנֵסִיּוֹת כּוּלָן וְעוֹשֶׂה אוֹתָן עֲטָרוֹת וְנוֹתְנָן בְּרֹאשׁוֹ שֶׁל הַקָּדוֹשׁ בָּרוּךְ הוּא — *After all synagogues have completed all their prayers, He (Sandalfon) takes all the prayers which were prayed, at all Houses of Worship everywhere, and makes them into crowns and places them (as it were) at the head of the Holy One, blessed be He* [Exod. Rabbah 21:4].*Or: (the prayers are) wreathed into a crown.* The prayers are wreathed or tied into a crown as is done when making a wreath or laurel.

[For a continuation of the description of the crown made of Israel's prayers, see the quote from the *Pesikta Rabbasi, Piska* 20, in the comm. to v. 27.]

לח קַבֵּל יְקַר טוֹטַפְתָּא,

יְתִיבָא בִּקְבִיעוּתָא:

לט וְרִשִׁימָא הִיא גוּפָא,

בְּחָכְמְתָא וּבְדַעְתָּא.

LEXICAL NOTES

38. קַבֵּל — *Beside, opposite;* (equivalent to the Hebrew כְּנֶגֶד, לְעֻמַּת, מוּל).

טוֹטַפְתָּא — *Tefillin,* literally: *frontlets,* i.e., an ornament worn on the forehead, as in *Deut.* 6:8: לְטֹטָפֹת. Onkelos renders: לִתְפִלִּין, *for tefillin.*

COMMENTARY

38. קַבֵּל יְקַר טוֹטַפְתָּא — *Beside His precious Tefillin.* This verse is a continuation of the previous one. The crown that has been wreathed from Israel's prayers rests in its permanently preassigned place alongside Hashem's Tefillin.

That Hashem puts on Tefillin is taught in the following Talmudic passage:

א"ר אָבִין בַּר רַב אַדָא א"ר יִצְחָק מְנַיִן שֶׁהַקָּדוֹשׁ בָּרוּךְ הוּא מַנִּיחַ תְּפִילִין שֶׁנֶּאֱמַר נִשְׁבַּע ה' בִּימִינוֹ וּבִזְרוֹעַ עֻזּוֹ בִּימִינוֹ זוֹ תּוֹרָה שֶׁנֶּאֱמַר מִימִינוֹ אֵשׁ דָּת לָמוֹ עֻזּוֹ אֵלּוּ תְּפִילִין שֶׁנֶּאֱמַר ה' עֹז לְעַמּוֹ יִתֵּן וּמְנַיִן שֶׁהַתְּפִילִין עֹז הֵם לְיִשְׂרָאֵל דִּכְתִיב וְרָאוּ כָּל עַמֵּי הָאָרֶץ כִּי שֵׁם ה' נִקְרָא עָלֶיךָ וְיָרְאוּ מִמֶּךָּ וְתַנְיָא רַבִּי אֱלִיעֶזֶר הַגָּדוֹל אוֹמֵר אֵלּוּ תְּפִילִין שֶׁבָּרֹאשׁ.

— *Rav Avin bar Ada cited Rav Yitzchok:* — *From where do we know that the Holy One, blessed be He, puts on Tefillin?* — *as it is said:* HASHEM *has sworn by His right hand, and by the arm of His strength* (Isaiah 62:8). *'By his hand'* means Torah, as it is said: At His right hand was a fiery law to them (Deut. 33:2) 'By the arm' of His strength means Tefillin, as it says: The Lord will give strength to His people (Psalms 29:11). But from where is it derived that the Tefillin are a strength to Israel? As is written: And all the people of the earth shall see that the Name of HASHEM is called upon you, and they shall be afraid of you (Deut. 28:10). And there is a dictum: Rabbi Eliezer the Great says: These are the Tefillin of the head. [Berachos 6a; see the notes to v. 40, for the continuation of this passage.]

It should again be emphasized that the passages quoted in this verse and the previous one, are not to be taken in the literal, anthropomorphic sense. The crown is analogous to Israel's prayers. Hashem is crowned and exalted by Israel's prayers and praise of Him, as in the words of the Sephardic

³⁸ *Beside His precious Tefillin,*

        it rests with regularity.

³⁹ *This is inscribed therein,*

        with wisdom and with knowledge:

יְתִיבָא — *It rests,* from יְתֵב, *to sit.*

בִּקְבִיעוּתָא — See *v.* 31.

39. רְשִׁימָא — *Inscribed,* from רָשַׁם. See also *v.* 8.

גּוּפָא — *Within it;* [*itself*] i.e., in the body or housing of the *tefillin* themselves.

COMMENTARY

Ritual of the Sabbath Mussaf *Kedushah* ... כֶּתֶר יִתְּנוּ לְךָ ה', *A crown have they given you, HASHEM* ...

Similarly Hashem's donning of Tefillin can be interpreted to mean that Hashem continually keeps Israel first and foremost in His considerations. Rav Hai Gaon (*Otzar HaGeonim, Berachos,* p. 12) says that the Talmud means that Hashem's *exhibits* or *shows* Tefillin, as we find, *Hashem showed Moses the knot of His Tefillin* (*Menachos* 35b). For, indeed, just as our Tefillin contain our assertion of faith in Hashem and our love and readiness to serve Him, so do His Tefillin contain the declaration of Israel's uniqueness among all the nations. However, the difficulty of anthropomorphism still remains, unfortunately, and the reader is directed to the commentaries. [See *comm.* to *v.* 40 for the verses found in God's Tefillin.]

39. רְשִׁימָא הִיא גּוּפָא — *This is inscribed within it* (I.e. Hashem's Tefillin).

An alternate and more literal translation is: *Indeed, inscribed within* [*Hashem's Tefillin*] *themselves.* In addition to the honor of Israel's having their prayers serve as a crown for Hashem, they also have the distinction of having their praises inscribed within Hashem's Tefillin (*Yad Aharon*).

בְּחָכְמְתָא וּבְדַעֲתָא — *With wisdom and with knowledge.*

The poet uses the word *wisdom* as a reference to the Tefillin of the head since it is the head in which wisdom resides, and from which it emanates. *Knowledge* refers to the Tefillin of the arm, for knowledge and understanding (בִּינָה) come from the heart which is next to the Tefillin of the arm. [See *Zohar III,* 256a; *ibid. III* 262a; *Tikkunei Zohar* 21] (*Yad Aharon*).

מ רְבוּתְהוֹן דְּיִשְׂרָאֵל,
קָרָאֵי בִּשְׁמַעְתָּא:

מא שֶׁבַח רִבּוֹן עָלְמָא,
אֲמִירָא דַכְוָתָא.

LEXICAL NOTES

40. רְבוּתְהוֹן — *The magnitude* [lit. *their greatness*], as in *Targum* to *Psalms* 145:3, וְלִרְבוּתֵיה *and to His greatness.*

קָרָאֵי — *Who recite* [*the Shema*], from קָרָא, (to recite, especially from the Torah).

בִּשְׁמַעְתָּא — *Of the Shema,* (*Deut.* 6:4). The *Shema* is a statement of the most fundamental principle of Judaism, which all others must presuppose — the uniqueness, unity, and oneness of God. See the notes to *v.* 32 above; also *Rambam, Yesodei HaTorah 1:7.*

COMMENTARY

40. ... רְבוּתְהוֹן דְּיִשְׂרָאֵל — *The magnitude of Israel, reciters of the Shema.*

God is glorified, lauded, and exalted by Israel's worship and praise of Him. Likewise, Israel is made great through its total acceptance of God and His commandments.

Verses describing the greatness of Israel are inscribed in Hashem's Tefillin, as the Talmud states:

א"ל רַב נַחְמָן בַּר יִצְחָק לְרַב חִיָּיא בַּר אָבִין הָנֵי תְּפִילִין דְּמָרֵי עָלְמָא מַה כְּתִיב בְּהוּ א"ל וּמִי כְּעַמְּךָ יִשְׂרָאֵל גּוֹי אֶחָד בָּאָרֶץ וּמִי מִשְׁתַּבַּח קוּב"ה בְּשִׁבְחַיְיהוּ דְיִשְׂרָאֵל אִין דִּכְתִיב אֶת ה' הֶאֱמַרְתָּ הַיּוֹם (וּכְתִיב) וַה' הֶאֱמִירְךָ הַיּוֹם אָמַר לָהֶם הקב"ה לְיִשְׂרָאֵל אַתֶּם עֲשִׂיתוּנִי חֲטִיבָה אַחַת בָּעוֹלָם ...

— *Rav Nachman ben Yitzchok said to Rav Chiyya bar Avin: Those Tefillin of the Lord of the Universe, what is written in them? He answered him: And what nation is like Your people Israel, a unique na-*

tion on the earth? (*I Chron.* 17:21. See also *comm.* to *v.* 38). *Does the Holy One, blessed be He, laud Himself with the praise of Israel? — Yes. For it is written:* You have avouched HASHEM this day (*and it is also written:*) And HASHEM has avouched you this day (*Deut.* 26:17-18) *The Holy One, blessed be He, says to Israel:* 'You have made Me the sole (unique) object of your love in the world ...' (*Berachos* 6a; this passage is continued in the *comm.* to *v.* 32, see there.)

[The verses found in Hashem's Tefillin are: *Deut.* 4:7, 8; 33:29; 4:34; and 26:19; and *I Chron.* 17:21.]

41. The poet now proceeds to laud the greatness of Israel by telling of its firm and adamant stand against the attempts of the nations of the world to convert them to other religions.

⁴⁰ *The magnitude of Israel,*

reciters of the Shema.

⁴¹ *Praise of the Lord of the Universe*

is a pure saying,

LEXICAL NOTES

41. אֲמִירָא — *Saying, statement, from* אָמַר.

דְכְוָתָא — I. *Purity, from* דְכוּתָא (plural: דַּכְוָותָא), *and from* דְכִי. II. *The like of* [*which*], *from* כְּוָת, *like, as in the Targum Onkelos to Exod.* 9:14: אֲרֵי לֵית דִּכְוָתִי, *for there is none like me; also Onkelos Exod.* 9:18 (*Mateh Levi*).

אֲמִירָא דַכְוָתָא — *An Aramaic rendition of Psalms* 12:7: אִמְרוֹת ה׳ אֲמָרוֹת טְהֹרוֹת, *the sayings of HASHEM are pure sayings* (*Yad Aharon; Shnei HaMe'oros*).

COMMENTARY

Verses 41-54 give a synoptic account of both sides of the arguments given during the religious disputations (וִכּוּחִים) and polemical debates that were so common between Christians and Jews throughout the Middle Ages (8th-15th centuries).

שְׁבַח רִבּוֹן עָלְמָא ... — (*The*) *praise of the Lord of the Universe, is a pure saying.*

Kinyan Tov interprets this verse as: The praise that we offer to Hashem, when we say that we love Him with all our heart and with all our soul (*Deut.* 6:5), is not idle talk. Rather, it is a pure, sincerely meant statement. We have demonstrated our sincerity by giving up our lives for Him throughout the bloody persecutions, inquisitions and pogroms that comprise our history. (See *v.* 46).

אֲמִירָא דַכְוָתָא — *Is a pure saying.*

The praise of God is pure, and free of all falsehood. This refers to the statements or words of the Torah and the Ten Commandments which are pure and holy statements from God and which are to be accepted and heeded totally because they are perfect in every way.

Also: *The praise of Hashem is, pure,* i.e., His word is pure, totally true and trustworthy. For when Hashem makes a statement or a promise we know that it will be fulfilled. He has the power to carry out His will — unlike man who may be unable to keep his word or who may be lying outright.

An alternative translation is: *The praise of Hashem is a statement, the like of which* ... *is good and fitting for me to tell before the kings of the world.* See next verse. [*Heidenheim; M'vo HaShir; Mateh Levi*].

עֲלֵיהּ מב שְׁפַר *עֲלַי לְחַוּוֹיֵהּ,

בְּאַפֵּי מַלְכְּוָתָא:

מג תָּאִין וּמִתְכַּנְּשִׁין,

כְּחֵזוּ אִדְוָתָא.

LEXICAL NOTES

42. עֲלַי — I. *Upon me, for me.* Other texts of the Akdamus read II. עֲלֵיהּ — *Upon him, upon it.* Comm. discusses how the readings affect the translation.

לְחַוּוֹיֵהּ — *To declare it,* from חֲוָה, as in *Daniel* 2:10; 3:32; and 5:15. See below.

בְּאַפֵּי — *In the presence of,* from אַפָּא.

43. וּמִתְכַּנְּשִׁין — *And they gather,* from כְּנַשׁ, (see *v.* 7).

COMMENTARY

42. שְׁפַר עֲלַי לְחַוּוֹיֵהּ — *It behooves me to declare it,* i.e., *Hashem's praise,* or: *It is fitting for it to be declared.*

The previous verse as well as this phrase is closely based on *Daniel* 3:32, which reads: אָתַיָּא וְתִמְהַיָּא דִי עֲבַד עִמִּי אֱלָהָא עִלָּאָה שְׁפַר קָדָמַי לְהַחֲוָיָה, *It is good for me to declare the signs and wonders that God on high has done with me* (Shnei HaMe'oros; Berger).

בְּאַפֵּי מַלְכְּוָתָא — *In the presence of kings.*

This verse is a continuation of the previous one. Israel is proud to declare in the presence of the kings of the world the greatness of Hashem, so that the world's monarchs will know the loyalty and devotion of a people to their God. Again, the poet is referring to the

religious debates, at which kings, cardinals and other high dignitaries were usually present. Verses 43-53 now proceed to describe this dialogue in detail (*Zos Nechemosi*).

Hashem desires that Israel should declare His praise among the nations, as we find in *Yalkut Shimoni, Tehillim* 146:

אָמַר רַבִּי אֱלִיעֶזֶר: אָמַר לָהֶם מֹשֶׁה לֹא בְּמַעֲשֵׂיכֶם אַתֶּם נִגְאָלִין אֶלָּא לְמַעַן תְּסַפֵּר בְּאָזְנֵי בִנְךָ וגו' וְלִיתֵּן שֶׁבַח להקב"ה לְסַפֵּר גְּדוּלָתוֹ וּתְהִלָּתוֹ בֵּין הָעוֹ"א וְכֵן הוּא אוֹמֵר סַפְּרוּ בַגּוֹיִם כְּבוֹדוֹ.

— *Rabbi Eliezer said: Moses said to them (Israel): It is not for your deeds that you are being delivered, but rather that you shall tell it in the ears of your children … (Exod. 10:2), and so that you shall offer praise to the Holy One, blessed be He, to tell His greatness and praises*

⁴² *It behooves me to declare it*

in the presence of kings.

⁴³ *They come and they gather,*

appearing like waves

בְּחֵזוּ — *Appearing like*, as in *Targum Onkelos* to *Gen.* 33:10; *Numb.* 9:15 and *ibid.* 11:7 from חֶזְוָא, *appearance*, and חֲזָא, *to see.*

אַדְוָתָא — *Waves (of the sea)*, as in *Succah* 51b, דְמִיתְחֲזֵי כְּאַדְוָתָא דְיַמָא, [*the walls of Herod's temple] looked like the waves of the sea (Rashi)*. See also *Bava Basra* 4a.

COMMENTARY

among the idol worshipers. And so it is stated: Declare His glory among the nations [*Psalms* 96:3] *(Yad Aharon).*

43. בְּחֵזוּ אַדְוָתָא — *Appearing like waves (from the sea).*

The poet uses this phrase to refer to the wicked of the world who desire to destroy Israel. The wicked are likened to the waves of the sea, as is found in *Yalkut Shimoni, Isaiah* 490:

אָמַר יְשַׁעְיָה וְהָרְשָׁעִים כַּיָם נִגְרָשׁ מַה הַיָם הַגַל הָרִאשׁוֹן אוֹמֵר אֲנִי עוֹלֶה וּמֵצִיף אֶת כָּל הָעוֹלָם כֻּלוֹ. וְכֵיוָן שֶׁהוּא בָּא לַחוֹל הוּא כּוֹרֵעַ לְפָנָיו וְאֵין הַגַל הַשֵׁנִי לָמֵד מִן הָרִאשׁוֹן ...

— *Isaiah says:* The wicked are like the troubled sea [*which cannot rest*] *(Isaiah* 57:20). Just as the sea's first wave says: '*I will rise up and flood the entire world,*' yet upon reaching the shore (lit. *sand*) breaks (lit.

kneels) before it, still the second wave does not learn from the first [*and attempts the same thing*]. So, too, the wicked man sees his fellow stricken because of his wickedness, and does not repent [*Rashi; ibid*]. *(Yad Aharon).* [See also *Midrash Tehillim* 2:2 and Introduction to *Madreigas HaAdam* by Rabbi Yosaif Horovitz].

Another reason for the poet's use of the expression '*like waves from the sea*', is that the wicked are likened to water *(Isaiah* 17:12 and 57:20; see above), and Israel is likened to fire *(Obadiah* 1:18). I.e., just as it is the nature of water to extinguish fire, so the wicked constantly attempt to extinguish the 'fire' of Israel. But due to Israel's upholding the Torah and Hashem's protection, the wicked are kept from carrying out their intentions *(Zos Nechemosi).*

מד תִּמְהִין וְשַׁיְלִין לֵיהּ, בְּעֵסֶק אָתְוָתָא:

LEXICAL NOTES

44. תִּמְהִין — *They wonder, they are astounded,* from תְּמַהּ.

וְשַׁיְלִין — *And they ask,* from שַׁיֵּיל, שְׁאַל.

COMMENTARY

44. תִּמְהִין וְשַׁיְלִין לֵיהּ בְּעֵסֶק אָתְוָתָא — *They wonder and inquire of him, concerning the signs.*

The heathens ask Israel about God's wonders and miracles [i.e. *signs* as in *Deut.* 6:22: אוֹתֹת וּמֹפְתִים, *signs and wonders*]. During Medieval disputations, the heathens always pressed Israel for signs that would prove God's existence and power, and demonstrate that He is the God Who watches and protects Israel. Surely the very opposite seemed to be true, with Israel continuously being murdered and tortured without Hashem's intercession. Furthermore, they would ask, what proof did Israel have that their hoped-for Messiah is the true one (*M'vo HaShir*).

According to *Yad Aharon,* the poet refers to *Psalms* 74:4 and the *Midrash* thereon, as the verse reads: שָׁאֲגוּ צוֹרְרֶיךָ בְּקֶרֶב מוֹעֲדֶךָ שָׂמוּ אוֹתֹתָם אֹתוֹת, *Your enemies roared in the midst of your congregations, they set up their signs for signs (Psalms 74:4).*

The *Midrash* interprets this verse as follows:

שָׂמוּ אוֹתֹתָם אֹתוֹת אָמְרוּ יוֹם פְּלוֹנִי אָנוּ כוֹבְשִׁין אוֹתָהּ נָטְלוּ אוֹתוֹת בַּחִצִּים הָיוּ יוֹרִים בַּצָּפוֹן וְהָיָה הַחֵץ הוֹלֵךְ בַּדָּרוֹם שֶׁנֶּאֱמַר קִלְקֵל בַּחִצִּים וְכָל סִימָן שֶׁנָּתְנוּ הִצְלִיחוּ הֲוֵי שָׂמוּ אוֹתֹתָם אֹתוֹת.

— *They set up their signs for signs (Psalms 74:4): They [Israel's enemy] said: 'On such and such a day we shall conquer her [Jerusalem]!' They read signs in arrows,* — *for they shot an arrow to the north and the arrow went to the south [towards Jerusalem]. As it is written:* He [קִלְקֵל] *divined with arrows.* [*To shake; to shoot; esp. to shake for the purpose of divination (Rashi)] (Ezekiel 21:26). And every sign that they tried augured that they would succeed, therefore, they set up their signs for signs,* [*Midrash Tehillim* 74:2; *Yalkut Ibid.* 809]. (See also *Gittin* 56a-b).

As *Midrash Tehillim* continues with reference to 74:9:

Our signs we do not see, there is no longer any prophet (*Psalms* 74:9): *This refers to the sign which you have promised:* Behold I will bring them from the north country, and gather them from the uttermost parts of the earth, and with them the blind and the lame ... *(Jer.* 31:7): *The reference is also to the sign:* How beautiful upon the mountains are the feet of the messenger of good tidings ... that says unto Zion: 'Your God reigns!' *(Isaiah 52:7).*

It is concerning these signs — those indicating heathen success

LEXICAL NOTES

בְּעֵסֶק — I. *Concerning, regarding* as in *Targum* to *Exod.* 18:8, עַל עֵיסַק, *regarding,* (*Mateh Levi*). From the verb עֲסַק, *to be occupied with, to be busy.* II. From the noun עֵסֶק, *matter, affair,* (*Heidenheim*).

אָתְוָתָא — *The signs,* plural of אָת, אָתְוָא.

COMMENTARY

and the contradictory ones auguring Israel's redemption — that the nations of the world wonder and ask. They see that their signs have accurately foretold the destruction of Jerusalem. On the other hand, the signs boding the salvation of Israel have not materialized. It is for this failure that the nations taunt and mock Israel, and Israel asks of Hashem (in the Midrash quoted above):

וְאִם אֵין אַתָּה עוֹשֶׂה בִּשְׁבִילֵנוּ עֲשֵׂה לְמַעַן שִׁמְךָ הַגָּדוֹל שֶׁמִּתְחָרֵף וּמִנָּאֵץ בָּעוֹלָם. — *If You will not act for our sake, act for the sake of Your great Name which is being disgraced and blasphemed in the world* (*Yad Aharon*).

Shnei HaMe'oros comments that the *signs* refers to the signs which were on the flags of the camps of the twelve tribes in the wilderness. The nations of the world wonder at and resent Israel's aloofness from mundane affairs. As the Torah says: בְּאֹתֹת לְבֵית אֲבֹתָם, *according to the signs of their fathers' house* (*Num.* 2:2). The nations realize that the greatness, unity, and strength of Israel lie in their steadfast loyalty to the traditions and heritage of *their fathers' house,* and their refusal to

assimilate with the nations. It is due to these *signs* that Israel has been able to survive throughout history, for the signs of the Torah have kept her separate and holy. This concept accords with *Bamidbar Rabbah* 2:3:

אִישׁ עַל דִּגְלוֹ בְאֹתֹת לְבֵית אֲבֹתָם הה"ד מִי זֹאת הַנִּשְׁקָפָה כְּמוֹ שַׁחַר יָפָה כַלְּבָנָה בָּרָה כַּחַמָּה אֵימָה כַּנִּדְגָּלוֹת קְדוֹשִׁים וּגְדוֹלִים הָיוּ יִשְׂרָאֵל בְּדִגְלֵיהֶם וְכָל הָעכו"ם מִתַּכְּלִין בָּהֶם וּתְמֵיהִין וְאוֹמְרִים מִי זֹאת הַנִּשְׁקָפָה וגו' אוֹמְרִים לָהֶם הָעכו"ם שׁוּבִי שׁוּבִי הַשּׁוּלַמִּית הִדַּבְקוּ לָנוּ בֹּאוּ אֶצְלֵנוּ וְאָנוּ עוֹשִׂין אֶתְכֶם שִׁלְטוֹנִים הֶגְמוֹנִים דּוּכָסִין אַפַּרְכִין אִסְטַרְטְלִיטִין ... וְיִשְׂרָאֵל אוֹמְרִים מַה תֶּחֱזוּ בַּשּׁוּלַמִּית מַה גְּרוּלָה אַתֶּם נוֹתְנִים לָנוּ.

— *Each man with his own standard, according to the signs of their fathers' house* (*Numb.* 2:2). *In reference to this, it is written:* Who is this that gazes down like the dawn, beautiful as the moon, clear as the sun, awesome as an army with banners? (*Shir HaShirim* 6:10). *Holy and great were Israel beneath their standards! And all the nations looked upon them and wondered, saying:* Who is this that gazes ...? *The nations say to them:* Return, return O Shulamis [*Israel*]! (*Shir HaShirim* 7:1). [Israel is refer-

מה   מְנָן וּמָאן הוּא רְחִימָךּ,
שַׁפִּירָא בְּרֵיוָתָא.

45. מְנָן — *From whence?* Contraction of מִן אָן.

רְחִימָךּ — *Your beloved,* from רְחִימָא, *beloved;* and from רְחֵם, *to love.*

שַׁפִּירָא — The feminine form of שַׁפִּיר, *beautiful,* equivalent to the Hebrew יָפָה as in *Targum* to *Gen.* 12:14.

red to as שׁוּלַמִּית because it is שְׁלֵמָה *complete,* in its faith. Another interpretation is that שׁוּלַמִּית is a contraction of מְשַׁלֶּמֶת לְמִיתָה, *content to die* (for God's sake) (*Shir HaShirim Rabbah* 7:2. See notes to *v.* 46).] *Cling to us, come unto us* [see *vs.* 47-49] *and we shall make you governors, generals, magistrates, lieutenants, commanders ...! And Israel replies:* What will you see in *Shulamis* (*Shir HaShirim* 7:1)? *What greatness can you give me [that can compare with the greatness that Hashem gives me]?* (See *v.* 51) (*Shnei HaMe'oros*).

Concerning the signs. The nations wonder and ask why the Jewish people are so preoccupied with the keeping of the signs (i.e., the Mitzvos) of the Torah. In particular, they wonder about the commandments of Sabbath, Tefillin, and circumcision, all three of which the Torah calls *signs,* since they are the sign or foundation of being Jewish. [See *Tikkunei Zohar,* Introduction 2a and b] (*Yad Aharon*).

45. מְנָן וּמָאן — *From whence, and who is?*
So do the heathens ask Israel.

The tone of their questioning is mocking and derisive.

שַׁפִּירָא בְּרֵיוָתָא — *O beautiful one in appearance.*

This verse refers to Israel. Israel is allegorically referred to in *Shir HaShirim* by the expression הַיָּפָה בַּנָּשִׁים, *you most beautiful of women* (5:9; see below). The Hebrew words יְפַת תֹּאַר are rendered by *Onkelos* as: שַׁפִּירָא בְּרֵיוָא (*Gen.* 29:17). The poet here uses the phrase שַׁפִּירָא בְּרֵיוָתָא to allude to that description. (See further below).

מְנָן וּמָאן הוּא רְחִימָךּ ... — *From whence, and Who is your beloved, O beautiful one in appearance.*

The heathens ask Israel to explain to them what is so great about their God that they cling to Him so dearly. This verse through *v.* 50 is an account of the dialogue between Israel and the heathens as cited in the *Shir HaShirim* (which is an allegorical account of the love between Israel and Hashem and the heathens' attempt to lure Israel away from their beloved God). In this verse the poet paraphrases that account and the *Midrash* expounding upon it: מַה דּוֹדֵךְ מִדּוֹד הַיָּפָה בַּנָּשִׁים, *What makes your beloved*

From whence, and Who is your beloved,
O beautiful one in appearance,

בְּרֵינָתָא — *In appearance,* from רֵינָא.

שַׁפִּירָא בְּרֵינָתָא — *Beautiful in appearance,* this refers to Israel which is allegorically referred to as הַיָפָה בַּנָשִׁים, *you most beautiful of women (Shir HaShirim* 5:9; see below). The Hebrew words יְפַת תֹּאַר are rendered by *Onkelos* as שַׁפִּירָא בְּרֵינָא *(Gen.* 29:17).

better than another beloved, O you most beautiful of women? (5:9) As the *Midrash* interprets:

אוּמוֹת הָעוֹלָם אוֹמְרִים לְיִשְׂרָאֵל מַה
דּוֹדֵךְ מִדּוֹד — מַה אֱלוֹהַ הוּא מֵאֱלוֹהוּת
מַה פַּטְרוֹן הוּא מִפַּטְרוֹנִין?

— *The nations of the world say to Israel:* What makes your beloved better than another beloved? *Why is your God better than all other gods? What makes your protector better than other protectors? (Midrash* 5:5).

And as the *Midrash* says further in (5:10):

כַּךְ הָיוּ אוּמוֹת הָעוֹלָם שׁוֹאֲלִים לָהֶם מַה
דּוֹדֵךְ מִדּוֹד שֶׁכַּךְ אַתֶּם מוּמָתִים עָלָיו שֶׁכַּךְ
אַתֶּם נֶהֱרָגִים עָלָיו כְּעִנְיָן שֶׁנֶּאֱמַר עַל כֵּן
עֲלָמוֹת אֲהֵבוּךְ וְאוֹמֵר כִּי עָלֶיךָ הֹרַגְנוּ כָל
הַיּוֹם כּוּלְכֶם נָאִים כּוּלְכֶם גִבּוֹרִים בּוֹאוּ
וְנִתְעָרְבָה יַחַד וְיִשְׂרָאֵל אוֹמְרִים נֹאמַר
לָכֶם מִקְצָת שְׁבָחוֹ וְאַתֶּם מַכִּירִים אוֹתוֹ —
דּוֹדִי צַח וְאָדוֹם וְכוּ'.

— *Thus do the nations of the world ask Israel and say:* What makes your beloved better than another beloved *(Shir HaShirim* 5:9) *that you so die for Him, that you so allow yourselves to be killed for Him?, as is stated:* Therefore even unto death *(read* עַל-מָוֶת) do we love

you *(ibid.* 1:3). [The literal translation of the verse is, *therefore do young maidens love You.* The *Midrash* reads the word עֲלָמוֹת, *maidens,* as if it were two words עַל-מָוֶת, *unto death.* This word has been *Midrashically* interpreted in many other ways, see the notes to *v.* 73]. *And as it is written:* For it is for Your sake that we are killed all day [*we are counted as sheep for the slaughter*] *(Psalms* 44:23). *You are handsome! You are brave! Come, let us intermingle! And Israel replies: We will tell you but a little of His praise, and you will recognize Him. You will recognize His greatness,* — My Love is clear skinned and ruddy ... (*Shir HaShirim* 5:10). [*My Beloved is white* (צַח), i.e., Hashem purifies my sins; and ruddy (i.e., Hashem is ready to punish those who sin against Him). White symbolizes purity and forgiveness, and red the symbol of sin and punishment (*Rashi*). (See *Shir HaShirim,* ArtScroll ed. ad. loc. See also *Isaiah* 1:18).

[See *Shir HaShirim,* ArtScroll edition, for a complete presentation and explanation of all passages quoted in this *comm.*]

מו אֲרוּם בְּגִינֵיהּ סָפִית,

מְדוֹר אַרְיָוָתָא:

LEXICAL NOTES

46. אֲרוּם — *That; because; so that;* equivalent to the Hebrew כִּי, which has various meanings depending on the context.

בְּגִינֵיהּ — *For His [Hashem's] sake,* or: *on His account.* From בְּגִין.

סָפִית — I. *You are destroyed,* or: *you perish,* from סָפָה, as in *Gen.* 19:15, פֶּן תִּסָּפֶה בַּעֲוֹן הָעִיר, *Lest you be swept away* [i.e., *destroyed*] *because of the sins of the city* (also *ibid.* 18:23 and 19:17). Or from סוּף, *to come to an end, to be exterminated.* As in *Targum Yerushalmi* to *Numb.* 33:52, וּתְסוֹפוּן יָת כָּל טַעֲוָתְהוֹן, *And you should destroy all their carved images.* [See also *Vayikra Rabbah* 37:4; *Koheles Rabbah* 10:17; *Bereishis Rabbah* 60:3.], from the root אָסַף, *to be destroyed,* as in *I Sam.* 15:6 and *Ezekiel* 34:29 (*Berger; Yad Aharon; Mateh Levi*).

II. *You stand at the threshold,* from the Hebrew root סָפַף, as in *Psalms* 84:11, בָּחַרְתִּי הִסְתּוֹפֵף בְּבֵית אֱלֹהָי, *I choose to stand at the threshold of the house of my Lord* (*Mateh Levi; Heidenheim*).

COMMENTARY

46. Four alternative translations are offered for this verse: I. אֲרוּם בְּגִינֵיהּ — *That for His sake you perish in a lions' den.*

II. — *That for His sake you stand at the threshold of a lions' den.*

Israel stands surrounded on all sides by hostile nations, who are ready to destroy her at every opportunity. And yet, for Hashem's sake they prefer to suffer in this lions' den than accept heathen ways and be assimilated. (See *vs.* 47-48 below). This verse is an allusion to *Shir HaShirim* 4:8: אִתִּי מִלְּבָנוֹן תָּבוֹאִי ... מִמְּעֹנוֹת אֲרָיוֹת מֵהַרְרֵי נְמֵרִים *Come with me from Lebanon ... from the lions' dens, from the mountains of the leopards.* The Midrash expounds [*Sh'mos Rabbah* 23:6] that *the lions' dens* refers to Babylonia and Media, and *the leopards* refer to Edom (Rome).

(*Mateh Levi*). At the same time, the poet alludes to Daniel who allowed himself to be thrown into a lion's den rather than to cease his worship of God (*Daniel* 6:8 ff.; See also *Jeremiah* 50:17).

III. — *That for His sake you are afflicted in a lions' den.*

IV. — *That for His sake you are placed* [or: *you have placed yourselves*], *in a den of lions.*

אֲרוּם בְּגִינֵיהּ ... — *That for His sake you perish in a lions' den.*

The poet continues his account of the heathens' wonder at the Jews' loyalty to their religion, and heathen argumentation against it. *Vs.* 46-48, describe the attempts to convert Israel to pagan religions. This account is based on the following verse in *Shir HaShirim* and its *Midrashic* interpretation: שׁוּבִי ...

⁴⁶ *That for His sake you perish*
in a lions' den?

LEXICAL NOTES

III. *You are tormented, afflicted.* See *Matnos Kehunah* to *Eichah Rabbasi* 1:36 on תִּסָּפוּן which reads:

לְפִי הָעִנְיָן הוּא לְשׁוֹן הַבָּאָה וְיִסּוּרִין וְעַיֵּין עֶרֶךְ סָפַת, וּפִיּוּט אָקְדָּמוּת מִילִין — אֲרוּם בְּגִינֵיהּ סָפִית פִּירְשׁוּ בּוֹ — כִּי בִּשְׁבִילוֹ לָקִית

— *According to the context, this [word] is an expression of beating and affliction, see also the Aruch under* ספת, *and the poem Akdamus Millin:* אֲרוּם בְּגִינֵיהּ סָפִית, *which the commentator [i.e., Mateh Levi] explains: that for His sake you are stricken (Shnei HaMe'oros).* [Solomon Buber reads תכפון, *to starve, to be hungry.* See Buber: *Eichah Rabbasi* (Vilna, 1899 p. 36, n. 306)].

IV. *You are placed,* or *immersed,* from the root סָפַת, as in *Bava Metziah* 89b, סוֹפֵת בְּמֶלַח וְאוֹכֵל, *he dips it in salt and eats it.* (See *Aruch HaShalem* sub. סָפַת).

מְדוֹר — *Dwelling;* here: *den.*

אַרְיָוָתָא — *Lions,* plural of אַרְיָא or אַרְיָוָא.

COMMENTARY

שׁוּבִי הַשּׁוּלַמִּית שׁוּבִי וְנֶחֱזֶה בָּךְ, *Return, return, O Shulamis, return, return that we may gaze at you ... (7:1).* This verse is an allegorical depiction of the nations' attempts to entice and cajole Israel to turn from its faith in Hashem, as the *Midrash* beautifully describes:

וְנֶחֱזֶה בָּךְ אוּמּוֹת הָעוֹלָם אוֹמְרִים לְיִשְׂרָאֵל: עַד מָתַי אַתֶּם מֵחִים עַל אֱלֹקֵיכֶם וּמְשַׁלְמִין לוֹ הה''ד עַל כֵּן עֲלָמוֹת אֲהֵבוּךְ וְעַד מָתַי אַתֶּם נֶהֱרָגִין עָלָיו כִּדְכְתִיב: כִּי עָלֶיךָ הֹרַגְנוּ כָל הַיּוֹם בֹּאוּ לָכֶם אֶצְלֵנוּ וְאָנוּ מְמַנִּין אֶתְכֶם דּוּכְסִין אַפְטְכִין, וְאִיסְטַרְטְלִין. וְנֶחֱזֶה בָּךְ — וְאַתּוּן אִינּוּן מְחִזְיָתֵיהּ דְּעָלְמָא הה''ד וְאַתָּה תֶחֱזֶה מִכָּל הָעָם

— *That we may gaze at you (7:1): The nations of the world say to Israel: 'How long will you die for* **your God, and totally give yourselves over to Him?'** *As it is written:* Therefore unto death do

we love You (1:3) [see *comm.* to *vs.* 45 and 73.] *'And how long will you allow yourselves to be killed for Him?' As it is written:* For it is for Your sake that we are killed all day (Psalms 44:23). *'Come to us and we shall appoint you magistrates, lieutenants, and commanders, that we may gaze at You' (ibid. 7:1)* [meaning] *and you shall be the admiration of the world, as it is written:* and you shall be the example for all the people (Exod. 18:21). [Literally *Exod.* 18:21 is translated: וְאַתָּה תֶחֱזֶה, *and you shall provide. The Midrash* here interprets the word תֶחֱזֶה to be a form of the word מְחִזְיָתֵיהּ, *an object to be looked at or admired* (lit. *mirror* or *show*). (*Shir HaShirim Rabbah* 7:2; see also *Rashi* to *ibid.* 5:9; also compare with the passage from the *Sifrei* quoted in *comm.* to *v.* 45.]

מז 'קְרָא וְיָאָה אַתְּ,

תֵּעְרְבִי אִין *תַּעַרְבִי לְמַרְוָתָא.

נַעְבֵּד; נַעֲבַד מח רְ'עוּתֵךְ *נַעֲבִיד לִיךְ,
בְּכָל אַתְרְוָתָא:

מט בְּחָכְמְתָא מְתִיבָתָא לְהוֹן,

LEXICAL NOTES

47. וְיָאָה — *And handsome,* from יָאֱיתָא (root: יְאָה), *beauty,* equivalent to the Hebrew word נָאֶה.

אִין — *If,* (Hebrew אִם).

אִין תַּעַרְבִי — *If you will blend; mingle;* or alternatively: *if you will assimilate,* from עֲרַב. Here used especially in the sense of to assimilate, or merge together. (See comm.).

לְמַרְוָתָא — *Into our dominion,* or alternatively: *under our authority,* from מָרוּת, as in the *Targum Onkelos* to *Exod.* 18:10, מִתְּחוֹת מָרְוַת מִצְרָאֵי, *from under the dominion of the Egyptians.*

COMMENTARY

47. יְקְרָא וְיָאָה אַתְּ ... — *Honored and handsome would you be, if you would mingle into our dominion.*

This verse continues the heathen arguments against Judaism, and the attempt to entice Israel to abandon its faith in God and convert to other religions.

The poet here quotes almost verbatim the expression used in the *Midrashic* account of the Israel-heathen dialogue. As the *Midrash* outlines the heathen argument: כּוּלְכֶם נָאִים כּוּלְכֶם גְּבּוֹרִים, בּוֹאוּ וְנִתְעָרְבָה יַחַד, *The heathens say to Israel ... 'You are all handsome! You are all brave! Come let us intermingle!'* (*Sifrei* 343; see *comm.* to *v.* 45 for the complete text of the above quoted passage). And as the

Mechilta also quotes this dialogue: הֲרֵי אַתֶּם נָאִים הֲרֵי אַתֶּם גְּבּוֹרִים, בּוֹאוּ וְהִתְעָרְבוּ עִמָּנוּ ..., *Behold, you are handsome! Behold, you are brave! Come and mingle with us!* (*Mechilta, Shirasa, Parsha* 3). The above two passages should also be compared to the quotation from *Midrash Bamidbar Rabbah* 2:3 in *comm.* to *v.* 44 above; and with the passage from *Shir HaShirim Rabbah* 7:2 quoted in *comm.* to *v.* 46. (*Yad Aharon; M'vo HaShir*).

Israel realizes, however, that such assimilation should never, and must never, be — for its survival depends upon its maintaining its uniqueness. As *Shir HaShirim Rabbah* states:

⁴⁷ *Honored and handsome would you be,*

if you would mingle into our dominion.

⁴⁸ *Your desire would be done for you*

in every place!

⁴⁹ *With wisdom he replies to them*

LEXICAL NOTES

48. רְעוּתָךְ — *Your desire,* from רְעִי. (See *v.* 33).

נַעֲבִיד לִיךְ — *Shall be done for you,* or alternatively: *we shall do for you,* from עֲבַד. (See *v.* 32).

לִיךְ — *For/to you.*

בְּכָל — I. *In all;* II. *In every.*

אַתְרְוָתָא — *Places,* plural of אֲתַר, *place.*

49. בְּחָכְמְתָא — *With wisdom.*

מְתִיבָתָא לְהוֹן — I. *He [or: they] (i.e., Israel) replies to them,* from אֲתִיב, especially in the sense of replying to a question or objection, from תוּב, *to return;* or, II. מְתִיבָתָא may be a noun: *reply,* in which case the phrase would be rendered: *A wise reply to them.*

COMMENTARY

מַה הַשֶּׁמֶן הַזֶּה אֵין מִתְעָרֵב בִּשְׁאָר מַשְׁקִין כָּךְ יִשְׂרָאֵל אֵין מִתְעָרְבִים באוה״ע — *Just as oil cannot be mixed with other liquids, so Israel cannot mix with the nations of the world (Yad Aharon).*

48. ... רְעוּתָךְ נַעֲבִיד — *Your (every) desire would be done for you, in every place.*

בְּכָל אַתְרְוָתָא — I. *In every place* that Israel be located, or II. *In every place [or nation]* in the world. (See below).

This is a continuation of the argument presented in *vs.* 44-47. Since, as the *comm.* explains, the nations seek to entice Israel to join them by offering it choice positions of honor and authority -- it follows

that *in all places* where Jews live, they will be in a position to control their destiny and to fulfill their desires (*M'vo HaShir*).

49. בְּחָכְמְתָא מְתִיבָתָא — *With wisdom she [Israel] replies to them but partially, to let them know.*

As mentioned above, no one can ever recount more than a minute fraction of Hashem's greatness and glory. As *Pirkei d'Rabbi Eliezer*, 3, says:

מִי יְמַלֵּל גְּבוּרוֹת ה' יַשְׁמִיעַ כָּל תְּהִלָּתוֹ וְכִי יֵשׁ אָדָם בָּעוֹלָם שֶׁהוּא יָכוֹל לְמַלֵּל גְּבוּרָתוֹ שֶׁל הַקָּדוֹשׁ בָּרוּךְ הוּא אוֹ לְהַשְׁמִיעַ כָּל תְּהִלָּתוֹ אֲפִילוּ מַלְאֲכֵי הַשָּׁרֵת אֵינָן יְכוֹלִין לְסַפֵּר אֶלָּא מִקְצָת גְּבוּרוֹתָיו — *Who can recount the mighty acts of* HASHEM, *who can make known*

קְצָת לְהוֹדָעוּתָא.

נ יְדַעְתּוּן חַכְּמִין לֵיהּ,

בְּאִשְׁתְּמוֹדָעוּתָא:

נא רְבוּתְכוֹן מָה חֲשִׁיבָא,

LEXICAL NOTES

קְצָת — *A little, a small part.*

לְהוֹדָעוּתָא — *To inform,* literally: *for [their] information,* from הוֹדִיעַ, the *hifil* form of the root word יָדַע.

50. חַכְּמִין — I. *Wise men.* II. *Recognize,* or: *know,* especially in the sense of comprehending, from the third person plural form of חֲכִּים. As in the *Targum Yerushalmi* to *Gen.* 37:33: חֲכַם יָתָהּ, *He [Jacob] recognized it [Joseph's shirt].*

COMMENTARY

all His praise? *(Psalms 106:2) Is there any man in the world who can tell of the greatness of the Holy One, blessed be He, or be able to make known all His praise?* — Even the ministering angels can tell but a small bit of His greatness (*Yad Aharon.* See also *Yalkut Shimoni* n. 864, to *Psalms* 106).

קְצָת לְהוֹדָעוּתָא — *But partially, to let them know.*

Israel replies only by giving a description of a small part of Hashem's greatness, majesty, and glory. Since God is so exalted above all the rewards that can be offered by the nations, why should Israel trade divine splendor for earthly trinkets? But Israel's reply cannot be more than a *partial* one, because Hashem is infinite, hence a complete description is clearly impossible as the poet has already expressed in vs. 5-9 (*M'vo HaShir*).

Again, the poet employs almost verbatim the terminology used by

the *Midrash* in describing Israel's reply to the nations.

Israel replies, *'We will tell you but a little of His praise, and (perhaps) you will recognize Him'* (*Sifrei,* 343; see comm. to v. 45 for the complete text. Cf. also *Mechilta, Parsha* 3).

50. Israel now begins its reply to the proselytizers.

יְדַעְתּוּן חַכְּמִין לֵיהּ — I. *If your wise men could but know Him with total recognition* [traditional Yiddish translation].

II. *Would that you [truly] know and recognize Him, with (total) recognition (and understanding)* [*M'vo HaShir; Yad Aharon; Shnei HaMe'oros*].

M'vo HaShir loosely translates and interprets this verse as: *Would that you take the time and effort to make yourselves knowledgeable of Him with total recognition and awareness ... then you would*

but partially, to let them know:

50 *If your wise men could but know Him,*

with total recognition!

51 *Your greatness — of what value is it*

LEXICAL NOTES

בְּאִשְׁתְּמוֹדְעוּתָא — *With [total] recognition,* from אִשְׁתְּמוֹדַע. The word is used frequently by *Onkelos* as the translation of הִכִּיר (*to recognize;* root נָכַר). As in the *Targum Onkelos* to *Gen.* 42:8, וְאִשְׁתְּמוֹדַע יוֹסֵף יַת אֲחוֹהִי וְאִינוּן לָא אִשְׁתְּמוֹדְעֵה, *And Joseph recognized his brothers, but they did not recognize him.* (See also *Targum* to *Gen.* 38:26; and 42:7). Also: *to realize, or be made aware of;* in *Numb.* 17:24; *Onkelos* renders: וְאִשְׁתְּמוֹדַעוּ, *and they realized,* i.e., Israel was convinced of Aaron's right to the priesthood. [See also *Ramban* to *Exod.* 12:43] (*Heidenheim*).

51. רְבוּתְכוֹן — *Your greatness,* from רְבוּתָא.

מָה חֲשִׁיבָא — *Of what value is it?* Or alternatively: *what is its value/importance,* from חָשׁוּב, *to be valuable, important, of high regard or standing.*

COMMENTARY

realize that your offer of greatness — of what importance is it? (See next verse.) The implication is that Israel's tormentors hope to ensnare it because, in their foolishness, they can never conceive God's greatness.

If you wise men of the world would only be able to know and understand something of our God with complete and total awareness and knowledge — then you would realize that all your attempts to lure us away from our faith are futile. However, the nations can never hope to understand anything of the Holy One, blessed be He, without having first toiled long and hard in the study of the Torah, as Israel has been doing for centuries. Only Israel is privy to even a small part of this knowledge of Hashem, for Hashem has given them the capacity to truly understand Him. As it is written: מַגִּיד דְּבָרָו לְיַעֲקֹב

חֻקָּיו וּמִשְׁפָּטָיו לְיִשְׂרָאֵל, *He declares His word to Jacob, His statutes and ordinances to Israel (Psalms* 147:19). To Israel alone does He reveal something of Himself. The other nations cannot reach the same degree of understanding of Hashem's laws and decrees (*Yad Aharon*).

[Note that the poet here uses the Aramaic equivalent of the Hebrew word הִכִּיר, *to recognize,* in order to employ the same words found in the *Midrash,* in describing Israel's reply to the heathen questions and arguments. Thus he employs the phrase מַכִּירִין and וְאַתֶּם מַכִּירִים אוֹתוֹ אַתֶּם אוֹתוֹ as quoted in *comm.* to *v.* 49.]

51. רְבוּתְכוֹן מָה חֲשִׁיבָא — *Your greatness — of what value is it?*

The poet continues his paraphrase of the *Midrashic* account of Israel's reply to its attempted proselytizers:

מַה גְּדוּלָה אַתֶּם נוֹתְנִים לָנוּ שְׁמָא בְּמַחֲלַת הַמַּחֲנַיִם שְׁמָא יְכוֹלִים אַתֶּם לִיתֵּן לָנוּ

קַבֵּל הַהִיא שְׁבַחְתָּא.

נב רְ בוּתָא דְיַעֲבֵד לִי,

כַּד מַטְיָא יְשׁוּעֲתָא:

נג בְּמֵיתִי לִי נְהוֹרָא,

LEXICAL NOTES

קַבֵּל — *In comparison to.* The word usually means *beside, opposite,* or *corresponding to* (see vs. 22 and 38).

שְׁבַחְתָּא — *Praise,* as in the Targum to *Psalms* 33:1.

52. דְיַעֲבֵד לִי — *That He will do for me, from* עֲבֵיד.

מַטְיָא — *Arrive,* from מְטֵי (מְטָה), *to arrive* (in time or in place).

COMMENTARY

אַבְרָהָם יִצְחָק וְיַעֲקֹב עָבְדוּ עֲבוֹדָה זָרָה
שֶׁיַעַבְדוּ בְּנֵיהֶם אַחֲרֵיהֶם, וְלֹא אֲבוֹתֵינוּ
עָבְדוּ ע״ז וְלֹא אָנוּ נַעֲבֹד ע״ז אַחֲרֵיהֶם,
אֶלָּא מַה אַתֶּם יְכוֹלִין לַעֲשׂוֹת לָנוּ כְּחוֹלָה
שֶׁנַעֲשָׂה לְיַעֲקֹב אָבִינוּ כְּשֶׁיָצָא מִבֵּית לָבָן?
... אוֹ שֶׁמָּא יְכוֹלִין אַתֶּם לַעֲשׂוֹת לָנוּ
כְּחוֹלָה שֶׁעָתִיד הקב״ה לַעֲשׂוֹת לְצַדִּיקִים
לֶעָתִיד לָבוֹא וכו'
— *And Israel replies to them ... have
you in all your days, ever heard of
Abraham, Isaac and Jacob worshiping idols, that their children after
them should also worship? — Our
fathers did not worship idols, nor
shall we! And can you make for us
the same round-dance as was made
[by the angels] for Jacob when he
left the house of Laban? ... And can
you perchance make for us a round-
dance like the one that the Holy
One, blessed be He, is prepared to
make for the righteous in the time
to come?!* [Midrash Shir HaShirim
Rabbah 7:2 — continued from
comm. to v. 46; see also comm. to
vs. 70 and 71; see especially the

כִּגְדוּלָה שֶׁעָשָׂה לָנוּ הָאֱלֹקִים בַּמִּדְבָּר
שֶׁהָיִינוּ חוֹטְאִים וְהוּא מוֹחֵל לָנוּ וְאוֹמֵר
לָנוּ וְהָיָה מַחֲנֶיךָ קָדוֹשׁ.
— *What greatness will you confer
upon us — perhaps* כְּמַחֲלַת הַמַּחֲנַיִם,
like a dance of the camps (Shir
HaShirim 7:1)? *Can you then confer upon us any of the greatness
which Hashem did for us in the
wilderness when we would sin and
He would pardon us* (מָחוֹל), *and tell
us, and your camp shall be holy
(Deut. 23:15)* ... (Numbers Rabbah
2:3). See *comm.* to *v.* 44 for the
beginning text of the above
Midrash. [The Midrash homiletical-
ly reads כְּמַחֲלַת הַמַּחֲנַיִם, *Like a
round-dance of the camps,* as if it
were vocalized כִּמְחוּלַת הַמַּחֲנַיִם, *as
the forgiveness (that Hashem
forgave) the camps (of Israel).* A
homiletical reading of this kind is
an oft-used tool in Midrashic ex-
egesis.]
    And as another *Midrash* says:
וְיִשְׂרָאֵל מְשִׁיבִין לָהֶם, שְׁמַעְתֶּם מִימֵיכֶם

52 The great things He will do for me

when redemption shall arrive;

53 When He shall bring me light,

יְשׁוּעָתָא — *Redemption, when the Messiah will come.*

53. בְּמֵיתֵי לִי — *When He (Hashem) shall bring to me*, or alternately: *when to me shall be brought*, from מֵיתֵי, *to bring*, from the root אֲתָא, *to come*. Some commentators *(Yad Aharon; Heidenheim)* translate מֵיתֵי, *to come*, and hence this phrase is rendered: *when to me shall come (the light).*

נְהוֹרָא — *Light.*

ArtScroll edition of *Shir HaShirim*, 7: 1-2] *(Yad Aharon,* see also *Ta'anis* 31a).

קֵבֶל הַהִיא שְׁבַחְתָּא — *In comparison to that praise.*

The expression *that praise*, refers both to the past, and to the future. It refers to the praises and greatness of God and the act of Creation, as well as to the great miracles that He performed for Israel during their redemption from Egypt and their stay in the wilderness *(Yad Aharon).* It also refers to the great rewards that are in store for the righteous in the future when the Messiah will come. It is this point that the poet now proceeds to describe *(M'vo HaShir).*

52. כַּד מַטְיָא יְשׁוּעָתָא — *When redemption shall arrive.* A slightly less literal translation would be: *Upon the arrival of the redemption.*

[Some editions of the *Akdamus* read: כַּד מַטְיָא שַׁעְתָּא, *when the time*

shall arrive. However, as Heidenheim points out, the given reading is more likely, since *v.* 39 ends with the word שַׁעְתָּא, and it is not the practice of poets to conclude two verses with the same word. Old manuscripts and editions corroborate the reading of יְשׁוּעָתָא. (As, for example, the *Machzor Sabbionetta-Cremona,* 1559-61).]

53. בְּמֵיתֵי לִי נְהוֹרָא — *When He [i.e., God] shall bring me light.*

Light refers to the light of redemption when the Messiah will come. This phrase is based on the *Targum* to *Isaiah* 5:20, בְּמֵיתֵי, נְהוֹרָא לְצַדִּיקַיָא יַחֲשׁוּךְ לְרַשִׁיעַיָא *When the light shall be brought to the righteous, it shall be dark for the wicked* ...

The use of the expression אוֹר, *light* to denote the redemption, and the days of the Messiah's coming is very common in *Talmud* and *Midrash*, as well as in the Scrip-

וְתִתְחֲפֵי לְכוֹן בַּהֲתָא.

נד לְקָרְיֵה כַּד אִתְגְּלֵי,

בְּתָקְפָּא וּבְגֵינָתָא:

LEXICAL NOTES

וְתִתְחֲפֵי לְכוֹן — *And you will be covered*, from חָפָה (Aramaic חֲפָא), as in *Esther 7:8*, וּפְנֵי הָמָן חָפוּ, *and they covered the face of Haman*. Here, as in *Esther*, the word חָפָה is used to indicate shame and degradation.

בַּהֲתָא — *Shame.*

54. אִתְגְּלֵי — *Be revealed, made manifest;* from גְּלִי.

בְּתָקְפָּא — *With might,* from the Hebrew and Aramaic root word תָּקַף.

COMMENTARY

tures. As an example: קוּמִי אוֹרִי כִּי אוֹרֵךְ וּכְבוֹד ה' עָלַיִךְ זָרָח, *Arise, shine; for your light has come, and the glory of HASHEM has shone upon you (Isaiah 60:1).* For other instances of this implication of the word 'light', see *Michah 7:8-9.* As stated in *Yalkut Shimoni Isaiah 499:*

כִּי עִמְּךָ מְקוֹר חַיִּים בְּאוֹרְךָ נִרְאֶה אוֹר מַהוּ בְּאוֹרְךָ נִרְאֶה אוֹר — זֶה אוֹרוֹ שֶׁל מָשִׁיחַ

— *For with You is the source of life; by Your light shall we see light (Psalms 36:10) ... What is meant by: In Your light shall we see light? — This refers to the light of Messiah.* (See also *ibid.* 500; and *Pesikta Rabbasi 36-37,* Ish-Shalom ed.).

In another interpretation, *light,* refers to the great light that was created on the first day of creation and which was later set aside by Hashem for the righteous when the Messiah will come. As found in *Chagigah 12a:*

אָמַר רַבִּי אֶלְעָזָר אוֹר שֶׁבָּרָא הקב״ה בְּיוֹם רִאשׁוֹן אָדָם צוֹפֶה בּוֹ מִסּוֹף הָעוֹלָם וְעַד

סוֹפוֹ כֵּיוָן שֶׁנִּסְתַּכֵּל הקב״ה בְּדוֹר הַמַּבּוּל וּבְדוֹר הַפְלָגָה וְרָאָה שֶׁמַּעֲשֵׂיהֶם מְקוּלְקָלִים עָמַד וּגְנָזוֹ מֵהֶן שֶׁנֶּאֱמַר וְיִמָּנַע מֵרְשָׁעִים אוֹרָם וּלְמִי גְּנָזוֹ לַצַּדִּיקִים לֶעָתִיד לָבוֹא

— *Rabbi Elazar said: The light that the Holy One, blessed be He, created on the first day enabled Adam to see from one end of the world to the other. But when the Holy One, blessed be He, looked at the (future) generation of the flood, and at the generation of the Tower of Babel, and saw their corrupt and sinful deeds, He arose and hid it from them, as it is stated: And the light was withheld from the wicked (Job 38:15), And for whom did He hide it? — For the righteous in the time to come;* (see also *Bereishis Rabbah,* chapters 3, 11, 12, and 42, and also *Rashi* to Gen. 1:4) [*T'yul B'gan*].

וְתִתְחֲפֵי לְכוֹן בַּהֲתָא — *And you will be covered with shame,* literally: *and shame will cover you.*

This phrase has its basis in two passages from the prophets:

and you will be covered with shame;

54 When His glory will be revealed

with power and with grandeur.

LEXICAL NOTES

וּבְגֵיוָתָא — *And with grandeur, pride,* from גֵּיוָתָא, *gloriousness* from גֵּאֵי (Heidenheim; M'vo HaShir).

Many editions of the Akdamus read וּבִגְבוּרְתָא, *strength.* Heidenheim prefers וּבְגֵיוָתָא, for the same reason given in the *comm.* to יְשׁוּעָתָא, in v. 52.

Note, however, that the reading בְּתָקְפָּא וּבִגְבוּרְתָא, can be supported, since the same expression is used in *Esther* 10:2: וְכָל מַעֲשֵׂה תָקְפּוֹ וּגְבוּרָתוֹ, *and all the acts of his might and his strength.* On the other hand the *Targumim* to *Isaiah* 2:12 and *Eccles.* 5:7 support our reading.

COMMENTARY

I. *Targum* to *Obadiah* 1:10: מֵחֲטוֹף אֲהוֹךְ יַעֲקֹב תַּחְפִּינָךְ בַּהֲתָא וְתִשְׁתֵּיצֵי לְעָלַם, *For, because of your violence against your brother Jacob, shame shall cover you, and you shall be cut off forever* (see Hebrew text: *ibid*).

II. The verse in *Michah* 7:10: וְתֵרֵא אִיבָתִי וּתְחַסְּהָ בּוּשָׁה (תרגום יונתן: וְתַחֲפִינָהּ בַּהֲתָא) — *And my enemy shall see it (i.e., the redemption), and shame shall cover her* [which Targum Yonasan renders: תַחֲפִינָהּ בַּהֲתָא] (Heidenheim; Yad Aharon).

Some editions of the *Akdamus* read בַּהֲתָא (root: בָּהָה), *darkness, blindness.* And hence our phrase becomes: וְתַחֲפֵי לְכוֹן בַּהֲתָא, *And you will be covered with darkness.* The reading is based on *Isaiah* 60:2; as explained by *Sanhedrin* 99a: וְהַיְינוּ דְּאָמַר לֵיהּ הַהוּא מִינָא לְרַב אַבָּהוּ אֵימָתַי אָתֵי מָשִׁיחַ אָמַר לֵיהּ לְחִי חַפֵּי לְהוּ חֲשׁוּכָא לְהַנְהוּ אִינְשֵׁי אִ"ל מֵילַט קָא לַייטַת לִי אִ"ל קְרָא כְּתִיב: כִּי הִנֵּה הַחשֶׁךְ יְכַסֶּה אֶרֶץ וַעֲרָפֶל לְאָמִּים וְעָלַיִךְ יִזְרַח ה' וּכְבוֹדוֹ עָלַיִךְ יֵרָאֶה — *And so a certain apostate said to*

Rav Abahu: 'When will the Messiah come?' He replied: 'When darkness will cover those people,' [meaning the heretic]. 'Do you curse me?!', he exclaimed. Answered he: 'No, it is a verse!, as it is written (Isaiah 60:2): 'For, behold, the darkness shall cover the earth, and a thick darkness the people: but HASHEM shall shine upon you, and His glory shall be seen upon you' (Yad Aharon).

54. יְקָרֵיהּ כַּד אִתְגְּלֵי — *When His glory will be revealed.*

The combination of words in this phrase is commonly found in the *Targum,* as for example in *Onkelos* to *Exod.* 4:27 וְעַרְעֵהּ בְּטוּרָא דְּאִתְגְּלִי עֲלוֹהִי יְקָרָא דַה', *And he met him at the mountain,* [i.e. Sinai upon which the glory of HASHEM was revealed. See also *Onkelos* to *Exod.* 16:10; 20:17; *Num.* 10:33; and *Deut.* 33:2.

This verse is a continuation of the previous one which paraphrases *Isaiah* 60:2 as mentioned in the *comm.* In this stanza, the poet con-

נה יְשַׁלֵם גְּמֵלַיָּא,

לְסַנְאֵי וְנַגְוָתָא.

נו צִדְקָתָא לְעַם חֲבִיב,

וְסַגִּיא זַכְוָתָא:

LEXICAL NOTES

55. יְשַׁלֵם גְּמֵלַיָּא — *Repay recompense, retaliate. He [God] will repay,* from שׁלם. *Retaliation for an evil deed.*

גְּמֵלַיָּא — *Recompense;* or alternately: *the deeds* from גְּמוּל.

לְסַנְאֵי — *To the enemies,* the plural construct of סַנְאָה.

וְנַגְוָתָא — *And the isles,* the plural of נַגְוָא, The *Targumic* equivalent of אִיִּים, *islands.* which appears frequently in *Isaiah, Ezekiel,* and *Jeremiah.* This word does not denote islands exclusively, but can also refer to a peninsula or to coastlands.

The poet uses the word 'isles' to subtly allude to the heathen and idolatrous enemies surrounding Israel. In the Scriptures the term *islands* invariably denotes an enemy of Israel, and the poet here uses the word broadly to designate all haters of Jews, as *Rashi* explains the word אִיִּים *isles,* in *Isaiah* 41:1, 5, *as the islands of idol worshipers.*

COMMENTARY

tinues his paraphrase of the *Targum* which reads as follows: וּבִיךְ יִשְׁרֵי שְׁכִנְתָּא דַה' וִיקָרֵה עֲלָךְ יִתְגְּלֵי, *And within you shall rest the Shechina of HASHEM and His glory shall be revealed upon you.* See the comm. to previous verse for the Hebrew text of *Isaiah* 60:2 (*Yad Aharon*).

55. יְשַׁלֵם גְּמֵלַיָּא — *He will repay recompense.* Other equally valid translations are: *He will repay the [evil] deeds,* or: *He will avenge the [evil] deeds.*

The sense of the verse is that Hashem will punish Israel's enemies for the evil that they have done it.

Basically, this phrase יְשַׁלֵם גְּמוּל

indicates that one will be dealt with commensurate with his deeds, whether for good or evil. The phrase appears several times in the Scriptures, as in (*Isaiah* 66:6), מְשַׁלֵם גְּמוּל לְאֹיְבָיו, *He repays recompense to His enemies.* Compare also with *Isaiah* 3:11. See comm. below.

לְסַנְאֵי וְנַגְוָתָא — *To the enemies and the isles.* The poet succinctly gives an Aramaic paraphrase of *Isaiah* 59:18, which reads, כְּעַל גְּמֻלוֹת כְּעַל יְשַׁלֵם חֵמָה לְצָרָיו גְּמוּל לְאֹיְבָיו לָאִיִּים גְּמוּל יְשַׁלֵם, *According to their deeds will He repay — rage to His tormentors, recompense to His enemies; to the islands He will repay recompense.*

⁵⁵ *He will pay recompense,*

to the enemies and the isles;

⁵⁶ *Righteousness to His beloved people,*

and abundant merits.

LEXICAL NOTES

However, more specifically, the word *isles* in the Scriptures, refers to various countries depending on the time, place, and context;
1). the Greeks, or Cypriots (i.e., the Kittim); See *Jer.* 2:10 and *Ezekiel* 27:6; and *Rashi* to *Isaiah* 11:11.
2). Italy, (and in post-Biblical times the Romans), as in the *Targum* to *Ezekiel* 27:7; also Apulia (אֲפוּלְיָא, an area Southeast of Italy), see *Targum Ezekiel* 27:6.
3). Crete; Macedonian Greece; and the coastlands of the Mediterranean Sea. As in *Jer.* 2:10; and *Ezekiel* 39:6.
4). the isles of Cappadocia, as in the *Targum* to *Jer.* 47:4; Tyre (צוֹר), see *Psalms* 72:10 and *Rashi, ibid.*

56. צִדְקָתָא — *Righteousness, justice;* צֶדֶק and צְדָקָה.

זַכְוָתָא — *Merits; virtue; the protecting influence resulting from good deeeds; the* plural of זְכוּתָא.

COMMENTARY

Compare the above quote, and our verse to *Isaiah* 3:11, אוֹי לְרָשָׁע רָע כִּי גְמוּל יָדָיו יֵעָשֶׂה לּוֹ, *Woe to the wicked his wickedness, for according to the deeds* [lit. *recompense*] *of his hands shall be done to him (Yad Aharon).*

56. ... צִדְקָתָא לְעַם חֲבִיב — *[And] righteousness to His beloved people . . .*

This is a continuation of the previous verse. As Hashem repays the wicked for their evil deeds, He will repay His beloved people with righteousness and many merits.

וְסַגִּיא זַכְוָתָא — I. *And abundant merits.*

The verse is to be read as a continuation of the previous one, as

follows: [. . . and Hashem will repay] 'His beloved people, with righteousness and abundant merits.' I.e., in reward for their worthiness, Hashem will repay them with many merits and advantages (*Heidenheim; Eshel Avrohom*).

II. *Who possess many/great merits,* or: *and (who are) of great merit.* Accordingly the entire verse is read as follows: [... And Hashem will repay] 'Righteousness to His beloved people, who are of great merit, or: *Who possess many virtues.* I.e., Israel has earned great and numerous merits for their sacrifices in upholding of the Torah (*Mateh Levi; M'vo HaShir; Shnei HaMe'oros*).

חֲדוּ שְׁלֵמָא בְּמֵיתֵי,

וּמָנֵי *דְּכִיתָא.

וּמָנָא; וּמָנָא; דַּכְוָתָא

LEXICAL NOTES

57. שְׁלֵמָא — *Total, complete:* from שָׁלֵם.

וּמָנֵי — I. *And the vessels;* The plural of מָנָא, (also מָאן) the usual *Targum* translation of the Hebrew כְּלִי (plural כֵּלִים, כְּלֵי). As in *Targum Onkelos* to *Num.* 3:31:
וּמָנֵי קוּדְשָׁא *and the holy vessels;* other examples are *Exod.* 27:19; 31:7; *Lev.* 15:22;
Num. 4:9,12,15,20,26,32.

COMMENTARY

57. חֲדוּ שְׁלֵמָא בְּמֵיתֵי — *When He
brings total joy,* i.e. when the Messiah will come.

Only then will there be truly
complete joy, for then the joy will
continue forever without any
hindrance.

The phrase *total joy* alludes to the
following allegory from *Shir
HaShirim Rabbah* 1:31:
לְמַטְרוֹנָה שֶׁהָלַךְ הַמֶּלֶךְ בַּעְלָהּ וּבָנֶיהָ
וְחַתְנֶיהָ לִמְדִינַת הַיָּם. וּבָאוּ וְאָמְרוּ בָּאוּ
בָּנַיִךְ אָמְרָה מַה אִיכְפַּת לִי תִשְׂמַחֲנָה
כַּלּוֹתַי, כֵּיוָן שֶׁבָּאוּ חַתְנֶיהָ אָמְרוּ לָהּ בָּאוּ
חַתְנַיִךְ אָמְרָה מַה אִיכְפַּת לִי תִשְׂמַחֲנָה
בְנוֹתַי. אָמְרוּ לָהּ בָּא הַמֶּלֶךְ בַּעֲלֵךְ אָמְרָה
הָאי חֶדְוָתָא שְׁלֵימָה חֲדוּ עַל חַדוּ. כַּךְ
לֶעָ״ל בָּאִין הַנְּבִיאִים וְאוֹמְרִים לִירוּשָׁלַיִם
בָּנַיִךְ מֵרָחוֹק יָבֹאוּ וְהִיא אוֹמֶרֶת לָהֶם מַה
אִיכְפַּת לִי. וּבְנֹתַיִךְ עַל צַד תֵּאָמַנָה אָמְרָה
מַה אִיכְפַּת לִי כֵּיוָן שֶׁאָמְרוּ לָהּ הִנֵּה מַלְכֵּךְ
יָבוֹא לָךְ צַדִּיק וְנוֹשַׁע הוּא אָמְרָה הָא
חֶדְוָתָא שְׁלֵמָה וכו'
— *A queen* [lit. *lady*] *whose husband the king, sons, and sons-in-
law, all went overseas.* [*Subse-
quently*] *they* (*messengers*) *came
and told her: 'Your sons have
returned!' Said she: 'What matters
it to me? Let my daughters-in-law
rejoice!' Upon the return of her
sons-in-law, they announced:*

'*Your sons-in-law have come!' Said
she, 'What concern is it of mine? Let
my daughters rejoice!' [But] when
they told her, 'Your husband the
king has arrived!' she said, 'This is a
complete joy, joy upon joy!'
Similarly, in the time to come, the
prophets will come and tell to
Jerusalem: 'Your sons come from
afar (Isaiah 60:4).' She will tell
them, 'What matters it to me?' [The
prophets will then say], 'And your
daughters are being carried on the
side (ibid.)'. She will again reply,
'What matters it to me?' But when
they will announce: 'Behold, your
king [i.e. Messiah] is coming to you,
He is just and deserving (Zechariah
9:9),' then she will say: 'This is
complete joy! ... ' (Shnei
HaMe'oros).*

M'vo HaShir explains the phrase
complete joy, by pointing out that it
is only when the Messiah will come,
that Jews will actually be allowed to
experience total joy, as found in
(*Berachos* 31a):
א״ר יוֹחָנָן מִשּׁוּם רשב״י אָסוּר לְאָדָם
שֶׁיְּמַלֵּא שְׂחוֹק פִּיו בְּעוֹלָם הַזֶּה שֶׁנֶּאֱמַר אָז
יִמָּלֵא שְׂחוֹק פִּינוּ וּלְשׁוֹנֵנוּ רִנָּה אֵימָתַי
בִּזְמַן שֶׁיֹּאמְרוּ בַגּוֹיִם הִגְדִּיל ה' לַעֲשׂוֹת עִם
אֵלֶּה

57 When He brings total joy,

and holy vessels ...

LEXICAL NOTES

II. *Share, portion* (as in *v.* 74). See *comm.*

דַּכְיָתָא — *Holy, clean* (as opposed to טְמֵא, *unclean*), the plural of דְּכֵי (and דַּכִיתָא).

LEXICAL NOTES

COMMENTARY

— *Rabbi Yochanan said in the name of Rabbi Shimon Ben Yochai: It is forbidden for a man's mouth to be filled with laughter in this world, because it is written:* Then will our mouths be filled with laughter, and our tongue with singing. — *When? — at the time when* they will say among the nations: 'HASHEM has done great things with them' (i.e., *when the Messiah will come*) (Psalms 126:2).

וּמָנֵי דַכְיָתָא — I. *And holy* [*lit. pure*] *vessels.*

The poet refers to the gold and silver vessels that Nebuchadnezzar took from the Temple during his seige and sacking of Jerusalem (see *II Kings* 24, especially *v.* 13; also *Jer.* 27:18; 28:6). These same vessels were subjected to defilement and desecration during the feast of Belshazzar, as found in *Daniel* 5:2-3:

בֵּלְשַׁאצַּר אֲמַר בִּטְעֵם חַמְרָא לְהַיְתָיָה לְמָאנֵי דַהֲבָא וְכַסְפָּא דִּי הַנְפֵּק נְבוּכַדְנֶצַּר אֲבוּהִי מִן הֵיכְלָא דִּי בִירוּשְׁלֶם וכו'. בֵּאדַיִן הַיְתִיו מָאנֵי דַהֲבָא דִּי הַנְפִּקוּ מִן הֵיכְלָא דִּי בֵית אֱלָהָא דִּי בִירוּשְׁלֶם וְאִשְׁתִּיו בְּהוֹן מַלְכָּא וְרַבְרְבָנוֹהִי שֵׁגְלָתֵהּ וּלְחֵנָתֵהּ

— *Belshazzar said, upon tasting the wine, to bring the gold and silver vessels which his father Nebuchadnezzar had removed from the Temple which was in Jerusalem ... Then they brought the golden vessels that were removed from the Temple of the House of God, which was in Jerusalem; and the king, his nobles, his wives, and his concubines, drank from them (Daniel 5:2-3).*

These vessels were ordered returned to Jerusalem by Cyrus (*Ezra* 5:14-15 and *ibid.*, 6:5). They were, however, looted by Titus during the second destruction of Jerusalem (*Berger*). When the Messiah will come, these vessels will be returned permanently to Jerusalem by the Holy One, blessed be He.

II. *And a pure portion.*

Zos Nechemosi and *Kinyan Tov* explain this to mean: חֵלֶק טוֹב זַךְ, *A* וְנָקִי שִׂמְחָה וְטוֹבָה בְּלִי שׁוּם עֶצֶב כְּלָל, *good portion, pure and clean; joy and goodness without the slightest sadness or grief.* The joy that Hashem will bring at the time of the redemption will be totally pure and complete, unlike the joys of this world which are always tinged with continuous everyday problems and cares.

נח קְרִיתָא דִירוּשְׁלֶם,
כַּד יְכַנֵּשׁ גָּלְוָתָא:

עֲלֵיהּ נט לְקָרְיה מַטִּיל עֲלַהּ,
בְּיוֹמֵי וְלֵילְוָתָא.

LEXICAL NOTES

58. קְרִיתָא — *To the city*, from קִרְיָא, *city, town, village*. The accusative locative form of the noun קִרְיָא, used to express *direction towards*, or *motion to a place*, is common in Biblical Hebrew formed by appending הָ to the noun, as for example, in Gen. 28:10: וַיֵּצֵא יַעֲקֹב מִבְּאֵר שָׁבַע וַיֵּלֶךְ חָרָנָה, *And Jacob went out from Beer-Sheva, and went to Charan*, and as in I Kings 14:17: וַתָּבֹא תִרְצָתָה, *And she came to Tirzah.*

יְכַנֵּשׁ — *Gather*; see vs. 7 and 43.

גָּלְוָתָא — *The exiled community of Israel.*

COMMENTARY

58. קְרִיתָא דִירוּשְׁלֶם — *To the city of Jerusalem.*

This verse concludes the previous one, and is to be read as follows: *When He will bring complete joy and the pure vessels to the city of Jerusalem, as He gathers in the Exile.*

כַּד יְכַנֵּשׁ גָּלְוָתָא — *As He gathers in the Exile.*

This expression, the ingathering of the Exile, is frequently used in the *Targum* to refer to the End of Days, when the Messiah will come, and the Holy One, Blessed be He, will gather in the Diaspora, and bring them to the city of Jerusalem. It is found, for example, in the *Targum* to *Michah* 7:12: בְּעִדָנָא הַהִיא יִתְכַּנְשׁוּן גָּלְוָתָא, *At that time [when the Messiah will come], the exiled will be gathered up* ...

59. לְקָרְיה מַטִּיל עֲלַהּ — I. *His Shechinah will protect* [lit. *cast a*

shadow over] *her* [i.e. *Jerusalem*]; or II. *His Shechinah will rest upon her.*

According to either translation, the basic sense is the same, i.e., Hashem's *Shechinah* (Presence) shall provide shade, shield, and protect the city of Jerusalem.

This verse is taken almost verbatim from *Targum Yonasan* to *Isaiah* 4:5 which foretells the events to come upon Jerusalem during the time of the redemption. The *Targum* reads:

וְיִבְרֵי ה' עַל כָּל מִקְדַּשׁ טוּרָא דְצִיּוֹן וְעַל אֲתָר בֵּית שְׁכִנְתֵּיהּ עֲנַן יְקָר יְהֵא מַטִּיל עֲלוֹהִי בִּימָמָא וְאָמִטְתָא וַחֲזוֹר כְּאֶשָּׁא שַׁלְהוֹבֵי בְּלֵילְיָא, אֲרֵי יַתִּיר מִן יְקָרָא דַאֲמִיר לְאֵיתָאָה עֲלוֹהִי שְׁכִנְתָּא תְּהֵי מִגְנָא עֲלוֹהִי בִּגְנוֹן

— *And HASHEM will create on every holy mountain of Zion, and upon the dwelling place of His Shechinah, His glorious cloud which will protect it during the day, and [He will create] a dense cloud*

58 To the city of Jerusalem,

as He gathers in the Exile.

59 His Shechinah will protect her

during days and nights.

LEXICAL NOTES

59. מַטִּיל — There are two opinions among the commentators as to the root of this word. I. *Shade* or *shield*, from טְלַל, and from טוּל, *to shade* (*Shnei HaMe'oros; Yad Aharon*). II. *Was placed*, from מוּטָל, being the participle of the *Hofal* (הָפְעַל) form of the verb נָטַל, *to move; to take*. An example of this usage is found in the Mishnah *Berachos* 17b: מִי שֶׁמֵתוֹ מוּטָל לְפָנָיו, *He whose dead lies* [i.e., *has been placed*] *before him* (Berger).

Most commentators, however, prefer the first definition, a view that is supported by the *Targum* quoted in the *comm.*

עֲלַהּ — *Upon her*. Other editions read עֲלֵיהּ, *upon it*, or *upon him*.

COMMENTARY

shining as a flaming fire at night; because in addition to the glory that He promised to bring upon her, the Shechinah will shield her as a canopy.

The 'clouds' refer to the *pillar of cloud* (עַמּוּד עָנָן), and *the pillar of fire* (עַמּוּד אֵשׁ), mentioned in *Exodus* 13:21-22. These clouds led Israel and shielded it from the Egyptians during the exodus from Egypt. See the *comm.* to *v.* 62 for the Hebrew text of the above verse in *Isaiah*.

Both *Rashi* and *Radak* explain that Jerusalem will require the shading and shielding of the *Shechinah* in order to protect the righteous within the city from the great heat of the sun which Hashem will allow to shine in all its full force in order to punish the wicked in the time to come. See *Radak* to *Isaiah* 4:5; and the *Rashi* to 4:6. This is based on the passage from *Avodah Zarah* 3b-4a:

אֵין גֵּיהִנֹּם לֶעָתִיד לָבֹא אֶלָּא הַקָּדוֹשׁ בָּרוּךְ הוּא מוֹצִיא חַמָּה מִנַּרְתְּקָהּ וּמַקְדִּיר רְשָׁעִים נִידוֹנִין בָּהּ וְצַדִּיקִים מִתְרַפְּאִין בָּהּ. רְשָׁעִים נִידוֹנִין בָּהּ דִּכְתִיב כִּי הִנֵּה הַיּוֹם בָּא בֹּעֵר כַּתַּנּוּר וְהָיוּ כָל זֵדִים וְכָל עֹשֵׂה רִשְׁעָה קַשׁ וְלִהַט אֹתָם הַיּוֹם וכו'. צַדִּיקִים מִתְרַפְּאִין בָּהּ דִּכְתִיב: וְזָרְחָה לָכֶם יִרְאֵי שְׁמִי שֶׁמֶשׁ צְדָקָה וּמַרְפֵּא בִּכְנָפֶיהָ וכו'

— *The Gehinnom in the World to Come will be nothing else, but that the Holy One, blessed be He, will remove the sun from its encasement, and allow it to flame forth. The wicked will be punished by it, and the righteous will be healed by it. The wicked will be punished by it, as it is written* (Malachi 3:20): For, behold!, the day comes, that it shall burn as an oven and all the proud, and all who do wickedness, shall be straw, and the day that comes shall consume them ... *and the righteous will be healed thereby, as it is written: It shall shine for you*

ס גְּנוּנֵהּ לְמֶעְבַּד בַּהּ,

בְּתוּשְׁבְּחָן כְּלִילָתָא:

סא דִּזְהוֹר עֲנָנַיָּא,

60. גְּנוּנֵהּ — I. *His* (Hashem's) *canopy*, from גְּנוֹן, גְּנוּנָא, *canopy, shade*, II. *Chupah* or *bridal canopy.*

לְמֶעְבַּד — *To be built*; literally, *to be made*, from the root עֲבַד, *to make*. Here used in the sense of building i.e. *the Temple*. See *vs.* 32, 48, and 52.

בַּהּ — *In her* [Jerusalem].

that fear my name, the sun of righteousness, with healing in his wings ... (*Shnei HaMe'oros; Yad Aharon*).

The above quoted passage also gives a deeper understanding of *v.* 53. I.e., the very same sunshine that will bring about the healing of the righteous, will simultaneously result in the punishment of the wicked (*Yad Aharon* to v. 53).

60. גְּנוּנֵהּ לְמֶעְבַּד בַּהּ — I. *His canopy to be built* [lit. *made*] *in her* [i.e., Jerusalem].

The poet here continues to paraphrase the *Targum* to *Isaiah* 4:5, begun in the previous verse. As the *Targum* concludes: שְׁכִנְתָּא תְהֵי מְגִנָּא עֲלוֹהִי כְּגָנוֹן, *the Shechinah will shield her* (Jerusalem) *as a canopy.* See the notes to the previous verse for the complete text of the *Targum.* (*Shnei HaMe'oros*).

II. *His Chupah*; or *bridal canopy*, as in the *Targum* to *Psalms* 19:6, הֵיךְ חֲתָנָא דְּנָפַק מִגְּנוּנֵיהּ (Hebrew text: וְהוּא כְּחָתָן יֹצֵא מֵחֻפָּתוֹ), *as a*

bridegroom coming out of his bridal chamber (or: 'canopy').

Kinyan Tov explains the 'bridal canopy', to be an allegorical reference to the Temple which will once again be erected when the Messiah will come. The Temple will be like a *chupah* in the allegorical wedding of Hashem and Israel. Depiction of God as the bridegroom and Israel as the bride is, of course, by no means uncommon in the Scriptures. The whole of *Shir HaShirim* is based on this theme. It is also found in *Hosea* (2:21), *Isaiah* (54:5) and *Jeremiah* (2:2). Accordingly, the verse is rendered: [In order] that His *chupah* be made in her (Jerusalem), wreathed out of praise.

בְּתוּשְׁבְּחָן כְּלִילָתָא — I. *With praise to be crowned* or *crowned with glory and praise.*

The canopy that Hashem will erect in Jerusalem will be crowned with the praises of Israel, as well as with the glory of the *Shechinah.*

⁶⁰ *His canopy to be built in her*

with praise to be crowned —

⁶¹ *Of brilliant clouds*

LEXICAL NOTES

בְּתוּשְׁבְחָן — *Praises*, the plural of תּוּשְׁבַּחְתָּא.

כְּלִילָתָא — I. *crowned*; or II. *wreathed*, from כְּלִילָא, *crown, wreath.*

61. דְּזֵהוֹר — *(Made) of brilliant clouds*, from זֵיהוֹרָא, *brilliance*, and זָהַר, *to shine.*

עֲנָנַיָּא — *Clouds*, plural of עֲנָן.

COMMENTARY

II. *Wreathed with praise(s).*

God's *chupah* will be 'wreathed' out of Israel's praises. It is appropriate to use the word *wreath* when referring to a *chupah*, since a *chupah* is indeed wreathed, i.e., woven out of material, or flowers and plants. As in *Gittin* 7a: *Mar, bar Rav Ashi* — דַּהֲוָה גָּדִיל כְּלִילָא לִבְרַתֵּיה, *twisted (wreathed) a bridal wreath for his daughter* [*Kinyan Tov; Shnei HaMe'oros*].

גְּנוּנֵהּ לְמֶעְבַּד בַּהּ ... — *That His [God's] canopy be built* [lit. *made*] *in her* [Jerusalem], *crowned with praise.* An alternate translation would be: *In order to make His canopy in her* [Jerusalem], *crowned with praise.*

While the verse continues the themes expressed in the *Targum* to *Isaiah* 4:5, the entire verse is also a close paraphrase of the *Targum* to *Isaiah* 28:5, which describes the rewards of the righteous upon the advent of the Messiah. The Hebrew text reads: *In that day shall HASHEM of hosts be* לַעֲטֶרֶת צְבִי

וְלִצְפִירַת תִּפְאָרָה, *for a desirable crown, and for a diadem of beauty.* *Targum* renders the Hebrew quote as לִכְלִילָא דְּחֶדְוָא וּלְכֶתֶר דְּתוּשְׁבָּחָא, *for a wreath of joy, and for a crown of praise.* Note the similarity in the wording of our verse to the wording of the *Targum* [*Shnei HaMe'oros*].

On the day that the Torah was given on Mount Sinai, the Jews were likened to a bride on the day of her betrothal, while God was analogous to the groom, as mentioned before. This is expressed in *Jeremiah* 2:2, זָכַרְתִּי לָךְ ... אַהֲבַת כְּלוּלֹתָיִךְ, *I [God] remember to you ... the love of your chupah.* (See the *Radak's* and *Rashi's* commentaries ad. loc.).

61. דְּזֵהוֹר עֲנָנַיָּא — [*Made*] *of brilliant clouds.*

This verse continues the paraphrase of *Isaiah* 4:5 and the *Targum* thereof. The *cloud* refers to the pillar of clouds that protected Israel during the exodus from Egypt. See *v.* 59. See also the *Midrash Tanchuma* quoted below.

לְמִשְׁפַּר כִּילָתָא.

סב לְפוּמֵיה דַעֲבִידְתָּא,
עֲבִידָן מְטַלַלְתָּא:

סג בְּתַכְתְּקֵי דְהַב פִּיזָא,

LEXICAL NOTES

לְמִשְׁפַּר — *To beautify*, from שְׁפַּר, *to beautify*, and from שֶׁפֶּר, *beauty*.

כִּילָתָא or כִּילְתָא — *Chupah, bridal canopy*, frequently used by the *Targum* for to translate the Hebrew חוּפָּה (chupah), as in the *Targum* to *Job* 15:32.

62. לְפוּמֵיה דְ־ — *According to his*, from the construction לְפוּמָא דְ־, *according to*, the root being פּוּמָא, פּוּם.

עֲבִידְתָּא — *Labor, toil*, root עֲבַד.

עֲבִידָן — *Will be made*, literally: *will they make* (his canopy).

מְטַלַלְתָּא — *Canopy*. Actually this word means: *a hut, shelter*. It is the *Targum* of סוּכָּה, *the type of booth built for the festival of Succos (Tabernacles)*, as in *Jonah* 4:5: וַיַּעַשׂ לוֹ שָׁם סֻכָּה, *Targum*: וַעֲבַד לֵיה תַּמָּן מְטַלַלְתָּא, *and he there made for himself a succah* [as a shelter from the sun].

COMMENTARY

לְמִשְׁפַּר כִּילָתָא — *To beautify the chupah* or alternatively: *For the beautification of the chupah* [that will be made for the righteous in the Time to Come]. The *chupah* will be composed of God's *Shechinah*. (See *comm.* below, and to the following verse).

This verse is bound to the subsequent one, and refers to the *canopy* that God will make for each righteous person as part of his reward in the World-to-Come. The verse is based on *Tanchuma, Pinchas* 14:

עָתִיד הַקָּדוֹשׁ בָּרוּךְ הוּא לַעֲשׂוֹת לְכָל צַדִּיק וְצַדִּיק חֻפָּה מֵעַנְנֵי כָבוֹד, שֶׁנֶּאֱמַר: וּבָרָא ה' עַל כָּל מְכוֹן הַר צִיּוֹן ... וְאוֹמֵר כִּי עַל כָּל כָּבוֹד חֻפָּה

— *The Holy One, blessed be He, shall make a chupah for each and ever one of the righteous, from the cloud of His glory.* As is stated: And HASHEM will create on every dwelling place of Mount Zion ... (Isaiah 4:5) and as the verse says further: For upon all the glory shall be a chupah (Yad Aharon. See also Tanchuma, Va'yakheil 10; and Tzav 12].

62. לְפוּמֵיה דְעֲבִידְתָּא — *For each according to his labor.*

Each person's reward will be in proportion to the amount of labor and toil that each person devotes to the studying and upholding of the Torah. This is summed up succinct-

to beautify the canopy ...

⁶² *For each according to his labor*

will the canopy be made.

⁶³ *Upon armchairs of purest gold*

LEXICAL NOTES

Here, however, the word is used more in the literal sense of מְטַלַּלְתָּא, *that which gives shade or covering* to that is: *a canopy*. See the notes to *v.* 59 for the meaning of טַלַל.

63. בְּתַכְתְּקֵי — Plural of תַּכְתְּקָא, *arm-chair, stool*, also spelled תכטקא, תכתכא תבטקא, טכטקא; See *Aruch HaShalem*, also see the notes to תבי in *v.* 81.

דְּהַב פִּיזָא — *Pure or refined gold*, the Aramaic translation of כֶּתֶם פָּז (*Shir Hashirim* 5:11), *the purest and rarest gold* in the world, being so refined that it shines with the brilliance of a diamond. (See *Rashi* to *Job* 28:17).

COMMENTARY

ly in the last *Mishnah of Avos 5*, לְפֻם צַעֲרָא אַגְרָא, *according to the labor* [lit. *pain*], *is the reward (Shnei HaMe'oros)*.

The verse is based on the following passage from *Bava Basra 75a*:
עָתִיד הקב״ה לַעֲשׂוֹת שֶׁבַע חוּפּוֹת לְכָל צַדִּיק וְצַדִּיק שֶׁנֶּאֱמַר: וּבָרָא ה' עַל כָּל מְכוֹן הַר צִיּוֹן וְעַל מִקְרָאֶהָ עָנָן יוֹמָם וְעָשָׁן וְנֹגַהּ אֵשׁ לֶהָבָה לָיְלָה כִּי עַל כָּל כָּבוֹד חֻפָּה מְלַמֵּד שֶׁכָּל אֶחָד וְאֶחָד עוֹשֶׂה לוֹ הַקָּדוֹשׁ בָּרוּךְ הוּא חוּפָּה לְפִי כְבוֹדוֹ
— *The Holy One, blessed be He, shall in the time to come, make seven chupas for each and every one of the righteous. As is stated: And HASHEM will create upon every dwelling place of Mount Zion, and upon her assemblies, a cloud and smoke by day, and the shining of a flaming fire by night; for upon all the glory shall be a chupah (Isaiah*

4:5). From this we learn that the Holy One, blessed be He, shall make for each and every one a chupah according to his honor (i.e., according to the honor that he deserves) [Heidenheim].

The poet uses the term מְטַלַּלְתָּא, the Aramaic equivalent of the Hebrew *succah*, rather than גְּנוּנָה or כִּילְתָא, the *Targumic* equivalents of חוּפָּה, *chupah*, because he wished to allude to *Bava Basra 75a:* עָתִיד הקב״ה לַעֲשׂוֹת סוּכָּה לַצַּדִּיקִים מֵעוֹרוֹ שֶׁל לִוְיָתָן, *In the time to come, the Holy One, blessed be He, will make a succah for the righteous from the hide of the Leviathan.* (See *vs.* 75-80).

63. בְּתַכְתְּקֵי דְּהַב פִּיזָא — *Upon* (lit. *with) arm-chairs of purest gold.*

In Paradise, the righteous will all

וּשְׁבַע מַעֲלָתָא.

סד תְּחִימִין צַדִּיקֵי,

קֳדָם רַב פְּעֲלָתָא:

סה וְרֵיוֵיהוֹן דָּמֵי,

לְשָׁבְעָא חֶדְוָתָא.

LEXICAL NOTES

וּשְׁבַע — And [into] seven [categories of distinction].

מַעֲלָתָא — I. Elevations, categories, the plural of מַעֲלָה. II. Step, ascent.

64. תְּחִימִין — Be positioned; from תְּחַם, to mark the limits; and from תְּחוּם, border, equivalent to the Hebrew noun גְּבוּל, boundary, וְהִגְבַּלְתָּ אֶת הָעָם סָבִיב, And you shall set bounds unto the people [confine them to within certain marked limits. Rashi] (Ex. 19:12) (Shnei Ha-Me'oros).

[Berger translates תְּחִימִין as מְסוּבִּים from סָבַב, to recline at a meal or banquet. He bases his translation on the fact that both תְּחִימִין and מְסוּבִּים are derived from roots having similar meanings, the former being from חָמָה, to surround; encircle, and the latter from סָבַב, to encircle; surround; also: to sit around a table for a meal. Hence, according to Berger תְּחִימִין צַדִּיקֵי is translated the righteous sit around a table for a meal. (See vs. 80, 81).]

COMMENTARY

sit upon armchairs of pure gold. This description is based on Kesubos 77b: ר' שִׁמְעוֹן בֶּן יוֹחַאי דַּהֲוָה יָתִיב עַל תְּלַת עֶשֶׂר תַּכְטְקֵי פִּיזָא [Bar Levai saw that]: Rabbi Shimon ben Yochai was sitting upon thirteen armchairs of pure gold [in paradise] i.e., thirteen chairs were set aside for his use].

וּשְׁבַע מַעֲלָתָא — I. And seven elevations.

The righteous in Paradise will be classified into one of seven categories each according to his merit. This is in accordance with Yalkut Shimoni Tehillim 879:

שִׁיר לַמַּעֲלוֹת ... לְמִי שֶׁעָתִיד לַעֲשׂוֹת מַעֲלוֹת לַצַּדִּיקִים לֶעָתִיד לָבֹא זוֹ לְמַעֲלָה מִזּוֹ ...
— A song of degrees (Psalms 121:1) ... [read] to Him who is prepared in the time to come to make different degrees (of elevations) for the righteous, one higher than the other (Yad Aharon).

It also follows:
שֶׁבַע מַעֲלוֹת הַצַּדִּיקִים הֵן בְּגַן עֵדֶן, כְּשֶׁבַע חֻפּוֹת נִפְרָדוֹת אֵלּוּ מֵאֵלּוּ כְּפִי מַעֲלָתָם
— There are seven categories into which the righteous will be divided in Gan Eden [Paradise], and with seven canopies will they be dis-

and seven elevations ...

⁶⁴ *Will the righteous be positioned*

before Him of many achievements,

⁶⁵ *And their appearance shall resemble*

someone sated with joy:

LEXICAL NOTES

קְדָם — See *v.* 21.

רַב — *Many.* An alternative translation is *great.* The word *many* can be used either in the quantitative or the qualitative sense. (See commentators to II *Sam* 23:20).

פְּעֶלָתָא — *Achievements;* literally, *deeds,* plural of פְּעוּלָה, *deed, labor.*

65. וְרֵיוְיהוֹן — *And their appearance;* plural of רֵיוָא. See *v.* 45 above.

דָמֵי — *Resemble, be considered as.*

לְשָׂבְעָא — From שְׂבַע. *To be sated, satisfied.*

חֶדְוָתָא — *Joy.* See *v.* 57 above.

COMMENTARY

tinguished one from the other, each according to his (individual) merit [*Bais HaMidrash, Jellinek, III. 133*] (*Berger*).

See also *Vayikra Rabbah* 30:2 cited in *comm.* to *v.* 65 above.

II. — *And elevated seven steps high.*

Each of the previously mentioned golden armchairs will be elevated seven steps high.

64. תְּחִימִין צַדִּיקֵי — *Will the righteous be positioned* or: *arranged* [i.e., in paradise] or alternatively: *will the righteous be appointed to his respective positions.*

This is a continuation of the previous verse. The righteous in Paradise will be arranged each in his respective, predesignated position,

before God, each sitting on an armchair of the finest gold, according to his merit.

קְדָם רַב פְּעֶלָתָא — *Before Him of many achievements.* (i.e., the Holy One, blessed be He).

This is an Aramaic translation of the phrase רַב פְּעָלִים in II *Sam.* 23:20 and I *Chron.* 11:22. It indicates one whose accomplishments are many and diverse. It has the further connotation of valorous achievements in the sense that they are of great merit.

65. לְשָׂבְעָא חֶדְוָתָא — *Sated with joy(s).*

This verse is taken almost verbatim from the *Targum* to *Psalms* 16:11, תְּהוֹדַע לִי אוֹרְחָא דְחַיֵּי שׂוֹבְעָא

סו רְקִיעָא בְּזֵיהוֹרֵיהּ,
וְכוֹכְבֵי זִיוָתָא:

סז הֲדָרָא דְּלָא אֶפְשַׁר,
לְמִפְרַט בְּשִׂפְוָתָא.

סח וְלָא אִשְׁתְּמַע וְחָמֵי,
נְבִיאָן חֶזְוָתָא:

66. רְקִיעָא — *The firmament*; lit. *the expanse [of the heavens].*

בְּזֵיהוֹרֵיהּ — *With its splendor.* See v. 61.

וְכוֹכְבֵי — *And (to) the stars*, plural of כּוֹכָב.

זִיוָתָא — From זִיו, *brightness, glory.*

67. הֲדָרָא — *Beauty,* or *honor.*

דְּחֶדְוָתָא קֳדָם אַפָּךְ, being the *Targum* translation of שֹׂבַע חַיִּים אֹרַח תּוֹדִיעֵנִי שְׂמָחוֹת אֶת פָּנֶיךָ וכו', *Let me know the path of life, the fullness of joy in your presence ... Ibn Ezra* comments that this psalm describes *the reward of the righteous.* Rashi explains succinctly what is meant by שֹׂבַע שְׂמָחוֹת, *a fullness of joy,* as follows: שִׂמְחָה שֶׁאֵין לָהּ קֵץ וְתִכְלָה הִיא, הַשִּׂמְחָה שֶׁל עָתִיד, *A joy to which there is no end or limit, this is the joy of the World to Come.* Since all pleasures will be spiritual, unhampered by the physical body, joy will be full and complete *(Radak, ibid).*

This and the following verse are based on *Vayikra Rabbah* 30:2 שֹׂבַע שְׂמָחוֹת אֶת פָּנֶיךָ [אַל תְּהֵי קוֹרֵא

שֹׂבַע אֶלָּא שֶׁבַע] אֵלּוּ שֶׁבַע כִּתּוֹת שֶׁל צַדִּיקִים שֶׁעֲתִידִים לְהַקְבִּיל פְּנֵי שְׁכִינָה, וּפְנֵיהֶם דּוֹמוֹת לַחַמָּה וְלַלְּבָנָה לָרָקִיעַ וְלַכּוֹכָבִים לַבְּרָקִים וְלַשּׁוֹשַׁנִּים וְלַמְּנוֹרָה הַטְּהוֹרָה שֶׁהָיְתָה בְּבֵית הַמִּקְדָּשׁ ...
— *The fullness* (שֹׂבַע) *of joy in Your presence — don't read 'sova'* (שֹׂבַע, *fullness, satiety) but 'sheva'* (שֶׁבַע) *seven. This applies to the seven classes of righteous men who will welcome the presence of the Shechinah; whose faces will be like the sun, the moon, the firmament, the stars, lightnings, lilies, and [the brightness of] the pure Menora that stood in the Temple.*
Some manuscripts of the *Akdamus* read לְשִׁבְעָא (with a *shin*, שׁ) and hence לְשִׁבְעָא חֶדְוָתָא, *To sevenfold joys* as in the above

⁶⁶ *As the firmament in its splendor*

and the stars in brightness.

⁶⁷ *Beauty it is not possible*

to specify with lips.

⁶⁸ *And which was neither heard nor seen*

by prophets in their visions.

LEXICAL NOTES

דְלָא אֶפְשָׁר — *Which is impossible.*

לְמִפְרַט — From פָּרַט, *To specify, to describe, in detail.*

בְּשִׂפְוָתָא – *With lips* or alternatively: *by (human) speech,* from שָׂפָה, *lip; speech.*

68. אִשְׁתְּמַע — *To be heard,* a form of the verb שְׁמַע, *to hear, listen.*

וְחָמֵי — From חָמָא, חֲמִי. *To see, observe.*

נְבִיאָן — Plural of נְבִיָא, *prophet.*

חֶזְוָתָא — *Visions,* (here: prophecies); plural of חֲזוּתָא, *vision.*

COMMENTARY

Midrash. Still other manuscripts read חֶזְוָתָא (instead of חֶדְוָתָא), the plural of חֲזוּתָא, *appearance, sight.* Thus, לְשִׁבְעָא חֶזְוָתָא, *to seven (different) appearances,* which also accords with the above *Midrash.* However these readings are unlikely, since, as stated above, the verse is almost certainly a reference to *Psalms 16:11 (Yad Aharon).*

66. רְקִיעָא בְּזֵיהוֹרֵיה ... — *As the firmament in its splendor, ...*

The verse continues the description of the faces of the righteous in the World to Come; as expressed in the latter half of the above cited *Midrash:* לָרְקִיעַ מִנַּיִן שֶׁנֶּאֱמַר: וְהַמַּשְׂכִּלִיל יַזְהִרוּ כְּזֹהַר הָרָקִיעַ לְכוֹכָבִים מִנַּיִן שֶׁנֶּאֱמַר: וּמַצְדִּיקֵי הָרַבִּים כַּכּוֹכָבִים

לְעוֹלָם וָעֶד, *From whence do we know that they* [the faces of the righteous] *will be like the firmament? — Because it is stated:* And they that are wise shall shine as the brightness of the firmament *(Daniel 12:3). From where do we know that they will resemble the stars? — As it is stated (ibid.):* And they that turn the many to righteousness [shall shine] as the stars forever and ever *(Heidenheim).*

68. וְלָא אִשְׁתְּמַע וְחָמֵי — *And which was neither heard nor seen.*

This verse continues the adumbration of the indescribable glory and honor that will be accorded the righteous in the world to

סט   בְּלָא שָׁלְטָא בֵּיהּ עַיִן,

בְּגוֹ עֵדֶן גִּנְּתָא.

ע   מְטַיְּלֵי בֵּי חִנְגָּא,

לְבַהֲדֵי דִשְׁכִינְתָּא:

עא   עֲלֵיהּ רָמְזֵי דֵין הוּא,

בְּרַם בְּאֶמְתָּנוּתָא.

LEXICAL NOTES

69. שָׁלְטָא — *Reigned (cf. v. 9).*

בְּגוֹ — *The midst, the inside.*

גִּנְּתָא — *Garden.*

70. מְטַיְּלֵי — From טַיֵּיל, *to promenade, to walk about, to enjoy oneself.*

בֵּי — *In, at, with.*

COMMENTARY

come which was begun in verse 61. The greatness awaiting the righteous is far beyond even the visions of the prophets.

The poet refers to *Berachos 34b:* כָּל הַנְּבִיאִים כּוּלָן לֹא נִתְנַבְּאוּ אֶלָּא לִימוֹת הַמָּשִׁיחַ אֲבָל לָעוֹלָם הַבָּא עַיִן לֹא רָאָתָה אֱלֹהִים זוּלָתְךָ — *All the prophets prophesied only until the days of the Messiah, but as for the World to Come 'No eye has seen it, except for You, oh God, (Isaiah 64:3) (Heiden-heim).*

69. בְּלָא שָׁלְטָא בֵּיהּ עַיִן — *Over which no eye has reigned.*

No living creature has ever seen Eden. The poet refers to *Berachos 34b:*
מַאי עַיִן לֹא רָאָתָה? רַבִּי שְׁמוּאֵל בַּר

נַחְמָנִי אָמַר: זֶה עֵדֶן שֶׁלֹּא שָׁלְטָה בּוֹ עַיִן כָּל בְּרִיָּה שֶׁמָּא תֹּאמַר אָדָם הָרִאשׁוֹן הֵיכָן הָיָה? — בְּגָן, וְשֶׁמָּא תֹּאמַר גָּן הוּא עֵדֶן — תַּלְמוּד לוֹמַר וְנָהָר יֹצֵא מֵעֵדֶן לְהַשְׁקוֹת אֶת הַגָּן
— *What is the meaning of 'No eye has seen'? (Isaiah 64:3) ... Rabbi Samuel ben Nachmani said: This is Eden (Paradise), which has never been seen by the eye of any creature. Perhaps you will say the first man Adam, where was he? — In the garden! And should you say, the garden and Eden are the same? — Not so! For the Torah says: And a river went out of Eden to water the garden (Gen. 2:10) — the garden is separate and Eden is separate. (Berachos 34b). Note the close similarity between the wording of*

⁶⁹ *Over which no eye has reigned*

> *the midst of the Garden of Eden.*

⁷⁰ *Therein they'll dance in a circle*

> *before the Shechinah's presence.*

⁷¹ *At Him, they will point: "That is He!"*

> *but with trepidation.*

LEXICAL NOTES

חִנְגָּא — *A round-dance, a circle;* the usual *Targum* rendering of the Hebrew מָחוֹל, *round-dance, to dance in a circle.* (See *Judges* 21:21, and the *Targum* there; see also the *Mishna Ta'anis* 26b).

לְבַהֲדֵי — *Before the presence of, in the company of; with,* from the prefix ־הַד, *with.*

דִּשְׁכִינְתָּא — *Of the Shechinah;* literally *dwelling or (royal) residence,* used to designate God's Divine Presence.

71. רָמְזֵי — *They will point,* from רְמַז, *to point, to gesture.*

דֵּין — *This, that; here (there);* דֵּין הוּא, *That is He!*

בְּרַם — *But, however;* as in *Daniel* 4:12 and 5:17.

בְּאֵמְתָנוּתָא — *With trepidation; fear,* from the Aramaic אִימְתָנָא, אֵמְתָנִי, *fear-inspiring;* and the Hebrew אֵימָה.

COMMENTARY

עָתִיד הקב"ה לַעֲשׂוֹת מָחוֹל לְצַדִּיקִים בְּגַן עֵדֶן וְהוּא יוֹשֵׁב בֵּינֵיהֶם וְכָל אֶחָד וְאֶחָד מַרְאֶה בְּאֶצְבָּעוֹ שֶׁנֶּאֱמַר: וְאָמַר בַּיּוֹם הַהוּא הִנֵּה אֱלֹהֵינוּ זֶה קִוִּינוּ לוֹ וְיוֹשִׁיעֵנוּ וכו'

— *In the future, the Holy One, blessed be He, will arrange a round-dance for the righteous in the Garden of Eden. He will sit among them and each of the righteous will [be able to] point with his finger. As is stated:* And it shall be said on that day — Lo, this is our God, for whom we waited, that he might save us *(Isaiah 25:9). See comm. to v. 73.*

71. בְּרַם בְּאֵמְתָנוּתָא — *But with trepidation.*

When the righteous will point to

our verse and that of the passage cited.

בְּגוֹ עֵדֶן גִּנְּתָא — *The midst of the Garden of Eden.*

The Garden of Eden is merely a part of Eden, Paradise proper. There have been those who have seen the *Garden* of Eden, but none who has seen Eden itself. Compare with *Ezekiel* 28:13 and the *Targum ibid.* (Heidenheim).

70. מְטַיְלֵי בֵּי חִנְגָּא — *Therein they'll dance in a circle* or, more loosely: *Therein (in Eden) they will participate in a round-dance.*

Compare the poet's description in this line with *Ta'anis* 31a:

[123]   *Akdamus*

שַׂבַּרְנָא לֵיה בְּשִׁבְיָן,

תְּקוֹף הֵמָנוּתָא:

יַדְבַּר לָן עָלְמִין,

עָלְמִין מְדַמּוּתָא.

LEXICAL NOTES

72. שַׂבַּרְנָא — *We hoped*, from the Hebrew שָׂבַר, *to hope, to wait, to look out for* [Aramaic סָבַר]. As in *Ps.* 119:166. שַׂבַּרְנָא לֵיה, can also be translated: *We waited for Him* ...

בְּשִׁבְיָן — *In our captivity*, from שְׁבִי, *to capture*, and שְׁבָיְיתָא, *captivity*.

תְּקוֹף — *Strength, power.* See v. 54.

הֵמָנוּתָא — *Faith, confidence*, the usual *Targum* of אֱמוּנָה. (See e.g. *Psalms* 119:138).

73. יַדְבַּר לָן — *He will lead us*, from the root דְּבַר, the *Targum* of נָהַג, *to lead, to conduct, to join, arrange.* Cf. *Psalms* 47:4 and *Rashi*.

COMMENTARY

God they will not do so in a disrespectful manner. Rather, it will be done with great fear and reverence. The poet alludes to the following *Midrash*:

וְהִתְהַלַּכְתִּי בְּתוֹכְכֶם עָתִיד הקב״ה לְטַיֵּיל עִם הַצַּדִּיקִים בְּגַן עֵדֶן לֶעָתִיד לָבוֹא, וְצַדִּיקִים רוֹאִים אוֹתוֹ וּמִזְדַּעְזְעִים מִלְּפָנָיו. וְהַמָּקוֹם אוֹמֵר לָהֶם לְצַדִּיקִים מַה לָכֶם שֶׁאַתֶּם מִזְדַּעְזְעִים מִלְּפָנַי? הֲרֵי אֲנִי כַּיּוֹצֵא בָּכֶם. לְפִי שֶׁאֲנִי כַּיּוֹצֵא בָּכֶם יָכוֹל לֹא תְּהֵא מוֹרָאִי עֲלֵיכֶם — תַּלְמוּד לוֹמַר: וְהָיִיתִי לָכֶם לֵאלֹהִים וְאַתֶּם תִּהְיוּ לִי לְעָם

— *And I will walk among you (Lev. 26:12) The Holy One, blessed be He, will walk with the righteous in the Garden of Eden in the Time to Come. And the righteous will see Him and tremble before Him. And the Lord will ask the righteous — Why do you tremble before Me? Behold I am as one of you!*

However, should you think that because I am as one of you, you need not be in fear of Me? — Hence it says: And I will be your God, and you shall be My people (ibid.) (Sifra, Bechukosai; Yalkut Shimoni Ibid. 672).

[The text of the above quoted passage was taken from the Codex Vatican no. 31, of the *Sifra* published by *Makor Pub. Ltd.* 1972.]

72. שַׂבַּרְנָא לֵיה בְּשִׁבְיָן — *We hoped for Him in our captivity*, i.e., in exile.

73. יַדְבַּר לָן עָלְמִין — *He will lead us eternally.*

This verse, continuing the depiction of the righteous in the Garden of Eden, alludes to *Vayikra Rabbah* 11:9:

עָתִיד הקב״ה לִהְיוֹת רֹאשׁ חוּלָה לַצַּדִּיקִים לֶעָתִיד לָבוֹא, הָדָא הוּא דִכְתִיב

⁷² *We hoped for Him in our captivity*

with a powerful faith.

⁷³ *He will lead us eternally*

resembling vigorous youths (in a round-dance).

The reason for the poet's use of the word יַדְבַּר is to be consistent with the *Targum's* translating of יְנַהֲגֵנוּ עַל־מוּת into יַדְבְּרִינָנָא כְּיוֹמֵי טַלְיוּתָנָא, *He will lead us as in the days of our youth (Ps. 48:15).* The poet refers to the *Midrashic* exposition of this verse in the Psalms. See *commentary.*

עָלְמִין — *Eternally, forever.* See *commentary.*

עָלְמִין — *Vigorous youths, young maidens.*

מְדַמּוּתָא — *Resembling as,* from דָּמָה.

שִׁיתוּ לִבְּכֶם לְחֵילָה לְחוֹלָה כְּתִיב וְהֵן חֹלִין לְפָנָיו בְּעַלְמוּת וּמַרְאִין עָלָיו כְּאִלּוּ בְּאֶצְבַּע וְאוֹמְרִין כִּי זֶה אֱלֹהִים אֱלֹהֵינוּ עוֹלָם וָעֶד הוּא יְנַהֲגֵנוּ עַל־מוּת בְּעַלְמוּת. בְּזְרִיזוּת. עַלְמוּת — כְּאִילִּין עוּלֵימָתָא כְּדָכְתִיב בְּתוֹךְ עֲלָמוֹת תּוֹפֵפוֹת (שם סח:כו) תִּרְגֵּים עֲקֵילָס אַתָנָסִיאָה — עוֹלָם שֶׁאֵין בּוֹ מוּת. עַלְמוּת — בִּשְׁנֵי עוֹלָמוֹת יְנַהֲגֵנוּ בָּעוֹלָם הַזֶּה וִינַהֲגֵנוּ בָּעוֹלָם הַבָּא. — *In the Time to Come, the Holy One, blessed be He, will be the leader of the round-dance of the righteous — as it is written:* Mark you well her walls (לְחֵילָה) *(Psalms 48:14).* [Read as if] *it is written* cholah (לְחוֹלָה, *round-dance). And they will dance around Him with vigor* (בְּעַלְמוּת) *and point to Him, as it were, with a finger, saying:* 'This is the God, our God, for ever and ever; He will lead us almus (עַל־מוּת) *(ibid. 48:15) —* with (עַלְמוּת) *or*

alomos (עַלְמוּת), youthfulness,' *as* young maidens, *as is written:* In the midst of (עֲלָמוֹת) damsels playing upon timbrels *(ibid. 68:26). Or as translated by Aquila* (עַל־מָוֶת), athanasia [*i.e. a world in which there is no death*]. *Or olomos* (עוֹלָמוֹת) *in two worlds. He will lead us in this world and He will lead us in the world to come (Vayikra Rabbah 11:9).*

Thus, according to this *Midrash,* there are four different interpretations for the word עַל־מוּת 1). youthfulness, quickness, dexterity, עַלְמוּת, (*Rashi Exod.* 2:8). 2). Young maidens, עֲלָמוֹת: 3). immortality, athansia — עַל־מָוֶת, above death; 4). two worlds — עוֹלָמוֹת. The poet uses the dual word play of עָלְמִין עָלְמִין so that all the above meanings can be inferred.

מְנָת דִּילָן דְּמִלְּקַדְמִין, עד
פָּרֵשׁ בַּאֲרָמוּתָא:

74. מְנָת — *Share, portion.*

דִּילָן — *Which is ours,* or more literally: *which is to us.*

פָּרֵשׁ — *To set aside, to separate off, to dedicate,* as for example in *Mishna Terumos* 4:1: הַמַּפְרִישׁ מִקְצָת תְּרוּמָה, *if one sets aside part of the Terumah.*

74. מְנָת דִּילָן דְּמִלְּקַדְמִין — *Our share which from before.*

The *share* refers to the share to be awarded the righteous when the Messiah will come. This reward was already set aside by God *from the beginning,* i.e., prior to and during the six days of Creation. The poet refers to 1). The Garden of Eden, and 2). the banquet of the Leviathan and the Behemoth. These rewards are mentioned in the *Midrash:* שִׁבְעָה דְּבָרִים קָדְמוּ לְעוֹלָם אַלְפַּיִם שָׁנָה הַתּוֹרָה, וְכִסֵּא כָּבוֹד, וְגַן עֵדֶן, וְגֵיהִנָּם, וּתְשׁוּבָה, וְהַבֵּית הַמִּקְדָּשׁ שֶׁל מַעֲלָה, וְשֵׁם מָשִׁיחַ — *Seven things preceded [the creation of] the world by two thousand years: the Torah, the throne of glory, the Garden of Eden, Gehinnom, repentance, the heavenly sanctuary and the name of the Messiah (Midrash Tehillim 90:12).*

The creation of the Behemoth and Leviathan: וַיִּבְרָא אֱלֹהִים אֶת הַתַּנִּינִם: רַב פִּנְחָס מִשֵּׁם רַב אִידִי (נ״א אַחָא) תַּנִּינַם כְּתִיב זֶה בְּהֵמוֹת וְלִוְיָתָן שֶׁאֵין לָהֶם בֶּן זוּגוֹת — *And God created the great sea-creatures (Gen. 1:21) Rav Pinchas said in the name of Rav Idi — it is written: sea*

creatures [תנינם, without a second yod. The Torah reads תנינם, in the defective spelling (חסר), instead of the *plene* form (מלא) of תנינים. Rav Idi deduces that because the word תנינם is spelled defectively it] refers to the Behemoth and Leviathan who likewise [are defective because they] lack mates. (See *Bava Basra* 74b, and the notes to the next six verses). *(Bereishis Rabbah 7:21).*

That this share has been set aside for Israel is expressed in the following *Midrash:*

אָמַר רַב בְּרַכְיָה שָׁמַיִם וָאָרֶץ לֹא נִבְרְאוּ אֶלָּא בִּזְכוּת יִשְׂרָאֵל דִּכְתִיב: בְּרֵאשִׁית בָּרָא אֱלֹקִים וְאֵין רֵאשִׁית אֶלָּא יִשְׂרָאֵל שֶׁנֶּאֱמַר: קֹדֶשׁ יִשְׂרָאֵל לַה׳ רֵאשִׁית תְּבוּאָתה

— *Rav Berechiah says: Heaven and earth were created only for the benefit of Israel, as is written: In the beginning of God's creation* (בְּרֵאשִׁית) *(Gen. 1:1); and the word* רֵאשִׁית [lit. *first or beginning*] *can signify only Israel as it is written: Holy is Israel unto HASHEM the* (רֵאשִׁית) *first fruits of his harvest (Jer. 2:3) [Vayikra Rabbah 36;4].*

74 Our share, which from before
was set aside with elevation.

LEXICAL NOTES

בַּאֲרָמוּתָא — From אֲרָמוּתָא, *elevation, raising up;* or *Terumah (heave-offering)* i.e. *that which is lifted or separated,* being that which an Israelite sets apart from his possessions in order to donate as a contribution to the Sanctuary, (see *Exod.* 25 1-7).

COMMENTARY

פְּרֵשׁ בַּאֲרָמוּתָא — *Was set aside [by God] with [special] elevation.* This can be alternatively translated as: *He [God] set aside as (one sets aside) Terumah.*

Paradise and the Leviathan and the Behemoth were especially created and set aside by God, for the enjoyment of the just in the world to come (see the *comm.* to the next six verses below).

The term פְּרֵשׁ is used by the *Targumim* in the translation of the Hebrew word תְּרוּמָה *setting aside or separating for a sacred purpose;* while אֲרָמוּתָא is used to render תְּנוּפָה, *Raising and elevating of something, especially as Terumah [Lev.* 10:15, and the *Targum* there.] Both words denote the elevation and sanctification of something to a status of importance and holiness.

75. The Leviathan and the Behemoth

◄§ The Leviathan

According to the Aggadah of the *Talmud* and *Midrash,* the לִוְיָתָן, *Leviathan,* is a giant fish created on the fifth day of creation and is the ruler of all the creatures of the sea.

Originally, it was created male and female, as were all other species. However, God saw that if the two fish were allowed to mate and multiply, they would destroy the entire world because of their great strength and numbers. God, therefore, killed the female and preserved it in brine, to be eaten by the righteous at the banquet that will be prepared for them in the Time to Come.

The Leviathan is so enormous that all the waters that flow from the Jordan river into the sea, can scarcely quench its thirst. It is not only large and powerful, but also very beautiful. Its fins are so radiant that they outshine the sun. Its eyes are so bright, that they sometimes illuminate the entire sea.

The *Talmud (Avodah Zara* 3b) says that the Leviathan is, as it were, the 'plaything' of God, with which He 'amuses' Himself.

◄§ The Behemoth

The Behemoth (בְּהֵמוֹת; also

טְלוּלֵה עה **טְלוּלָא דְלִוְיָתָן,**

וְתוֹר טוּר רָמוּתָא.

75. טְלוּלָא — *Sport, amusement,* as in *Eruvin* 68b: כחוכא ואטלולא, *as amusement and sport.* The word טלולא is used to designate the amusement and sport of hunting.

וְתוֹר — *Ox,* the Aramaic for the Hebrew שׁוֹר.

known in hebrew as שׁוֹר הַבָּר, and in Aramaic as תּוֹר בְּרָא, *wild ox)* was created on the sixth day of the creation of the world. The Behemoth is a gigantic ox, and like the Leviathan, possesses enormous strength. It, too, was created male and female, and like the Leviathan, had to be prevented from multiplying, lest the world be destroyed. God therefore neutered the male and eliminated the female's desire to propagate.

The Behemoth is so monstrous, that he requires the produce of a thousand hills for its daily food. Its need for water is so great, that all the water that flows from the Jordan River for one day, is enough for but one gulp. God therefore provided him with the exclusive use of the River Yubal that flows from Paradise to quench its thirst.

When the Messiah shall come, God will summon the angels to enter into battle against the Leviathan, for the amusement of the righteous. But the Leviathan will cast one glance upon them, and the angels will run in fear and dismay from the field of battle. They will return to attack him with swords,

but to no avail, since steel is as straw to his scales. Equally futile will be the throwing of spears and stones, as they will bounce off him without any effect.

Disheartened, the angels will give up the battle, and Hashem will signal to the Leviathan and Behemoth to enter into battle with each other. The result will be that the Leviathan will slaughter the Behemoth with a cut from his very sharp fins. At that moment the Behemoth will kill the Leviathan with a blow from his tail, or alternatively: his horns. (Another version reads that Hashem himself will kill the Leviathan. See *comm.* to *v.* 79).

From the beautiful skin of the Leviathan, God will construct canopies to shelter the righteous from the sun. They will eat the meat of the Behemoth and the Leviathan amid great joy and merriment, at a huge banquet that will then be given for them.

The above is but a very brief synopsis of the Aggadah on the Leviathan and Behemoth. The main sources for the above account of the Behemoth and the Leviathan are to

LEXICAL NOTES

טור — *Mountain.*

רָמוּתָא — *High, lofty;* from רום, *high;* רָמוּתָא specifically designates *loftiness, pride, grandeur.*

COMMENTARY

be found in the following *Talmudic* and *Midrashic* sources: *Shabbos* 77b; *Bava Basra* 74a-75b; *Avodah Zarah* 3b; *Chulin* 57b; *Vayikra Rabbah* 13:3,22; *Bamidbar Rabbah* 21:18,22; *Pesikta d'Rav Kahana* 6,29; *Pesikta Rabbasi* 16, 23:5, 48:3; *Tanchuma Chaye Sarah* 3, *Shemini* 6, end of *Pinchas*; *R'ei* 6; *Nitzavim* 4; *Pirkei d'Rabbi Eliezer* 9-11; *Yalkut Shimoni Isaiah* 501, *Yonah* 550; *Tehillim* 882, *Iyov* 957; *Shmuel* 161.

For an allegorical explanation see also the Zohar II 34, 108, 223b; III 217a; 240a, also Zohar I, 18b.

The Behemoth and Leviathan are mentioned in the scriptures in the following places; *Isaiah* 27:1; *ibid.* 30:6; *Psalms* 50:10, 73:22, 104:26; *Job* 3:8; 40:15,25.

טְלוּלָא דְלִוְיָתָן — *Sport with the Leviathan.*

The poet is referring to the following: בְּהֵמוֹת וְלִוְיָתָן הֵן קַנִיגִין שֶׁל צַדִּיקִים לֶעָתִיד לָבוֹא, *The Behemoth and Leviathan will be the game in a hunt for [the amusement of] the righteous in the time to come (Vayikra Rabbah* 13, 3; see comm. to verses 77 and 78 below).

The Leviathan is often described in *Talmud* and *Midrash* as having been created for the entertainment and diversion of both God and the righteous. Until the destruction of the Temple, God amused Himself, as it were, with the Leviathan as is stated in *Avodah Zarah* 3b: רְבִיעִיוֹת יוֹשֵׁב וּמְשַׂחֵק עִם לִוְיָתָן שֶׁנֶּאֱמַר לִוְיָתָן זֶה יָצַרְתָּ לְשַׂחֶק בּוֹ, *One quarter of each day God sports with the Leviathan, as it says:* Leviathan which you created to sport with *(Psalms* 104:26).

This daily pastime came to an end with the destruction of the Temple. However, when the Messiah will come, the entertainment will resume — as *Targum* translates the above verse: לִוְיָתָן דֵין בָּרֵיתָא לְמִגְחָךְ בֵּיהּ בְּסְטוֹדַת בֵּית מְדוֹרֵיהּ, *The Leviathan which You created to sport with for the righteous at the banquet [to be held] at the House of Your dwelling [i.e. when the Messiah will come.]*

וְתוֹר טוּר רָמוּתָא — *And the ox of lofty mountains.*

This phrase is from the *Targum* to *Psalms* 50:11, וְתוֹר בָּר דְּרָעֵי בְּכָל יוֹמָא בְּטוּרִין אַלְפָא, *And the wild ox which grazes every day upon a thousand mountains.* This verse re-

עו וְחַד בְּחַד כִּי סָבִיךְ,
וְעָבֵד קְרָבוּתָא:

עז בְּקַרְנוֹהִי מְנַגַּח בְּהֵמוֹת,
בְּרַבְרְבוּתָא *בִּרְבוּתָא.

עח יְקַרְטַע נוּן לְקִבְלֵיה,
בְּצִיצוֹי בִּגְבוּרְתָא:

LEXICAL NOTES

76. וְחַד בְּחַד — *And one with the other; as in the Targum of Job 41:8,* חַד עִם חַד, מְקָרְבִין, *One will draw near to the other.*

סָבִיךְ — *Interlock, from* סָבַךְ, *to interlace, entangle. See* comm.

קְרָבוּתָא — *Battle, confrontation, from* קְרָב.

וְעָבֵד קְרָבוּתָא — *And engage in battle, literally, and they will make war.*

77. בְּקַרְנוֹהִי — *With his horns, from* קֶרֶן, *horn.*

COMMENTARY

fers to the following *Midrash:* בַּשִּׁשִׁי הוֹצִיא מִן הָאָרֶץ בְּהֵמוֹת שֶׁהוּא רָבוּץ בְּהַרְרֵי אֶלֶף וּבְכָל יוֹם נָיוֹם מַרְעִיתוֹ אֶלֶף הָרִים וּבַלַּיְלָה הֵם נִצְמְחִין מֵאֲלֵיהֶן כְּאִלוּ לֹא נָגַע בָּהֶם, *On the sixth day He brought forth from the earth the Behemoth which lies stretched out on a thousand hills, and every day it grazes on the verdure of a thousand hills, and overnight it [the verdure] grows back by itself as though he had not touched it. (Pirkei de-Rabbi Eliezer, II).*

76. וְחַד בְּחַד כִּי סָבִיךְ — *When one with the other will interlock.*

This description of the battle is from the *Pesikta d'Rav Kahana, Piska 29:*

אֶחָד בְּאֶחָד יִגַּשׁוּ וְרוּחַ לֹא יָבֹא בֵינֵיהֶם אַל תִּקְרִי וְרוּחַ אֶלָּא וְרֶוַח ... בְּהֵמוֹת וְלִוְיָתָן מִדַּבְּקִין זֶה עִם זֶה. שֶׁנֶּאֱמַר אִישׁ בְּאָחִיהוּ יְדֻבָּקוּ וּמִשֶּׁהֵן מְדַבְּקִין זֶה עִם זֶה אֵינָן מִתְפָּרְשִׁין זֶה מִזֶּה שֶׁנֶּאֱמַר: יִתְלַכְּדוּ וְלֹא יִתְפָּרָדוּ — *One will draw near to the other and no air can come between them (Job 41:8). Do not read 'ruah'* (רוּחַ), *air, but 'revach'* (רֶוַח) *space ... The Behemoth and the Leviathan will be joined to each other (in battle), as is written:* They are joined one to another *(ibid. 41:9). And once joined they will not be sundered, as is said:* They cleave to each other and cannot be sundered *(ibid.).*

בְּקַרְנוֹהִי ... יְקַרְטַע ... **77-78.** — *With his horns ... Will leap ...*

76 When one with the other will interlock

and engage in battle.

77 With his horns the Behemoth

will gore with might.

78 The fish will leap to meet him

with his fins, with power.

מְנַגַּח — *To gore, to butt,* especially with horns.

בִּרְבוּתָא — From רְבוּתָא, *greatness, strength.*

78. יְקַרְטַע — From קַרְטַע, *to leap, to jump, to spring.*

נוּן — *Fish,* as in *Targum Gen.* 9:2, וּבְכָל נוּנֵי יַמָּא, *And with all the fish of the sea.*

לְקַבְלֵיה — *To meet him,* from קַבֵּל, *to receive, greet, meet.*

בְּצִיצוֹי — *With his fins.*

בִּגְבוּרְתָא — From גְּבוּרָה, *power, strength.*

The source of *vs.* 77 and 78 is the following *Midrash:*

אָמַר רַב יוּדָן בְּרִ׳ שִׁמְעוֹן בְּהֵמוֹת וְלִוְיָתָן
הֵן קִנִיגִין שֶׁל צַדִּיקִים לֶעָתִיד לָבוֹא, וְכָל
מִי שֶׁלֹּא רָאָה קִינִיגִין שֶׁל אוּמּוֹת הָעוֹלָם
בָּעוֹלָם הַזֶּה זוֹכֶה לִרְאוֹתָן לָעוֹלָם הַבָּא,
כֵּיצַד הֵן נִשְׁחָטִין — בְּהֵמוֹת נוֹתֵץ לְלִוְיָתָן
בְּקַרְנָיו וְנוֹחֲרוֹ וְלִוְיָתָן נוֹתֵץ לִבְהֵמוֹת
בִּסְנַפִּירָיו וְקוֹרְעוֹ

— *Rav Judan son of Rabbi Simeon said: The Behemoth and Leviathan will be the hunting-sport of the righteous in the time to come, and all those who did not participate in the hunts of the nations of the world, in this world will be privileged to see them in the World to Come. How will they be* slaughtered? — *The Behemoth will attack the Leviathan with his horns and gore him, and the Leviathan will cut the Behemoth with his fins and rend him (Vayikra Rabbah 13:3).* [The Behemoth will kill the Leviathan by goring, since fish do not require ritual slaughtering. However, the Behemoth, being an ox, requires proper slaughter, therefore the Leviathan will ritually slaughter him through the use of his very sharp fins. The *Midrash* says that God will issue a special ruling that the Behemoth slaughtered in this manner is kosher for eating, for, ordinarily, ritual slaughter is acceptable only if it is performed by a qualified human being.]

עט מְקָרֵב לֵיהּ בָּרְיֵהּ,

בְּחַרְבֵּיהּ *רַבְרְבוּתָא.

פ אַרסטוֹן לְצַדִּיקֵי יְתַקֵּן,

וְשֵׁרוּתָא:

רַבְרְבָתָא: בְּרַבְרְבוּתָא

---

79. מְקָרֵב — From קָרֵב, *to approach*; also *to intercede*.

לֵיהּ — *Them*, literally, *him*.

בָּרְיֵהּ — *Their* (lit. *his) Creator*, as in *Targum Prov.* 17:5, לְבָרְיֵהּ, *to his Creator*.

בְּחַרְבֵּיהּ — From חֶרֶב, *sword*.

COMMENTARY

79. מְקָרֵב לֵיהּ בָּרְיֵהּ בְּחַרְבֵּיהּ — *Their [or: The] Creator will approach [them] with His sword;* This verse alludes to the following *Aggadah:* כִּי אָתָא רַב דִּימִי א״ר יוֹנָתָן עָתִיד גַּבְרִיאֵל לַעֲשׂוֹת קְנִיגְיָא עִם לִוְיָתָן שֶׁנֶּאֱמַר: תִּמְשֹׁךְ לִוְיָתָן בְּחַכָּה וּבְחֶבֶל תַּשְׁקִיעַ לְשׁוֹנוֹ וְאִלְמָלֵא הקב״ה עוֹזְרוֹ אֵין לוֹ שֶׁנֶּאֱמַר: הָעֹשׂוֹ יַגֵּשׁ חַרְבּוֹ — *When Rav Dimi came, he said in the name of Rav Yonasan: In the future Gabriel will arrange a hunt of the Leviathan — for it is said: Can you draw out Leviathan with a fish hook? Or press down his tongue with a rope? (Job 40:25) And if the Holy One, blessed be He, will not help him, he will be unable to prevail over him, as it is written: He Who has made him, shall draw near His sword (Job 40:19) (Bava Basra 74b-75a).*

There appears to be a contradiction between the previous two verses and the present one. The first two verses state that the Behemoth and Leviathan will kill each other in battle, yet this verse says that God Himself will use his sword to kill them. *Maharsha* explains that Leviathan and Behemoth, both of them being the creations of God, will be the sword of God. Each animal will be God's tool which God will use to kill the other. The *Maharsha* reads the verse in *Job* 40:19: *He Who has made him shall draw near His sword* as follows — *He Who has created (the Leviathan) shall draw near His sword (which is the Behemoth).* (*Aggadot Maharsha* to וְאִלְמָלֵא הקב״ה עוֹזְרוֹ — *Bava Bathra* 75a). The wording of the Pesikta d'Rav Kahana clearly supports this explanation.

מָה הקב״ה עוֹשֶׂה? — רוֹמֵז לְלִוְיָתָן וְהוּא מַכֶּה אֶת הַבְּהֵמוֹת בְּסַנְפִּירָיו וְשׁוֹחֲטוֹ וְרוֹמֵז לִבְהֵמוֹת וְהוּא מַכֶּה לְלִוְיָתָן בִּזְנָבוֹ וּמְמִיתוֹ — *What will the Holy One, blessed be He, do? — He will signal to the Leviathan and it will strike the*

אקדמות [132]

79 Their Creator will approach them

with His mighty sword.

80 A banquet will He prepare for the righteous

and a dinner.

LEXICAL NOTES

רַבְרְבוּתָא — From רַבְרְבָא, *mighty, great;* also from רַבָּא, *great, large.*

80. אֲרִסְטוֹן — *Banquet, principal meal,* from the Greek apistov = *morning meal, breakfast.*

יְתַקֵן — *Will He (God) prepare,* from תְּקֵן, *to prepare, establish.*

COMMENTARY

Behemoth with its fin and slaughter it. He will signal to the Behemoth and it will strike Leviathan with its tail and kill it (*Pesikta d'Rav Kahana, Piska 29*).

Hence it is through God's signal, that each creature will become the tool or sword of God, and will effect the slaughter of the other.

Another explanation for this difficulty is that after the Behemoth and Leviathan will kill one another, God will approach with His sword in order to divide their meat for distribution to the righteous (*Yad Aharon*).

80. אֲרִסְטוֹן — *A banquet.*

The reference is to the meal to be served to the righteous in the Time to Come, after the final redemption has found in the following *Midrashic* sources:

רַב בְּרַכְיָה בְּשֵׁם רַב יִצְחָק אֲרִסְטוֹן גָּדוֹל
עָתִיד הקב״ה לַעֲשׂוֹת לַעֲבָדָיו צַדִּיקִים
לֶעָתִיד לָבוֹא

— Rav Berachia said in the name of Rav Isaac: The Holy One, blessed be He, shall make a great banquet for His servants, the righteous, in the Time to Come (*Vayikra Rabbah 13:3*).

אָמַר רַבָּה אָמַר רַב יוֹחָנָן עָתִיד הקב״ה
לַעֲשׂוֹת סְעוּדָה לְצַדִּיקִים מִבְּשָׂרוֹ שֶׁל
לִוְיָתָן.

*Rabbah said in the name of Rav Yochanan: The Holy One, blessed be He, will make a banquet for the righteous from the meat of the Leviathan (*Bava Basra 75a*). See also Jellinek, Beth Hamidrash, vol. VI, pages 150-1, Eisenstein (*Ozar Midrashim*, vol. I, page 90 — מדרש סעודת לויתן).*

וּשְׁרוּתָא — *And a meal.*

See *Rashi* to Gen. 43:16. The poet probably uses the word שִׁירוּתָא because it is the same word used by the *Targum* with reference to the feast of the Leviathan to be given for the righteous: יַעְבְּדוּן עֲלוֹי חַכִּימַיָא

LEXICAL NOTES

81. מְסַחֲרִין — From סְחַר, *to encircle*; used often, in the sense of: *to recline and/or dine around a table*, as exemplified in the *Targum*: to Kings 13:20: ... וַהֲוָה עַד דְּאִינוּן מְסַחֲרִין עַל פָּתוֹרָא, *And it was, as they were still sitting and dining around the table, that ...*

תַכֵּי — From תַכָּא, *table; chair or stool, tray*; קָרִיבוּ תַכָּא קַמֵיה, *they placed a tray before him (Bava Metziah 86a)*, used to denote any three- or four-legged, four-cornered table, chair or serving tray. See *Talmudische Archaologie*, I, p. 59, and קדמוניות התלמוד, vol. 2 part 1, pg. 25., both by Samuel Krauss. Also Kohut's, *Aruch Ha-Shalem* under תַכְּתָה.

דְּכַדְכֹד — From כַּדְכֹד (*Isaiah 54:12), Precious stones, gems*. The exact meaning of this word is not clear. Some translate: *rubies*.

COMMENTARY

שֵׁירוּתָא יְפַלְגוּנֵיה בֵּין תַּגָּרַיָא, *The scholars [righteous] shall make a feast upon him [the Leviathan] and they shall divide him among the merchants (Targum Job 40:30).* This verse is explained by the *Talmud* as follows: After the main portions will have been served to the righteous ... *The rest [of the Leviathan] will be divided up and used as merchandise to be sold in the streets of Jerusalem as it is said (ibid.): They will divide him among the Kena'anim [merchants] (Bava Basra 75a).*

וְהַשְׁאָר מְחַלְקִין אוֹתוֹ וְעוֹשִׂין בּוֹ סְחוֹרָה בְּשׁוּקֵי יְרוּשָׁלַיִם שֶׁנֶּאֱמַר: יֶחֱצוּהוּ בֵּין כְּנַעֲנִים.

Yad Aharon addresses himself to the question of why the poet in this verse, employs two words, אֲרִסְטוֹן and שֵׁירוּתָא, which have very similar meanings. He answers that אֲרִיסְטוֹן, which generally refers to breakfast, indicates the feast of the Leviathan, which is more properly eaten for breakfast since it is fish, a lighter food. However, שֵׁירוּתָא, refers to the main banquet, when the meat of the Behemoth will be served *(Yad Aharon; ad. loc.)*.

81. מְסַחֲרִין עֲלֵי תַכֵּי — *They will recline around tables.*

This phrase is from the following *Midrash*, describing the banquet for the righteous in Paradise in the Time to Come:

וְכָל אֶחָד יוֹשֵׁב כְּמֶלֶךְ עַל כִּסֵּא שֶׁל זָהָב וְלִפְנֵי כָּל אֶחָד וְאֶחָד שֻׁלְחָן שֶׁל מַלְגָּלִיּוֹת

⁸¹ They will recline around tables

of precious stones and gems.

⁸² Before them there will flow

balsam rivers,

LEXICAL NOTES

וְגוּמַרְתָּא — As with the previous word, the precise meaning is unclear. The root is from the Aramaic גְמַר with which the *Targum* translates the Hebrew word אֶקְדָּח (in *Isaiah* 54:12), a kind of precious stone, perhaps a carbuncle (a kind of black pearl). In the *Talmud* the word גּוּמַרְתָּא is used to mean a burning, glowing coal, as in *Chulin* 11a — דְּמָנַח גּוּמַרְתָּא עֲלֵיה, *He placed a coal upon it*. It may be a precious stone of a brilliance as dazzling as a glowing coal. Some modern translators speculate that אֶקְדָּח means *beryl*.

82. נְגִידִין — *There will flow* corresponding to the Hebrew מָשַׁךְ: from the Biblical Aramaic word נְגַד, *to flow, to stream*. As in *Daniel* 7:10: ... נְהַר דִּי נוּר נָגֵד וְנָפֵק מִן, *A river of fire flowed and emanated from him* ... קֳדָמוֹהִי

קַמֵּיהוֹן — *Before them*, from קֳמֵי, *before, in the presence of*. As in *Targum Yonason* to *Genesis* 33:3.

אֲפַרְסְמוֹן — *Balsam* [oil].

נַהֲרָתָא — From נַהֲרָא, *river stream*; the feminine plural form is נַהֲרָוָתָא.

COMMENTARY

— *And each and every one [of the righteous] will sit like a king on a throne of gold, and before each one shall be a table of precious stones.* (*Osios d'Rabbi Akiva*, version A).

מְסַחֲרִין עֲלֵי תַּבֵּי ... — *They will recline around tables.*

The poet derived this description of Paradise from the prophecy in *Isaiah* (54:12) depicting the World to Come. וְשַׂמְתִּי כַּדְכֹד שִׁמְשֹׁתַיִךְ וּשְׁעָרַיִךְ לְאַבְנֵי אֶקְדָּח, *And I will embed the frames of your windows with rubies, and your gates with stones of carbuncle* (Rashi, Radak, and *Ibn Ezra*), which *Targum* renders: וְאֲשַׁוֵּי בְמַרְגְּלִין אָעָךְ וְתַרְעָיִךְ לְאַבְנֵי גְמַר, *And I will place precious stones in your wooden utensils, and*

stones of carbuncle in your [cities'] gates. *Targum* does not interpret the Hebrew word שִׁמְשֹׁתַיִךְ, as derived from שֶׁמֶשׁ, *sun* [thus meaning window-frames, i.e., places exposed to the sun]. Rather, the *Targum* interprets the verse as if it read תִּשְׁמוֹשָׁתַיִךְ, *the things which you handle and use every day:* from שַׁמֵּשׁ, *to handle, to use*. It is to the above *Targumic* interpretation of the verse in *Isaiah* that the poet refers in this verse of the *Akdamus* — that in the Time to Come, even the everyday utensils used by the righteous will be made of precious stones and gems (*Yad Aharon*).

82. אֲפַרְסְמוֹן נַהֲרָתָא — *Balsam Rivers.*

וּמִתְפַּנְּקִין וְרָווּ,

בְּכַסֵּי רְוָיָתָא.

פד חֲמַר מְרַת דְּמִבְּרֵאשִׁית,

נְטִיר בֵּי נַעֲוָתָא:

LEXICAL NOTES

83. וּמִתְפַּנְּקִין — *And they will delight;* from אִתְפַּנֵּיק, *to enjoy oneself, to take pleasure.* The *Targum's* rendering of the Hebrew תִּתְעַנָּגוּ *(Isaiah 57:4).* See also the *Targum* to Psalms 37:4, 11. From: פָּנַק, *to live in luxury,* פְּנַק, *to indulge oneself.*

וְרָווּ — I. From רָוָה, *to drink one's fill (especially wine).* II. from רְוֵי, *to drink until intoxicated.* וּשְׁתִי מִן חַמְרָא וּרְוִי, *and he drank wine and became drunk. (Targum, Genesis 9:21).* III. from רִינָּה, *to refresh* (Hebrew הִתְרַוָּה, *to be refreshed).*

84. חֲמַר — *Wine.*

מְרַת — *Juice,* (especially from grapes).

COMMENTARY

There are tens of *Midrashim* that mention the rivers of balsam oil flowing in the Garden of Eden, whose fragrance and beauty will be enjoyed by the righteous as part of their reward in the World to Come. For sources on this theme see: *Midrash Konen, Bayis 5,* in Jellinek, *Bais HaMidrash* p. 29 (Eisenstein, *Otzar Midrashim Vol. I,* p. 256); *Seder Gan Eden,* loc. cit. pp. 52-53 *(Ibid,* p. 84); *Ma'aseh d'Rav Yehosha ben Levi,* in Eisenstein, loc. cit. 211; *Yalkut Shimoni, Bereishis,* 20.

One of the best known accounts is that of Eliezer son of Pedas who was poor and suffered hunger all his life. As a reward for his righteousness, the Holy One, blessed be He, promised him that:

יָהֵיבְנָא לָךְ לְעָלְמָא דְאָתֵי תְּלֵיסְרֵי נַהֲרָוָתָא דְמַשְׁתָא אַפַּרְסְמוֹן דַּכְיָין — *In the World to Come, I will give you thirteen rivers flowing with pure balsam oil [around which the righteous will be able to promenade, and in which they will bathe (Rashi)] (Ta'anis 25a).*

83. וּמִתְפַּנְּקִין — *And they will delight.*

The poet possibly refers to the following *Targum,* which gives a description of what will happen to the righteous when the Messiah will come. Note the similarity of the words used in this verse to those of *Targum Yonasan* to *Numbers* 11:26:

וְיִתְפַּנְּקוּן מִן טַוְורָא דְאִיצְטְנַע לְהוֹן מִן שֵׁירוּתָא וִיקַבְּלוּן אֲגַר עוֹבָדֵיהוֹן

⁸³ *And they will delight and drink their fill*

from overflowing goblets

⁸⁴ *Of sweet wine which, from the beginning*

was preserved in pressing tanks.

LEXICAL NOTES

חֲמַר מְרַת — *Sweet wine, the first flow of freshly squeezed grapes.* It is often used by *Targum* as the Aramaic rendering of the Hebrew עָסִיס [*the fine and sweet wine,* *Rashi*] as in the *Targum* to *Amos:* וְיִרְבּוּן טוּרַיָא חֲמַר מְרַת, *and the mountain will flow* [lit. *be filled with*] *sweet wine.*

נְטִיר — I. *To preserve,* as in the preservation of fruit, II. *to reserve.*

בֵּי — *In, at.*

נַעֲוָתָא — The plural of נַעֲוָא, *the hollowed-out tank in which grapes are pressed* (Hebrew יֶקֶב). (See *Targum* and *Rashi* to *Genesis* 49:12). As in the *Targum Yonason* to *Exodus* 22:28: חֲמַר נַעֲוָךְ, *The wine from the tank of your wine-press* (See also *Avoda Zara* 74b).

COMMENTARY

— *And they will enjoy themselves with [the feast of] the ox that was set aside for them from the beginning of time [see next verse] and they will accept the rewards of their labor (of their good deeds).*

בְּכַסֵּי רְוָיָתָא — *With overflowing goblets.*

This phrase is from *Psalms* 23:5: כּוֹסִי רְוָיָה, *My cup overflows.* In Aramaic, רְוָיָתָא *is an intoxicating drink.* Accordingly בְּכַסֵּי רְוָיָתָא can be translated: *With goblets filled with intoxicating drink.* Each one of the righteous will have his own cup at the feast in the Time to Come: וּבְיַד כָּל אֶחָד וְאֶחָד כּוֹס שֶׁל זָהָב מְרוּקָם בַּאֲבָנִים טוֹבוֹת וּמַרְגָּלִיוֹת. — *And in the hand of each and every one [of the righteous] will be*

a goblet of gold, set with precious stones and diamonds (Osios d'Rabbi Akiva, Version A).

84. חֲמַר מְרַת דְּמִבְּרֵאשִׁית — *Of sweet wine which, from the beginning.*

This verse should be read as a continuation of the previous verse. The righteous will take delight in drinking from cups overflowing with the wine that was preserved for them since the six days of creation. This verse refers to the following *Talmudic* passage:

מַאי עַיִן לֹא רָאָתָה? אָמַר רַבִּי יְהוֹשֻׁעַ בֶּן לֵוִי זֶה יַיִן הַמְשׁוּמָר בַּעֲנָבָיו מִשֵּׁשֶׁת יְמֵי בְרֵאשִׁית.

— *What [is the meaning of] No eye has ever seen (Isaiah 64:3)? — Rabbi Joshua ben Levi said: This is the*

פה ‏זַכָּאִין כַּד שְׁמַעְתּוּן,
שְׁבַח דָּא שִׁירָתָא.

LEXICAL NOTES

85. ‏זַכָּאִין — Plural of ‏זַכַּאי, *righteous, worthy;* also *guiltless* (= *innocent*).

‏כַּד שְׁמַעְתּוּן — *As you heard;* often used in the sense of *to obey, to pay heed.*

‏שִׁירָתָא — *Hymn, poem, song;* from ‏שִׁיר or ‏שִׁירָה.

COMMENTARY

— There was a jewel [of a saying] in the mouth of Rav: In the World to Come there is neither eating nor drinking; neither procreation nor transacting of business; no envy, nor hatred nor rivalry. Only the righteous sit with their crowns upon their heads, and they enjoy the radiance of the Shechinah; as is stated; And they beheld God and they ate and drank (Ex. 24:11) [i.e., they satiated themselves from the Shechinah as if they were eating and drinking (Berachos 17a)]. See also Rambam, Mishnah Torah, Sefer Mada, Hilchos Teshuvah.

Of the many answers that have been given to explain the apparent corporeality (‏גשמיות) of the pleasures of the righteous in Paradise as given in the *Akdamus,* the main replies are as follows:

1) That the feast which will be given to the righteous will indeed be physical, but one must realize that in this world, physical and the spiritual are closely interrelated. For it is through partaking of physical food that we obtain our sustenance

wine which has been preserved in its grapes from the six days of creation [for the righteous to drink, in the World to Come] (Berachos 34b). See also *Sanhedrin 99a,* and *Zohar, Midrash Ha-Ne'elam,* I, pp. 135b and 192a; also *ibid.* II, pp. 39-40.

‏חֲמַר מְרַת דְּמִבְּרֵאשִׁית נָטִיר — I. *The wine was preserved; and then* II. *reserved for the righteous; and* III. *guarded by God, until the Time to Come.*

Several commentators address themselves to the poem's depiction of the physical pleasures that are to be enjoyed by the righteous (*Yad Aharon; M'vo HaShir; T'gul B'gan; Heidenheim*). They note that the account of the rewards of the righteous in the World to Come seems to be in conflict with *Berachos* 17a:

‏מַרְגְּלָא בְּפוּמֵיהּ דְּרַב: הָעוֹלָם הַבָּא אֵין בּוֹ
‏לֹא אֲכִילָה וְלֹא שְׁתִיָּה וְלֹא פְּרִיָּה וְרִבְיָה
‏וְלֹא מַשָּׂא וּמַתָּן וְלֹא קִנְאָה וְלֹא שִׂנְאָה
‏וְלֹא תַחֲרוּת אֶלָּא צַדִּיקִים יוֹשְׁבִין
‏וְעַטְרוֹתֵיהֶם בְּרָאשֵׁיהֶם וְנֶהֱנִים מִזִּיו
‏הַשְּׁכִינָה שֶׁנֶּאֱמַר: וַיֶּחֱזוּ אֶת הָאֱלֹהִים
‏וַיֹּאכְלוּ וַיִּשְׁתּוּ.

אקדמות [138]

85 *O righteous ones, just as you heard*
the praise within this hymn ...

COMMENTARY

in order that our minds and bodies may function on the spiritual level *(Rashba, to Bava Basra 75a).*

2) Although the Banquet of the Behemoth and the Leviathan will indeed be physical, their feast will be the last physical meal to be eaten by the righteous. It will act as the transition between the base physical world and the eternal spiritual life to be enjoyed by the righteous as described in the above cited *Talmudic* passage *(M'vo HaShir).*

3) The eating of the Leviathan and the Behemoth, as well as the drinking of the wine set aside from the days of creation, are by no means to be considered base physical foods, since God Himself has set them aside for the righteous. They are therefore to be considered part of the spiritual rewards of the righteous in the World to Come *(Yad Aharon, p. 148).*

[It must be emphasized that *Yad Aharon* uses more than twenty closely printed pages in order to discuss this question, and it would be impossible to deal with this problem adequately in our commentary. The reader seeking further allegorical interpretations of verses 75-84, may consult the commentaries of *Rambam, Ramban, Rashba,* and *Maharsha* to the specific *Talmudic* passages mentioned in the text of

the commentary as well as the footnotes. Initially, the reader is referred to *M'vo HaShir* p. 40; *Yad Aharon,* pp. 135-148; and *T'yul B'gan* pp. 79-100].

85. Having completed the narrative and descriptive portions of his poem, the poet now concludes his words with a blessing for his audience *(vs. 85-88),* and a blessing on the Torah *(vs. 89-90).*

זַכָּאִין כַּד ... — *O righteous ones, just as you have heard.*

The poet tells his audience that, as a reward for their having listened to and also recited, the praises of God in this poem, so may they also be privileged to be among the righteous in Paradise. The poet refers to the following passages from *Talmud* and *Midrash:*

אָמַר רַבִּי יְהוֹשֻׁעַ בֶּן לֵוִי כָּל הָאוֹמֵר שִׁירָה בָּעוֹלָם הַזֶּה זוֹכֶה וְאוֹמְרָהּ לְעוֹלָם הַבָּא שֶׁנֶּאֱמַר: אַשְׁרֵי יוֹשְׁבֵי בֵיתֶךָ עוֹד יְהַלְלוּךָ סֶּלָה

— *Rabbi Yehoshua son of Levi said: Everyone who utters poems [or songs] of praise (for the Almighty) in this world, will be privileged to recite them in the World to Come, as is written:* Happy are those who dwell in Thy house, they will praise You yet again *(Ps. 84:5) [Sanhedrin 91b].* It is for this reason that this verse from *Psalms 84:3,* is said, prior to the saying of *Psalms 145* in

[139]   *Akdamus*

קְבִיעִין כֵּן תֶּהֱווֹן, פו

בְּהַנְהוּ חֲבוּרְתָא:

וְתִזְכּוּן דִּי תֵיתְבוּן, פז

בְּעֵלָּא דָרְתָא.

LEXICAL NOTES

86. קְבִיעִין — From קָבַע, *to be appointed, to be established*.

כֵּן תֶּהֱווֹן — *So may you be* (future second person of הֲוֵי, *to be*).

בְּהַנְהוּ — From הָן or הוֹן, *this one*, or *that one*.

חֲבוּרְתָא — *Company, party*; חֲבוּרָה is also the title given to the colleagues at the academy.

87. וְתִזְכּוּן — *And (you should) merit*; from זָכָה, *to merit reward, to be privileged*.

COMMENTARY

the daily prayers. *Berochos* 4b states that whoever recites *Psalm* 145 three times daily is assured of being among those of the World to Come. This *Psalm*, like the *Akdomus*, are both poems of praise and are likewise both written in acrostic form, in alphabetical order.

The following passage from *Osios d'Rabbi Akiva*, version A, expresses the high esteem in which God holds those who recite poems and hymns of praise: שֶׁאֶלְמָלֵא שִׁירָה וְזִמְרָה שֶׁהֵם אוֹמְרִים לְפָנַי בְּכָל יוֹם לֹא בָּרָאתִי אֶת עוֹלָמִי, *God says of Israel: that be it not for the hymns and songs that they say before Me every day, I would not have created My world (Eshel Avraham)*. [For

more on the value of reciting poems of praise see: the *Zohar* II, p. 54b כַּד בַּר נָשׁ דְּאָמַר וכו', and also *ibid. II*, p. 144a.

86. בְּהַנְהוּ חֲבוּרְתָא — *Among that company.*

The poet blesses his audience that as they have listened to and participated in the recounting of the praises of the Almighty in this poem, so may they also merit to be among the righteous in Paradise. This verse is to be read as the continuation of the previous one. (*Yad Aharon;* see notes to *v.* 85).

87. בְּעֵלָּא דָרְתָא — *In the foremost row.*

This description of the righteous

אקדמות [140]

⁸⁶ *So may you appointed be*

among that company.

⁸⁷ *And merit to be sitting*

in the foremost row ...

LEXICAL NOTES

דִּי — *That* [conjunction], as in *Daniel* 4:3: דִּי פְשַׁר חֶלְמָא, *that they should interpret the dream.*

תֵיתְבוּן — *(You should) be sitting.* The second person plural of יְתֵב, *to sit.*

בְּעֵלָּא — From בְּעֵלָּא, *height, from above;* and from עֵילָאָה, *uppermost, high(est).*

דְּרָתָא — From דָּרָא, *row.*

COMMENTARY

who will sit in rows before the Presence of God, is from *Succah* 45b and *Sanhedrin* 97b: אָמַר רָבָא תְּמָנֵי סְרֵי אַלְפֵי דָרָא הֲוַה דְקַמֵיה קוּדְשָׁא בְּרִיךְ הוּא שֶׁנֶּאֱמַר: סָבִיב שְׁמֹנָה עָשָׂר אָלֶף — *Rav said: There are eighteen thousand rows before the Holy One, blessed be He, as it is written: There shall be eighteen thousand all around [and the name of the city will be HASHEM is there] (Ezekiel 48:35).*

Although this verse in Ezekiel refers to Jerusalem in the future, the *Talmud* also interprets it to refer to the righteous sitting in rows around the presence of the Shechinah in heaven *(Eshel Avraham* following *Rashi).*

The righteous will also be divided into seven classes in accordance to their merit. The most deserving ones will sit in the uppermost rows, while the less meritorious ones will be further away from the Shechinah. This verse refers back to verses 63-64. *(Kinyan Tov).*

88. אֲרֵי תְצִיתוּן לְמִלּוֹי — *If you will listen to the words of God,* i.e., the Ten Commandments.

If you do so, you will have the privilege of sitting in the uppermost rows in Paradise *(Mateh Levi; M'vo HaShir).*

Some editions of the *Akdamus* read לְמִלַי, *to my words.* The poet tells his listeners that if they will

פח אֲרֵי תְצִיתוּן לְמִלּוֹי,
דְּנָפְקִין בְּהַדְּרָתָא:

פט מְרוֹמֵם הוּא אֱלָהִין,
בְּקַדְמָא בְּקַדְמָא וּבַתְרַיְתָא.

LEXICAL NOTES

88. אֲרֵי — *If;* (equivalent to the Hebrew כִּי which can also mean *when, that, because.*

תְצִיתוּן — *You shall listen,* especially in the sense of *to heed, to obey,* from צית. As in the *Targum* to Deut. 32:1, אֲצִיתוּ שְׁמַיָּא, *Listen you heavens.*

לְמִלּוֹי — *To His [God's] words,* or *to His commands;* from מִלָּא, *word, command.*

דְּנָפְקִין — *That emanate, that go out,* from נְפַק.

COMMENTARY

89. בְּקַדְמָא וּבַתְרַיְתָא — *In the beginning and at the end* or alternately: *at first and at last.*

God was the first King at the beginning of the world, before and during creation, and He will be the last King at the world's end. The phrase בְּקַדְמָא וּבַתְרַיְתָא, is an Aramaic translation of the reference in *Isaiah* to one of the characteristics and attributes of God, the verse reads as follows: אֲנִי רִאשׁוֹן וַאֲנִי אַחֲרוֹן וּמִבַּלְעָדַי אֵין אֱלֹהִים, *I am the first, and I am the last, and beside Me there is no other God* (Isaiah 44:6). Compare also with *Isaiah* 41:4.

Shir HaShirim Rabbah 1:45 expands upon the above-cited verse as follows:

אָמַר רֵישׁ לָקִישׁ וְלָמָה הוּא אֱמֶת? אֲלַ"ף

listen to his words, — meaning the words of the Ten Commandments, which will be read and explained by him after the reading of this poem — then they will be privileged to sit in the uppermost rows in Paradise (*Kinyan Tov, Zos Nechemosi*). The poet speaks of *his own words* because he is in fact the Meturgeman (מְתוּרְגְּמָן, *translator, interpreter*), whose function it is to translate and explain each verse of Scripture, subsequent to its being read by the reader of the Torah. (See Introduction).

דְּנָפְקִין בְּהַדְּרָתָא — *That emanate in beauty.*

This is an allusion to *Psalms* 29:4, קוֹל ה' בֶּהָדָר, *the voice of HASHEM is beautiful* [Heidenheim].

---

88 *If you shall listen to His words*

that emanate in beauty!

89 *Exalted is He — God —*

in the beginning and at the end.

LEXICAL NOTES

בְּהַדְרָתָא — *In beauty or with beauty, splendor, majesty, glory; from* הָדָר.

89. מְרוֹמָם — *Exalted, elevated; from* רום.

בְּקַדְמָא — *In (or at) the beginning, or alternately: at first, that is, at the time before and during creation. See comm. From* קַדְמָאה, *previous, in ancient times; and/or* קַדְמִין, *beginning, olden days.*

וּבְתַרְיָתָא — *And at the end, from* בַּתְרָא, *the last, the latest; and from* בָּתַר, *after. See Targum to Deut. 13:10.*

COMMENTARY

עֲשָׂרָה מְלָכִים מָלְכוּ מִסּוֹף הָעוֹלָם וְעַד סוֹפוֹ מֶלֶךְ הָרִאשׁוֹן זֶה הקב"ה הַשֵּׁנִי זֶה נִמְרוֹד הַשְּׁלִישִׁי זֶה יוֹסֵף הָרְבִיעִי זֶה שְׁלמֹה הַחֲמִשִׁי זֶה אַחְאָב מֶלֶךְ יִשְׂרָאֵל הַשִּׁשִּׁי זֶה נְבוּכַדְנֶצַּר הַשְּׁבִיעִי כּוֹרֶשׁ הַשְּׁמִינִי אֲלֶכְסַנְדְּרוֹס מוֹקְדוֹן הַתְּשִׁיעִי מֶלֶךְ הַמָּשִׁיחַ הַמֶּלֶךְ הָעֲשִׂירִי חוֹזֶרֶת הַמְּלוּכָה לִבְעָלֶיהָ מִי שֶׁהָיָה הַמֶּלֶךְ הָרִאשׁוֹן הוּא הַמֶּלֶךְ הָאַחֲרוֹן שֶׁנֶּאֱמַר: אֲנִי רִאשׁוֹן וַאֲנִי אַחֲרוֹן

— *Ten kings ruled [and will rule] from one end of the world to the other. The first one was the Holy One, blessed be He, the second was Nimrod ... the third was Joseph ... the fourth was Solomon ... the fifth was Ahab ... the sixth was Nebuchadnezzar ... the seventh was Cyrus ... the eighth was Alexander [the Great] of Macedonia ... the ninth will be the King Messiah ...*

בְּרֹאשׁ הָאוֹתִיּוֹת, מ"ם בָּאֶמְצַע, תי"ו בְּסוֹפָן. לוֹמַר: אֲנִי רִאשׁוֹן וַאֲנִי אַחֲרוֹן וּמִבַּלְעָדַי אֵין אֱלֹהִים אֲנִי רִאשׁוֹן שֶׁלֹּא קַבַּלְתִּי מַלְכוּתִי מֵאַחֵר וַאֲנִי אַחֲרוֹן שֶׁאֵינִי מוֹסְרָה לְאַחֵר שֶׁאֵינוּ בָּעוֹלָם

— *Resh Lakish said: and why is [the seal of God]* אֱמֶת, *truth? [Because]* Alef (א) *is the first of the letters,* Mem (מ) *is at the middle, [of the Aleph-Bais] and* Tav (ת) *is at the end. [God] says: I Am the first and I Am the last, and beside Me there is no other God (Isaiah 44:6) — I am the first in that I have not taken over My kingdom from another, and I am the last, in that I shall not give it over to another, for there is no other in the universe (Yad Aharon).*

Pirkei d'Rav Eliezer, 11, further expands on the above:

צ צְבִי וְאִתְרְעִי בָן,
וּמְסַר לָן אוֹרַיְתָא:

LEXICAL NOTES

90. צְבִי — *To desire, to choose, to take delight in.* See notes to verse 35 above.

וְאִתְרְעִי — I. *And He [God] chose (us)* ... as in *Targum to Psalm* 78:68, וְאִתְרְעִי יַת שֵׁבֶט יְהוּדָה, *And He chose the tribe of Judah.*

COMMENTARY

by the tenth king, the kingdom will return to its [proper] owner. [That is] He Who was the First King, shall be the last. As it is written (Isaiah 44:6): *I am the first and I am the last* (Yad Aharon).

90. צְבִי וְאִתְרְעִי בָן — I. *He desired and chose us;* or II. *He took delight in us and chose us,* ...

מְרוֹמַם הוּא — *Exalted is He* ...
... צְבִי וְאִתְרְעִי — *He desired and chose* ...

These final two verses are a paraphrase of the blessing recited before the reading of the Torah. Realizing that the *Akdamus* is a considerable interruption (הַפְסָקָה) of the reading of the Torah, he felt that the blessing should again be repeated, at least in the form of an Aramaic paraphrase. The parallel of these verses to the blessing is as follows:

מְרוֹמַם הוּא אֱלָהִין corresponds to בָּרוּךְ אַתָּה ה׳ אֱלֹהֵינוּ
Exalted is the Lord = Blessed are You, HASHEM our God.

90 *He desired and chose us*

and gave to us the the Torah!

LEXICAL NOTES

II. *To delight in,* as in the *Targum* to *Psalm* 22:9, פְּצָא יָתֵיהּ מְטוּל דְּאִתְרְעֵי בֵיהּ, [*Let the Lord*] *save him because He took delight in him.*
From: רְעֵי.

וּמְסַר לָן — *And He gave us;* from מְסַר, *transmit, to hand over.*

אוֹרַיְתָא (also אוֹרַיְיתָא) — *the Torah.*

COMMENTARY

☙ בְּקַדְמָא וּבְתְרַיְתָא corresponds to מֶלֶךְ הָעוֹלָם
[*He was*] *the first* [*king of the Universe*] *and* [*He will be*] *the last,* — (This translation is in accordance with the *Midrashim* cited in the *comm.* to *v.* 89 above) = *Our God, King of the Universe.*

☙ צְבִי וְאִתְרְעֵי בָן corresponds to אֲשֶׁר בָּחַר בָּנוּ מִכָּל הָעַמִּים
He desired and chose us = *Who has chosen us from all peoples).*

☙ וּמְסַר לָן אוֹרַיְתָא corresponds to וְנָתַן לָנוּ אֶת תּוֹרָתוֹ
(*And He gave us the Torah* = *and He gave us His Torah)* [*M'vo HaShir, Zos Nechemosi*].

תם ונשלם שבח לא־ל בורא עולם
ברוך ה׳ לעולם אמן ואמן

⌁§ *Bibliography*

Bibliography

The following commentaries on *Akdamus* were consulted in the preparation of this volume. Those cited in the commentary are referred to by the names shown.

Yad Aharon

ספר ''יד אהרן'' מאת אהרן דוד טיקאצינסקי בספר ''ברכת אברהם'' מאת אברהם אביש; ווארשא, תרצ''ד.

The most complete and comprehensive commentary ever written on the *Akdamus*. This commentary gives Scriptural and *Midrashic* sources for every verse, as well as Kabbalistic interpretations.

Shnei HaMe'oros

סדר ''פיוט אקדמות'' עם פרוש שני המאורות מאת שניאור זלמן משה פרידמאן; ווילנא, תרס''ב.

The commentary gives the *Targumic*, *Talmudic*, and *Midrashic* sources of every verse, as well as the Hebrew translations of all difficult Aramaic passages. An introduction gives an account of the life and times of Rabbi Meir of Worms, the author of *Akdamus*.

Heidenheim

''סדר אקדמות'' עם פירוש ותרגום מאת וואלף ב''ר שמשון היידנהיים, ב''מחזור לחג השבועות''; זולצבאך, תר''א; וגם וויען, תקפ''ז.

This commentary offers a German-Yiddish translation of the *Akdamus*, as well as a Hebrew commentary containing much material of a linguistic nature. This is the commentary found in the famous *Rodelheim Machzorim*.

Zos Nechemosi

ספר ''זאת נחמתי'' מאת שלמה ב''ר חיים חייקיל יאנאווסקי: ווארשא, תרפ''ג.

Kinyan Tov

ספר ''קנין טוב'' מאת שלמה ב''ר חיים חייקיל יאנאווסקי: פיעטרקוב, תרס''ד.

Both commentaries, were written by the same author. The former is brief and succinct, while the latter is rather extensive, stressing the moral teachings to be found in the *Akdamus*.

M'vo HaShir

''מבוא השיר'' מאת שמואל חיים יעלין (מווענגראב); פיעטרקוב, תרפ''ו.

An extensive commentary on the *Akdamus* giving insights into the specific *Midrashim* upon which many verses are based. It also deals with the verses which are not fully dealt with by *Mateh Levi*. A Yiddish translation of the *Akdamus* is also provided.

T'yul B'gan

ספר "טיול בגן" מאת ר' נתנאל
מזמושץ; פיעטרקוב, תרפ"ו.
Primarily a homiletical commentary on the *Akdamus*. The author's primary aim is to expound upon the moral and ethical teachings in the *Akdamus*.

Eshel Avraham

ספר "אשל אברהם" על אקדמות
מאת אהרן אשר ב"ר אברהם
וואלינעץ; נו יארק; תשט"ז
This commentary provides a Yiddish translation of the *Akdamus*, as well as *Midrashic* sources for some of the verses.

Tzvi V'chamid

ספר "צבי וחמיד" בהספר "עטרת
חכמים" מאת צבי בן ארי'
טאקסין; ווילנא, תרע"א
A commentary emphasizing the major thematic trends of the *Akdamus*. A Hebrew translation is also supplied.

Baumarin

"ספר אקדמות" עם פירוש הקצר
... והארך. מאת משה ב"ר
אברהם באמאן; ווארשא, תרס"ב
A commentary on the *Akdamus* written in two parts: 1) a short commentary giving the simple interpretation (פְשַׁט) of the words; and 2) a long homiletical commentary on various themes. The short commentary was reprinted recently in *Siddur*

Minchas Yerushalaim, 1972. (*Otzar HaPoskim* Publishing Co.)

Berger

"תולדותיה ומקורותיה של שירת
אקדמות" ד"ר נפתלי נתן ברגר;
בני-ברק, תשל"ג
A scholarly translation and commentary on the *Akdamus* written by Naftali Nathan Berger. It includes biographical and historical studies of the poet and the developing halachic treatment of *Akdamus* (see Introduction).

Mateh Levi/Bais Levi

"מחזור מטה לוי" — שבועות;
לעמבערג, תרס"ז
A brief commentary on the *Akdamus*. Found in all *Mateh Levi* Machzorim since their first printing in the mid-19th century. This anonymous commentary was composed in the 15th century and is found in mss. of the *Akdamus*. It was first printed in the *Machzor Sabbionetta-Cremona*, 1557-61.
This commentary, written in the 19th century gives the sources of the *Mateh Levi* commentary. First printed in the *M'vo HaShir* commentary.

Kol-Bo

מחזור "כל-בו" עם פירוש; ווילנא,
תרפ"ד
An anonymous commentary printed in the Cantor's *Machzor Kol Bo*, in 1924.

Moadim (Mipi Olalim)

"מועדים, ספר שבועות" — כרך
ד' בעריכת מ. ליפסון (מחזור "מפי
עוללים"); הוצאת "אמנת";
ירושלים, תל אביב, תש"ז
From the Sefer Moadim, for
Shavuos, edited by M. Lipsin.
The book contains what many
consider the finest and most
accurate Hebrew translation
of the Akdamus. This translation is also found in the Siddur and Machzor MiPi
Olelim, 1937.

* "באור שירת אקדמות" מאת
אהרן מיאדלער ווארשא, תרס"ד

* "ספר המועדים" — שבועות —
כרך ג' אסף מאת ד"ר יום־טוב
לוינסקי "דביר" ת"א, תשי"ג

* אקדמות — ב"סידור רנת
ישראל" ירושלים, תשל"ג

* מחזור לשלש רגלים עם באור
חספיק בלשון יהודית־אשכנזית
(יידיש־דייטש) ווילנא, תרל"ז

* מחזור מן שלש רגלים:
לעמבערג, תר"י.

Traditional Translation

אקדמות עם פירוש עברי טייטש
דפות "עץ חיים" תשכ"ה

Many Yiddish translations of
the Akdamus have been
published from 1721 up until
our present day. Although not
always completely accurate by
scholarly standards, these
translations represent the living oral tradition of the proper
translation of the Akdamus.

Talmudic, Midrashic, and Other Works
Quoted in the Commentary

Targum Onkelos
Targum Yonasan Ben Uziel
Targum Yerushalmi
Talmud Bavli
Talmud Yerushalmi
Midrash Rabbah
Midrash Tanchuma
Pirkei d'Rabbi Eliezer
Midrash Tehillim
Pesikta d'Rav Kahana
Bais HaMidrash (Yellinek)
Battei Midrashos (Wertheimer)
Yalkut Shimoni
Sifrei

Sifra
Mechilta
Pesikta Rabbossi
Midrash Lekach Tov
Zohar
Zohar Chadash
Tikkunei Zohar
Tosefta
Pirkei Avos
Avos d'Rabbi Nosson
Otzar HaGeonim:
    (B.M. Lewin)
    13 volume gaonic commentary
    on the talmud.

* These works are not quoted in the commentary.